TABLE OF CONTENTS

Top 20 Test Taking Tips	4
Algebraic Operations and Expressions	5
Equations and Inequalities	31
Complex Numbers	65
Functions and Graphing	70
Practice Test	106
Practice Questions	106
Answers and Explanations	134
Secret Key #1 - Time is Your Greatest Enemy	154
Pace Yourself	154
Secret Key #2 - Guessing is not Guesswork	154
Monkeys Take the Test	154
$5 Challenge	155
Secret Key #3 - Practice Smarter, Not Harder	156
Success Strategy	156
Secret Key #4 - Prepare, Don't Procrastinate	156
Secret Key #5 - Test Yourself	157
General Strategies	157
Special Report: How to Overcome Test Anxiety	163
Lack of Preparation	163
Physical Signals	163
Nervousness	164
Study Steps	166
Helpful Techniques	167
Special Report: Additional Bonus Material	171

Top 20 Test Taking Tips

1. Carefully follow all the test registration procedures
2. Know the test directions, duration, topics, question types, how many questions
3. Setup a flexible study schedule at least 3-4 weeks before test day
4. Study during the time of day you are most alert, relaxed, and stress free
5. Maximize your learning style; visual learner use visual study aids, auditory learner use auditory study aids
6. Focus on your weakest knowledge base
7. Find a study partner to review with and help clarify questions
8. Practice, practice, practice
9. Get a good night's sleep; don't try to cram the night before the test
10. Eat a well balanced meal
11. Know the exact physical location of the testing site; drive the route to the site prior to test day
12. Bring a set of ear plugs; the testing center could be noisy
13. Wear comfortable, loose fitting, layered clothing to the testing center; prepare for it to be either cold or hot during the test
14. Bring at least 2 current forms of ID to the testing center
15. Arrive to the test early; be prepared to wait and be patient
16. Eliminate the obviously wrong answer choices, then guess the first remaining choice
17. Pace yourself; don't rush, but keep working and move on if you get stuck
18. Maintain a positive attitude even if the test is going poorly
19. Keep your first answer unless you are positive it is wrong
20. Check your work, don't make a careless mistake

Algebraic Operations and Expressions

Real, natural, whole, integer, rational, irrational, imaginary, and complex numbers

The set of **real numbers** contains all numbers which have distinct locations on a number line. **Natural numbers** are real numbers used for counting: 1, 2, 3, 4, ... The set of **whole numbers** includes the counting numbers along with the number zero: 0, 1, 2, 3, 4, ... The set of **integers** includes whole numbers and their opposites: ..., -4, -3, -2, -1, 0, 1, 2, 3, 4, ... **Rational numbers** include any real number which can be expressed as a fraction in which the numerator is an integer and the denominator is a non-zero integer; rational numbers include integers, fractions, terminating, and repeating decimals. **Irrational numbers,** such as $\sqrt{2}$ and π, are real numbers which are not rational; in decimal form, these numbers are non-repeating and non-terminating, so any decimal (or fractional) representations of irrational numbers are only approximations. The set of **imaginary numbers** includes all numbers whose squares are negative and therefore excludes any real number; the imaginary number i is defined as the square root of -1. The set of **complex numbers** encompasses both the real and imaginary; a complex number can be written in the form $a + bi$, where a and b are real numbers, and i is the imaginary number.

Relationships among these sets of numbers

Below is an example of a diagram which shows that natural numbers are a subset of whole numbers, which are a subset of integers, which are a subset of rational numbers. All of these together with irrational numbers comprise the set of real numbers. Complex numbers include both real and imaginary numbers.

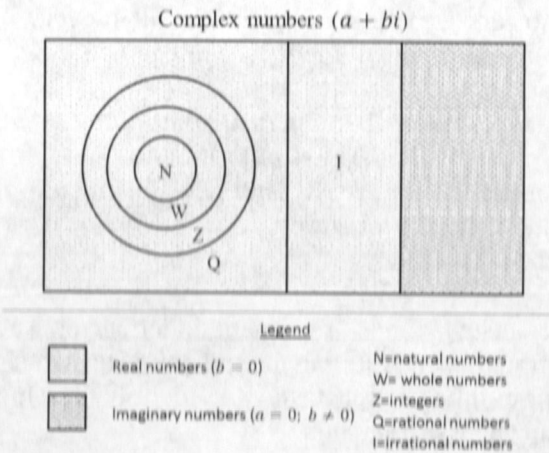

Note that the sizes of the boxes and circles do not reflect the sizes of each set. Each set contains an infinite number of elements.

Problem

Classifying each of the following numbers as a real, natural, whole, integer, rational, irrational, imaginary, and/or complex
1. π
2. −6
3. 22
4. i
5. $\frac{2}{3}$
6. $2 + 3i$

1. π is an irrational number, a real number, and a complex number
2. -6 is an integer, a rational number, a real number, and a complex number
3. 22 is a natural number, a whole number, an integer, a rational number, a real number, and a complex number
4. i is an imaginary number and a complex number
5. $\frac{2}{3}$ is a rational number, a real number, and a complex number
6. 2+3i is a complex number

Problem

Determining whether each statement is true
1. All natural numbers are real numbers.
2. Some integers are whole numbers.
3. Imaginary numbers are not real.
4. No integer is irrational.
5. All rational numbers are integers.

1. True; all natural numbers are real numbers.
2. True; some integers are whole numbers. Not all integers, however, are whole numbers, but all whole numbers are integers.
3. True; imaginary numbers are not real.
4. True; no integer is irrational. Integers are part of the set of rational numbers, and irrational numbers are not rational.
5. False; all rational numbers are NOT integers. All integers are rational, but not all rational numbers are integers.

Problem

In the statements below, * and ___ represent undefined operations. Name the properties illustrated in each statement and define for which operation(s) and ___ each of these statements is true. Also, identify for which sets of numbers these properties are true
1. $a * b = b * a$
2. $a * (b * c) = (a * b) * c$
3. $a * (b\_c) = a * b \_ a * c$
4. $a * b = a$

1. $a * b = b * a$ illustrates the commutative property, which is true for any complex numbers a and b when * represents addition or multiplication.

2. $a * (b * c) = (a * b) * c$ illustrates the associative property, which is true for any complex numbers a and b when * represents addition or multiplication.

3. $a * (b \_ c) = a * b \_ a * c$ illustrates the distributive property, which is true for any complex numbers a and b when * represents multiplication and _ represents addition or subtraction.

4. $a * b = a$ illustrates an identity, where the quantity a is unchanged by the operation * with the quantity b. This property is true for any complex number a when * represents addition or subtraction and when $b = 0$. This property is true for any complex number a when * represents multiplication or division and $b = 1$.

Note: The operation * can also represent "to the power of" when a is any complex number and $b = 1$ since, by definition, any number raised to the first power is that number.

Zero exponent and negative exponent properties

The **zero exponent property** states $a^0 = 1$ for all $a \neq 0$. The **negative exponent property** states $a^{-b} = \frac{1}{a^b}$ for all $a \neq 0$.

Consider the series ..., 2, 4, 8, 16, 32, ... Notice that each number is two times the previous number, so the series can be written $... 2, 2 \cdot 2, 2 \cdot 2 \cdot 2, 2 \cdot 2 \cdot 2 \cdot 2, 2 \cdot 2 \cdot 2 \cdot 2 \cdot 2...$, which can be more easily expressed using powers of 2: ..., $2^1, 2^2, 2^3, 2^4, 2^5, ...$

The exponent of each number is one more than the exponent of the previous number. Extend the series a few numbers to the left: ..., $\frac{1}{4}, \frac{1}{2}, 1, 2, 4, 8, 16, 32, ...$ Also, apply the pattern of exponents to the series written as powers of two: ..., $2^{-2}, 2^{-1}, 2^0, 2^1, 2^2, 2^3, 2^4, 2^5$, ... Compare the relative positions of newly written terms: $2^0 = 1$; $2^{-1} = \frac{1}{2} = \frac{1}{2^1}$; $2^{-2} = \frac{1}{4} = \frac{1}{2^2}$.

Product of powers and quotient of powers properties

The **product of powers** property states that when multiplying two monomials with like bases, add together the powers of that base; for example, $x^7 \cdot x^3 = x^{7+3} = x^{10}$ because $(x \cdot x \cdot x \cdot x \cdot x \cdot x \cdot x) \cdot (x \cdot x \cdot x) = x \cdot x \cdot x \cdot x \cdot x \cdot x \cdot x \cdot x \cdot x \cdot x = x^{10}$. The **quotient of powers** property states that when dividing two monomials with like bases, subtract the powers of that base; for example $\frac{x^7}{x^3} = x^{7-3} = x^4$ because $\frac{x \cdot x \cdot x \cdot x \cdot x \cdot x \cdot x}{x \cdot x \cdot x} = \frac{x}{x} \cdot \frac{x}{x} \cdot \frac{x}{x} \cdot x \cdot x \cdot x \cdot x = 1 \cdot 1 \cdot 1 \cdot x \cdot x \cdot x \cdot x = x^4$.

Power of a product, power of a quotient, and power of a power

The **power of a product** property states that when multiplying together two monomials with the same power but different bases, multiply the bases and keep the power the same; for example, $x^3 \cdot y^3 = (xy)^3$ because $x^3 \cdot y^3 = x \cdot x \cdot x \cdot y \cdot y \cdot y = x \cdot y \cdot x \cdot y \cdot x \cdot y = (x \cdot y) \cdot (x \cdot y) \cdot (x \cdot y) = (xy)^3$. (Notice the use of the commutative and associate properties of multiplication.) Similarly, the **power of a quotient** property states that when diving two monomials with the same power but different bases, divide the bases and keep the power the same; for example, $\frac{x^3}{y^3} = \left(\frac{x}{y}\right)^3$ because, $\frac{x^3}{y^3} = \frac{x \cdot x \cdot x}{y \cdot y \cdot y} = \frac{x}{y} \cdot \frac{x}{y} \cdot \frac{x}{y} = \left(\frac{x}{y}\right)^3$. Lastly, the **power of a power** property states that when raising a monomial to a power, multiply the power of each term in the monomial by the power to which the monomial is raised; for example, $(x^3y^2)^3 = x^{3\cdot3}y^{2\cdot3} = x^9y^6$ because $(x$^$3 \ y$^$2 \ )$^$3 = (x \cdot x \cdot x \cdot y \cdot y)(x \cdot x \cdot x \cdot y \cdot y)(x \cdot x \cdot x \cdot y \cdot y) = x \cdot x \cdot x \cdot x \cdot x \cdot x \cdot x \cdot x \cdot x \cdot y \cdot y \cdot y \cdot y \cdot y \cdot y = x^9y^6$ (Again, notice the use of the commutative and associate properties of multiplication.).

<u>Example</u>

Below is an example illustrating $\sqrt[n]{x} = x^{\frac{1}{n}}$.

$\sqrt{3} = 3^{\frac{1}{2}}$ In this example, $x = 3$ and $n = 2$.

$(\sqrt{3})^2 = (3^{\frac{1}{2}})^2$ The inverse operation of taking the square root is raising to the second power. Perform the same operation on both sides of the equation.

$3 = 3^{\frac{1}{2}\cdot 2}$ To raise a power to a power, multiply the powers.

$3 = 3^1$ Simplify. $\frac{1}{2} \cdot 2 = 1$.

$3 = 3$ Simplify. 3^1 = 3.

<u>Problem</u>

Simplifying the expression $\sqrt[6]{9x^4}$

$(9x^4)^{\frac{1}{6}}$ Rewrite the expression using rational exponents

$(3^2x^4)^{\frac{1}{6}}$ Substitute 3^2 for 9.

$3^{\frac{1}{3}}x^{\frac{2}{3}}$ Use the power of a power property of exponents.

$3^{\frac{1}{3}}x^{\frac{1}{3}}x^{\frac{1}{3}}$ Use the product of a power property to rewrite $x^{\frac{2}{3}}$ as the product of $x^{\frac{1}{3}}$ and $x^{\frac{1}{3}}$.

$(3xx)^{\frac{1}{3}}$ Use the product of powers property to rewrite the expression

$\sqrt[3]{3x^2}$ Simplify.

Problem

When two integers are added, subtracted, or multiplied, the resulting sum, difference, or product is also an integer; therefore, the set of integers is closed under these operations. Is the set of rational numbers closed under the same operations?

Given that $a, b, c,$ and d are integers and that b and d do not equal zero,
$$\frac{a}{b}+\frac{c}{d}=\frac{ad+bc}{bd} \text{ and } \frac{a}{b}-\frac{c}{d}=\frac{ad-bc}{bd} \text{ and } \frac{a}{b}\cdot\frac{c}{d}=\frac{ac}{bd}$$
$\frac{a}{b}$ and $\frac{c}{d}$ are rational numbers. The products $ad, bc,$ and bd are integers since the product of two integers is always an integer; likewise, since the sum or difference of two integers is always an integer, $ad + bc$ and $ad - bc$ must also be integers. Therefore, $\frac{ad+bc}{bd}, \frac{ad-bc}{bd},$ and $\frac{ac}{bd}$ represent ratios of two integers and are, by definition, rational. So, the set of rational numbers is closed under addition, subtraction, and multiplication.

Problem

Determine if the following statements are true or false. Provide an explanation for the true statement(s) and a counterexample for the false statement(s).
1. The sum of a rational number and an irrational number is always irrational.
2. The sum of two irrational numbers is always irrational

1. It is **true** that the sum of a rational number and an irrational number is always irrational. Consider for a moment that the statement is false; this would require the existence of some irrational number x that when added to rational number a would produce rational number b: $a + x = b$. Solving the equation for x yields $x = b - a$. The difference of b and a must be rational since the set of rational numbers is closed under subtraction. Since $x = b - a$, x must be a rational number; there is no such irrational number x that when added to a rational number yields a rational number. Therefore, the sum of a rational and an irrational number is always irrational.
2. It is false that the sum of two irrational numbers is always irrational. For example, the sum of irrational numbers $\sqrt{3}$ and $-\sqrt{3}$ is zero, which is rational.

Problem

Determine if the following statements are true or false. Provide an explanation for true statements and a counterexample for false statements
1. The product of a nonzero rational number and an irrational number is always irrational.
2. The product of two irrational numbers is always irrational.

1. It is **true** that the product of a nonzero rational number and an irrational number is always irrational. Consider for a moment that the statement is false; this would require the existence of some irrational number x that when multiplied by rational number a would produce rational number b: $ax = b$. Solving the equation for x yields $x = \frac{b}{a}; a \neq 0$. If x is equal to the

ratio of two rational numbers, it must also, by definition, be rational. (Note that the ratio of two rational numbers can be rewritten as the ratio of two integers.) So, there is no such irrational number x that when multiplied by a rational number yields a rational number. Therefore, the product of a rational and an irrational number is irrational.

2. It is false that the product of two irrational numbers is always irrational. For example, the product of irrational numbers $\sqrt{3}$ and $-\sqrt{3}$ is -3, which is rational.

Problem
Determine if the following statement is always true, sometimes true, or never true: an integer raised to a non-integer power is an integer.

It is **sometimes true** that an integer raised to a non-integer power is an integer. For example, $4^{\frac{1}{2}} = \sqrt{4} = 2$. However, it is not always true. For example, $3^{\frac{1}{2}} = \sqrt{3}$.

The expression $6s^2$ gives the surface area of a cube with edge length s. What is the coefficient of this expression?

A term is a product and/or quotient of a real number and one or more variables, each of which may be raised to a nonnegative integer exponent. The real number is the coefficient of the term. A polynomial expression is a term or sum of several terms. The expression $6s^2$ is therefore a single term, and the coefficient is the real number 6. Note that if a term is written, for example, as simply s^2, then the coefficient is 1, because $s^2 = 1s^2$. A coefficient may also be negative, such as in the term $-0.5ab$.

The expression $2W + 2L$ gives the perimeter of a rectangular frame with side lengths W and L. How many terms does this expression have?

A polynomial expression is the sum and/or difference of one or more terms. Each term is a product and/or quotient of one or more variables, each of which may be raised to a nonnegative integer exponent, and a real number. The expression $2W + 2L$ has 2 terms, one of which is $2W$ and the other of which is $2L$. It is important to realize that terms are separated by addition or subtraction. Therefore an expression such as $4xy$ has only 1 term. Also, since an expression such as $2x - 3y$ can be written as $2x + (-3y)$ the second term could be referred to as positive or negative.

What are the factors of the expression $x(5x + 2)(x - 4)$?

The factors of the expression $x(5x + 2)(x - 4)$ are the expressions x, $5x + 2$, and $x - 4$. To identify the factors of an expression, the expression must be written as a product of terms and/or expressions (with any expressions delineated by parentheses). The factors themselves may involve addition or subtraction of multiple terms, but if the expression is not written only as the product of terms or expressions, the expression is not in factored form. For example, the polynomial $x^2 + 2x + 8$ cannot be factored with real numbers, so it is considered to be one factor. The polynomial $x^2 + 6x + 8$ can be factored as $(x + 2)(x + 4)$, and therefore has two factors, $(x + 2)$ and $(x + 4)$.

Interpret the exponent in the expression $5000(1 + \frac{r}{12})^{12t}$. The expression gives the value of an account that earns annual interest rate r, after t years.

The exponent in the expression is $12t$. Since the variable t represents the number of years, the exponent represents the number of months in t years. For example, if $t = \frac{1}{2}$ or half a year, then $12t = 12 \cdot \frac{1}{2} = 6$ months. Similarly, if $t = 2$, then $12t = 12 \cdot 2 = 24$ months. This means that the exponent $12t$ converts the time since the initial deposit from years to months. Note that this relates to the expression $\frac{r}{12}$, in which 12 represents the number of times annually the interest is compounded (monthly, in this case). For $t = 1$, the initial amount 5000 is multiplied by the expression $(1 + \frac{r}{12})$ 12 times, corresponding the number of times the interest is compounded by one-twelfth the annual interest rate. [If the interest were compounded quarterly, the expression would read $5000\left(1 + \frac{r}{4}\right)^{4t}$].

In the expression $18,000(1 + r)^{20}$, what is the base of the exponent 20? Evaluate the expression for $r = 0.1, 0.4,$ and 0.7 and round to the nearest integer.

In the expression $18,000(1 + r)^{20}$, the base of the exponent 20 is $(1 + r)$, not 1 or r. This is because by the order of operations, the sum in parentheses is calculated first, and then this sum is raised to the power of 20. The last step is to then multiply this result by the coefficient 18,000. For $r = 0.1, 0.4,$ and 0.7, the expression is equal to the following values (to the nearest integer):

$$8,000(1 + r)^{20} = 18,000(1.1)^{20} \approx 121,095$$

$$18,000(1 + r)^{20} = 18,000(1.4)^{20} \approx 15,060,286$$

$$18,000(1 + r)^{20} = 18,000(1.7)^{20} \approx 731,561,653$$

Simplify the expression $\frac{2-x}{x-2}$.

To simplify a rational expression, factor both the numerator and denominator, and then simplify by noting that the ratio of identical factors equals 1. In this particular expression, the numerator is the opposite of the denominator. That is, $2 - x = -(-2 + x) = -(x - 2)$. Rewrite the numerator and then simplify:

$$\frac{2-x}{x-2} = \frac{-(x-2)}{x-2} = -1$$

The expression simplifies to -1. Note that the original expression is equal to -1 for all values of x except $x = 2$. This is because the original expression is not defined for $x = 2$: the denominator would be equal to zero in this case, and division by zero is undefined.

What is the role of the number 2 in the expression $\log_2 \frac{1}{8}$?

The given expression is a logarithm. A logarithm asks the question: "to what exponent does the base need to be raised to equal the argument?" The $\frac{1}{8}$ is the argument, and the 2 is the base of the logarithm. This means that the expression yields the value of the exponent to which 2 must be raised to equal $\frac{1}{8}$. Such an expression can be simplified using the identity $b^{(\log_b x)} = x$ as follows:

$$a = \log_2 \frac{1}{8}$$
$$2^a = 2^{\left(\log_2 \frac{1}{8}\right)}$$
$$2^a = \frac{1}{8} = \frac{1}{2^3} = 2^{-3}$$
$$a = -3$$
$$\log_2 \frac{1}{8} = -3$$

Write the leading term of the expanded form of $(3x - 1)^5$.

In order to expand a binomial that is raised to a power apply the binomial theorem. The number of terms will be equal to the exponent, which in this case is 5. The leading term contains the greatest occurring power of x, which will be x^5 in this case. Thus, to obtain the leading term, raise the x-term of the binomial to the 5th power: $(3x)^5 = 243x^5$. Then multiply the result by the first entry (corresponding to the leading term of the expansion) of the 5th row (corresponding to the exponent) of Pascal's triangle. In any row, though, the first entry is 1. Therefore the leading term of the expanded form of $(3x - 1)^5$ is $243x^5$.

How can 9 - (m + 1)² can be rewritten in factored form?

The expression 9 - (m + 1)² can be rewritten by first noting that the expression is a difference of squares. Since 9 = 3², the expression can be written as (3)² - (m + 1)². In general, a difference of squares is factored as a² - b² = (a + b)(a - b). In this case, a = 3 and b = m + 1:

$$9 - (m + 1)^2 =$$
$$3^2 - (m + 1)^2 =$$
$$(3 + m + 1)(3 - (m + 1)) =$$
$$(4 + m)(2 - m)$$

How x⁶ - y⁶ is both a difference of squares and a difference of cubes.

A difference of squares can be written as a² - b², and a difference of cubes can be written as a³ - b³. Both of these are factorable binomials. By using the property of exponents that states
(aᵐ)ⁿ = aᵐⁿ, the term x⁶ can be written as either (x²)³ or (x³)². The term y⁶ can be rewritten in a similar way. Therefore x⁶ - y⁶ = (x³)² - (y³)² and, equivalently, x⁶ - y⁶ = = (x²)³ - (y²)³. Regardless of which method is used, there is only one *completely* factored expression that is equivalent to x⁶ - y⁶. (Since one of the factors of the difference of squares method is x³ - y³,

which is itself a difference of cubes, the resulting expressions from either method are essentially equivalent).

Rewrite 2x² – 6xy – 2x + 6y in factored form.

The expression 2x² – 6xy – 2x + 6y has 4 terms, and therefore may be factorable by grouping. Group terms of like degree: group terms containing the square of a single variable or the product of two variables, for example. The GCF of the first two terms 2x² and 6xy is 2x. The GCF of the last two terms 2x and 6y is 2. Rewrite the expression as follows:
$$2x^2 - 6xy - 2x + 6y =$$
$$2x(x - 3y) - 2(x - 3y)$$

The factored parts of the expression have a common binomial factor, (x – 3y). Complete the factoring by factoring out (x – 3y):
$$2x(x - 3y) - 2(x - 3y) =$$
$$(x - 3y)(2x - 2)$$

Solve $4^{3x} = 2^{x+10}$.

Two exponential expressions are equal if they have the same base and exponent. To solve for x, rewrite the expressions so they have the same base, and then set the resulting exponents equal to each other. Because 4 = 2², rewrite 4^{3x} with a base of 2:

$$4^{3x} = 2^{x+10}$$
$$(2^2)^{3x} = 2^{x+10}$$
$$2^{6x} = 2^{x+10}$$
$$6x = x + 10$$
$$5x = 10$$
$$x = 2$$

What is the relationship between the linear factors (x – a) and (x – b) of a quadratic expression and the zeros of the related function?

If the linear factors of a quadratic expression are (x – a) and (x – b), then the quadratic function can be written as y = k(x – a)(x – b), where k is a nonzero constant. The zeros of this function are the values of x for which y = 0. Direct substitution of a or b for x makes the value of y equal to 0, so x = a and x = b are zeros of the quadratic function. Note that the value of k may affect the shape or direction of the graph of the function, but not the x-intercepts (the zeros of the function).

What are the zeros of the function y = 4x² – 10x?

The zeros of the function y = 4x² – 10x are the values of x for which y = 0. To find the zeros, factor the right side of the equation, and set y = 0:

$$y = 4x^2 - 10x$$
$$y = 2x(2x - 5)$$
$$0 = 2x(2x - 5)$$

Next, since a product is only equal to zero if at least one of the terms is zero, set the linear factors of the function $2x$ and $(2x - 5)$ equal to 0:

$$2x = 0 \qquad 2x - 5 = 0$$
$$x = 0 \qquad 2x = 5$$
$$x = \frac{5}{2}$$

The zeros of the function $y = 4x^2 - 10x$ are $x = 0$ and $x = \frac{5}{2}$.

Give an example of a quadratic function with zeros $x = 1$ and $x = -3$

If a is a zero of a quadratic function, then $(x - a)$ is a factor of the quadratic expression that defines the function. Therefore $(x - 1)$ and $(x + 3)$ are both factors of the quadratic function. Quadratic functions with these zeros therefore have the form $y = k(x - 1)(x + 3)$. The reason that this is just a form, and not a unique function, is because multiplying the two binomial factors by any nonzero constant results in another quadratic function with the same zeros. For example, the functions $y = -5(x - 1)(x + 3)$ and $y = 7(x - 1)(x + 3)$ have zeros $x = 1$ and $x = -3$.

Find the x-intercepts of $y = 9x^2 - 6x + 1$.

The x-intercepts of $y = 9x^2 - 6x + 1$ are the zeros of the function. These can be determined by first factoring the quadratic expression $9x^2 - 6x + 1$:

$$9x^2 - 6x + 1 = (3x - 1)(3x - 1) = (3x - 1)^2$$

The expression is a perfect square trinomial. Because the two factors are the same, there is only one x-intercept of the function. Set the factor equal to 0:

$$3x - 1 = 0$$
$$3x = 1$$
$$x = \frac{1}{3}$$

The x-intercept of $y = 9x^2 - 6x + 1$ is therefore $x = \frac{1}{3}$.

What is the technique of completing the square?

The quadratic expression $ax^2 + bx + c$ can always be written as the square of a linear binomial, plus some constant. This is useful to solve or graph quadratic equations or functions. The technique is as follows:

$a\left(x^2 + \frac{b}{a}x\right) + c =$ Factor a from the quadratic and linear terms.

$a\left(x^2 + \frac{b}{a}x + \frac{b^2}{4a^2}\right) + c - \frac{b^2}{4a} =$ Add the square of half the coefficient of x within the parentheses; subtract the product of that term and a outside the parentheses.

$$a\left(x + \frac{b}{2a}\right)^2 + c - \frac{b^2}{4a} =$$

Rewrite the trinomial as a perfect square.

$$a\left(x + \frac{b}{2a}\right)^2 + \frac{4ac-b^2}{4a} \qquad \text{Simplify.}$$

Complete the square to find the minimum value of $y = x^2 - 4x$.

To complete the square, first factor out the leading coefficient, the coefficient of x^2. This is 1, so no factoring is required. Next, add and subtract the square of half the coefficient of x. This value is $\left(\frac{-4}{2}\right)^2 = 4$. Finally, rewrite the first three terms as a square of a linear binomial.

$$y = x^2 - 4x$$
$$y = x^2 - 4x + 4 - 4$$
$$y = (x - 2)^2 - 4$$

The term $(x - 2)^2$ will never be negative; its minimum value is 0 (when $x = 2$). The minimum value of the function $y = (x - 2)^2 - 4$ can be found by substituting the minimum value of the squared binomial: $y_{min} = 0 - 4 = -4$.

Complete the square to find the maximum value of $y = -2x^2 + 6x$.

In order to determine the maximum value of the function, write the function in standard form by completing the square:

$$y = -2x^2 + 6x$$
$$y = -2(x^2 - 3x)$$
$$y = -2\left(x^2 - 3x + \frac{9}{4}\right) + 2 \cdot \frac{9}{4}$$
$$y = -2\left(x - \frac{3}{2}\right)^2 + \frac{9}{2}$$

Since the first term will always be negative unless it is zero (which happens at $x = 3/2$), the vertex of the graph of the function is $\left(\frac{3}{2}, \frac{9}{2}\right)$. The coefficient of x^2 is negative, so the parabola opens downward. Therefore the maximum value of the function is $\frac{9}{2}$.

The minimum value of $y = x^2 + 4bx$ is –1. Find two possible values of b.

In order to determine the vertex of the function, write the function in standard form by completing the square:

$$y = x^2 + 4bx$$
$$y = x^2 + 4bx + 4b^2 - 4b^2$$
$$y = (x + 2b)^2 - 4b^2$$

The vertex of the graph of the function is therefore $(2b, -4b^2)$. The coefficient of x^2 is positive, so the parabola opens upward. The minimum value is $-4b^2$, which must be equal to –1 in this case. Solving for b gives $b = \pm\frac{1}{2}$. The equation of the function is either $y = x^2 + 2x$ or $y = x^2 - 2x$.

The number of bacteria in a sample doubles approximately every hour. To the nearest million, by what factor does the number of bacteria increase in one day?

The situation is modeled by an exponential function. The bacteria count doubles every hour, so let t represent the number of hours. The equation $b = 2^t$ will give the number of bacteria b present after t hours. For now assume the actual number of bacteria is not important, so at $t = 0$ there is 1 bacterium. There are 24 hours in a day, so if d represents days, $t = 24d$, and the equation becomes
$b = 2^t = 2^{24d}$. This equation can be rewritten as $b = (2^{24})^d = 16{,}777{,}216^t$, which means that there are about 17 million times more bacteria each day.

Rewrite the expression 1.3^{2x} so that the only exponent present is $3x$.

In order to write the expression with an exponent of $3x$, use the properties of exponents. First, use the property $a^{mn} = (a^m)^n$ to write $1.3^{2x} = (1.3^2)^x$. The exponent can be changed to $3x$ if the expression is cubed, or raised to the power of 3. To do this without changing the value of the expression, also take the cube root, or raise to the power of $\frac{1}{3}$. This can be written as shown:

$$(1.3^2)^x = [(1.3^2)^{\frac{1}{3}}]^{3x}$$

Using a calculator, $(1.3^2)^{\frac{1}{3}} \approx 1.191$. So, $1.3^{2x} \approx 1.191^{3x}$. To check this, each expression can be evaluated for values of x to see that they are approximately equal.

The table shows the number of decibels for certain power ratios. By what factor does the power ratio increase for an increase of 1 decibel?

Decibels	Power Ratio
10	10
20	100
30	1,000

For each increase of 10 in the number of decibels, the power ratio increases by a factor of 10. Equivalently, the power ratio is equal to 10 raised to a power equal to the number of decibels divided by 10. If P represents the power ratio and d the number of decibels, then $P = 10^{\frac{d}{10}}$. To determine the factor for an increase of 1 decibel, rewrite the equation as $P = 10^{\frac{d}{10}} = (10^{\frac{1}{10}})^d$. Using a calculator, $10^{\frac{1}{10}} \approx 1.259$, so the power ratio increases by a factor of about 1.259 for an increase of 1 decibel.

A cable company has 12,000 current customers. They begin to lose 3% of their current customers each year. On average, about what percent of their customers do they lose each month?

The situation is modeled by an exponential decay function. The number of customers decreases by 3%, or equivalently is multiplied by 0.97 each year. The equation $c = 12{,}000(0.97)^t$ will give the number of customers c present after t years. There are 12 months in a year, so if m represents months, the equation becomes $c = 12{,}000(0.97)^{\frac{m}{12}}$. This equation can be rewritten as $= 12{,}000(0.97^{\frac{1}{12}})^m$ or $c \approx 12{,}000(0.997)^m$, which means that the cable company loses a factor of (1 − 0.997), or about 0.3%, of its current customers each month.

What is the common ratio of a geometric series?

A series is a sum (finite or infinite) of terms of a (finite or infinite) sequence. The series is called *geometric* if the ratio of any term to the preceding term is the same value. This value is called the *common ratio* of the geometric series. For example, in the finite sum 3 + 6 + 12 + 24 + 48, the ratio of any term to the previous term is 2. Therefore, the series is a finite geometric series with a common ratio of 2.

Derive the formula for the sum S of the first (n +1) terms of a finite geometric series given by the equation $S = a + ar + ar^2 + \ldots + ar^n$, where $r \neq 1$.

Write the equation for the sum, and then multiply each side by r:

$S = a + ar + ar^2 + \ldots + ar^n$
$rS = (a + ar + ar^2 + \ldots + ar^n)r$
$rS = ar + ar^2 + ar^3 + \ldots + ar^n + ar^{n+1}$

If the first equation above is subtracted from the third equation, many of the terms will cancel. In fact, the only unique terms are the term a in the first equation and the term ar^{n+1} in the other. Subtract the equations and solve for S to obtain the formula for the sum of the first (n + 1) terms of a finite geometric series:

$rS - S = ar^{n+1} - a$
$S(r - 1) = a(r^{n+1} - 1)$

$$S = \frac{a(r^{n+1} - 1)}{r - 1}$$

Is $8 - 8\left(\frac{1}{2}\right) + 8\left(\frac{1}{2}\right)^2 - 8\left(\frac{1}{2}\right)^3 + \cdots - 8\left(\frac{1}{2}\right)^7$ a finite geometric series?

Yes, the series $8 - 8\left(\frac{1}{2}\right) + 8\left(\frac{1}{2}\right)^2 - 8\left(\frac{1}{2}\right)^3 + \cdots - 8\left(\frac{1}{2}\right)^7$ is a finite geometric series with a common ratio of $-\frac{1}{2}$. When the common ratio of a geometric series is negative, the signs of the terms alternate. This is because even powers of a negative number result in a positive value, and odd powers of a negative number result in a negative value. Also, as required by a geometric series, the ratio of any term and the preceding term will always be $-\frac{1}{2}$, since the ratio has one positive and one negative term. (Any series that has consecutive negative terms must therefore have only negative terms. This occurs when the coefficient of each term is negative, not when the common ration is negative.)

In the formula below, x represents the monthly interest rate and L the loan amount for a 30-year mortgage with a monthly payment P.

$$L = P\left(\frac{1}{1+x} + \frac{1}{(1+x)^2} + \cdots + \frac{1}{(1+x)^{360}}\right)$$

Find the monthly payment for a $250,000 loan with an annual interest rate of 6%.

The part of the equation in parentheses is a geometric series with common ratio $\frac{1}{1+x}$. Use the general formula for the sum of the first n terms of a finite geometric series, $S_n = \frac{a(1-r^n)}{1-r}$, to rewrite the equation, where a is the first term and r is the common ratio. Then solve for P:

$$L = P\left(\frac{1}{1+x} + \frac{1}{(1+x)^2} + \cdots + \frac{1}{(1+x)^{360}}\right)$$

$$= P\left(\frac{\frac{1}{1+x}\left(1-\left(\frac{1}{1+x}\right)^{360}\right)}{1-\frac{1}{1+x}}\right) = P\left(\frac{\frac{1}{1+x} - \left(\frac{1}{1+x}\right)^{361}}{1-\frac{1}{1+x}}\right)$$

$$P = L\left(\frac{1-\frac{1}{1+x}}{\frac{1}{1+x} - \left(\frac{1}{1+x}\right)^{361}}\right)$$

Since x represents the monthly interest rate, $x = \frac{0.06}{12} = 0.005$. Substituting this for x and 250,000 for L gives $P = \$1498.88$, rounded to the nearest cent.

Polynomials are closed under multiplication.

For a set to have closure under a particular operation, applying the operation to two elements of the set must result in a member of the set. This means that the product of any two polynomials results in another polynomial. This is correct, because every term of a polynomial in x is of the form ax^n, where a is a real number and n is a nonnegative integer. The product of any two such terms would be $ax^m \cdot bx^n = abx^{m+n}$, where ab is a real number and $m + n$ is a nonnegative integer. The last statement relies on the fact that real numbers are closed under multiplication, and nonnegative integers are closed under addition.

Subtract the polynomial $3x^2 - 4x + 1$ from the polynomial $-2x^2 - x + 5$.

To subtract polynomials, subtract like terms. Like terms have the same variable part, such as $3x^2$ and $-2x^2$, which are both are x^2 terms. To find the difference of like terms, find the difference of the coefficients, and retain the same variable part. You can use the distributive property to first distribute the subtraction to each term of the polynomial that is being subtracted.

$$(-2x^2 - x + 5) - (3x^2 - 4x + 1) =$$
$$(-2x^2 - x + 5) - 3x^2 + 4x - 1 =$$
$$(-2x^2 - 3x^2) + (-x + 4x) + (5 - 1) =$$
$$-5x^2 + 3x + 4$$

Is the sum of two cubic polynomials also a cubic polynomial?

The sum of two cubic polynomials is not necessarily a cubic polynomial. However, it is either a cubic polynomial or a polynomial of lesser degree. The sum of two cubic polynomials of the form $ax^3 + bx^2 + cx + d$, where $a \neq 0$, will have the same form, however it is possible that individual like terms are opposites and have a sum of 0. For example, the sum of $-3x^3 + 2x - 3$ and $3x^3 + 5x^2$ is $5x^2 + 2x - 3$, which is a quadratic polynomial. (Notice that coefficients b, c, and d in the cubic polynomial form are each allowed to equal zero; that is, cubic polynomials can be missing any of the terms with degree less than 3.)

Multiply a binomial and a trinomial

To multiply a binomial and a trinomial, use the distributive property. Because a binomial has 2 terms and a trinomial has 3 terms, there will be 2·3 = 6 multiplications when multiplying the polynomials. In the example below, each term of the binomial is multiplied by the entire trinomial. Then, that multiplication is distributed to each term of the trinomial. In the final steps, like terms are combined and the answer is expressed in standard form, with terms written in order of descending degree.

$(x + 2)(x^2 - 3x + 9) = x(x^2 - 3x + 9) + 2(x^2 - 3x + 9) =$
$x^3 - 3x^2 + 9x + 2x^2 - 6x + 18 =$
$x^3 - x^2 + 3x + 18$

What is the Remainder Theorem for polynomials?

The Remainder Theorem for polynomials states that for a polynomial $P(x)$ and a real number a, the remainder when $P(x)$ is divided by $(x - a)$ is $P(a)$, the value of the polynomial evaluated at $x = a$. If there is no remainder, that is if the remainder equals 0, then $P(a) = 0$ and $(x - a)$ is a factor of the polynomial $P(x)$. For example, if $P(x) = (2x - 3)(3x + 1)$, this can be written as $P(x) = 6(x - \frac{3}{2})(x + \frac{1}{3})$. Here $P\left(\frac{3}{2}\right) = 0$ and $P\left(\frac{1}{3}\right) = 0$, so that the remainder is zero when $P(x)$ is divided by $(x - \frac{3}{2})$ and $(x + \frac{1}{3})$; $(x - \frac{3}{2})$ and $(x + \frac{1}{3})$ are therefore factors of $P(x)$.

On the other hand, the Remainder Theorem also can be used to obtain the remainder when the above $P(x)$ is divided by any binomial, such as $(x - 4)$:

$$\text{Rem}\left[\frac{P(x)}{x-4}\right] = P(4) = (2(4) - 3)(3(4) + 1)$$
$$= (8 - 3)(12 + 1) = 5 \cdot 13 = 65$$

When a polynomial $P(x)$ is divided by $(x + 2)$, the remainder is –4. What is the value of $P(-2)$?

To solve this question, apply the Remainder Theorem for polynomials. The Remainder Theorem states that for a polynomial $P(x)$ and a real number a, the remainder when $P(x)$ is divided by
$(x - a)$ is $P(a)$. Since $P(x)$ was divided by the factor $(x + 2)$, let $a = -2$ in the theorem. This means that $P(a) = P(-2)$, and this is equal to the remainder. Since the remainder is –4, it must be that
$P(-2) = -4$. Note that it is not required to explicitly know the polynomial $P(x)$ or even its degree to apply the remainder theorem.

Divide the polynomial $x^2 + 2x - 4$ by $(x - 3)$. Verify the Remainder Theorem by evaluating the polynomial at $x = 3$.

Divide the polynomial $x^2 + 2x - 4$ by $(x - 3)$ using synthetic or long division:

```
3 | 1  2  -4              x  -  5
    3  15          x - 3 | x² + 2x - 4
    1  5  11             - x² + 3x
                               5x - 4
                               5x + 15
                                    R 11
```

In either case, the remainder is 11. By the Remainder Theorem, for a polynomial $P(x)$ and a real number a, the remainder when $P(x)$ is divided by $(x - a)$ is $P(a)$. In this case, this means the remainder when $x^2 + 2x - 4$ is divided by $(x - 3)$ must be $P(3)$. Verify that $P(3) = 11$ by substituting $x = 3$ into the polynomial:
$(3)^2 + 2(3) - 4 = 9 + 6 - 4 = 11$

Let $P(x)$ be a cubic polynomial function such that $P(2) = P(-1) = P(4) = 0$. If the y-intercept of $P(x)$ is 2, what is the equation for $P(x)$?

By the Remainder Theorem, for a polynomial $P(x)$ and a real number a, the remainder when $P(x)$ is divided by $(x - a)$ is $P(a)$. This means that, since their remainders when divided into $P(x)$ are all zero, $(x - 2)$, $(x + 1)$, and $(x - 4)$ are factors of $P(x)$. Because $P(x)$ is a cubic polynomial function, it must then be of the form $P(x) = a(x - 2)(x + 1)(x - 4)$, where a is some real number. To determine a, use the fact that the y-intercept is 2, which means that $P(0) = 2$:

$$P(x) = a(x - 2)(x + 1)(x - 4)$$
$$P(0) = 2 = a(0 - 2)(0 + 1)(0 - 4) = 8a$$
$$2 = 8a$$
$$a = ¼$$

The equation for $P(x)$, then, is $P(x) = \frac{1}{4}(x - 2)(x + 1)(x - 4)$.

Find the zeros of $y = 2x^2 + 3x - 5$ by factoring.

The zeros of $y = 2x^2 + 3x - 5$ are the values of x for which $y = 0$. These are also the x-intercepts of the graph of the function. Factor $2x^2 + 3x - 5$ and rewrite the equation as $y = (2x + 5)(x - 1)$. In factored form, the zeros are found by setting each linear factor equal to zero:

$2x - 5 = 0$ $x - 1 = 0$
$2x = 5$ $x = 1$
$x = \frac{5}{2}$

The zeros of $y = 2x^2 + 3x - 5$ are $x = 1$ and $x = \frac{5}{2}$.

Long division for polynomials.

Long division for polynomials is similar to long division of integers. For example, when dividing 385 by 12, you first determine how many times 12 goes into 38 (and write 3 as the corresponding digit of the quotient). Then you subtract 36 from 38, giving 2, and the 5 is brought down to form 25, and so on. With polynomial division, the first term written for the quotient is equal to the first term of the dividend divided by the first term of the divisor. For example, if $5x^2 + 10x + 3$ is being divided by $x - 2$, the first term for the quotient is $\frac{5x^2}{x} = 5x$. $5x$ times $x - 2$ is $5x^2 - 10x$, and then $5x^2 - 10x$ is subtracted from $5x^2 + 10x$, yielding $20x$; the 3 is then brought down to form $20x + 3$. This process continues until the remainder is determined.

Find the remainder when $2b^2 + 3b + 2$ is divided by $2b + 1$.

The remainder when $2b^2 + 3b + 2$ is divided by $2b + 1$ can be found by long division. To divide polynomials using long division, find the first term of the quotient by dividing $2b^2$ by $2b$, which gives b. Multiply this by the divisor to get $2b^2 + b$, and then subtract this result from the first two terms of the dividend to obtain $2b$. Then bring down the $+2$ to form $2b + 2$, and continue in this way. The complete division is shown below.

When the degree of the result after a subtraction is less than that of the divisor, the result is the remainder. So, the remainder is 1, and $2b^2 + 3b + 2$ divided by $2b + 1$ is equal to $b + 1 + \frac{1}{2b+1}$.
(Note: synthetic division cannot be used in this case, since the divisor is not a linear factor.)

Rewrite the rational expression $\frac{3x^3 + 2x^2}{x}$ by inspection.

The rational expression has a monomial for a denominator. This means that when each term of the numerator is divided by the denominator, the result of each division can be found by applying properties of exponents. In particular, the property $\frac{x^n}{x^m} = x^{n-m}$ can be used to rewrite each term as shown:

$$\frac{3x^3 + 2x^2}{x} = \frac{3x^3}{x} + \frac{2x^2}{x} = 3x^2 + 2x$$

The polynomial $3x^2 + 2x$ is equivalent to the original rational expression. Note that the only exception is the value $x = 0$, because the original rational expression is undefined for $x = 0$.

Add the expressions $\frac{1}{x+1} + \frac{x}{x+1}$ and simplify the result.

To add rational expressions, first obtain a common denominator. Then add the numerators, and keep the same denominator. Since the denominator of each expression is $x + 1$, the expressions can be added directly:

$$\frac{1}{x+1} + \frac{x}{x+1} = \frac{1+x}{x+1}$$

The expressions 1 + x and x + 1 are equivalent. By dividing the numerator and denominator by x + 1, the expression can be further simplified:

$$\frac{1+x}{x+1} = \frac{x+1}{x+1} = 1$$

The sum of the rational expressions is equal to 1. This is true for all values of x except x = −1, since the original expressions are undefined for x = −1.

What is the least common denominator of $\frac{3x}{x^2-x-6}$ and $\frac{2x}{x^2-6x+9}$?

To determine the least common denominator, or LCD, of two rational expressions, factor the denominators completely. The LCD is equal to the product of the greatest occurring power of each unique factor.

$x^2 - x - 6 = (x - 3)(x + 2)$
$x^2 - 6x + 9 = (x - 3)^2$

The unique factors are (x + 2) and (x − 3). The greatest occurring power of (x − 3) is 2. Therefore the LCD of the two expressions is
$(x + 2)(x - 3)^2$.

Multiply the expressions $\frac{1-x}{x^2+2x+1}$ and $\frac{5}{x^2-1}$. Simplify the result.

To multiply two rational expressions, multiply the numerators to obtain the new numerator, and multiply the denominators to obtain the new denominator:

$$\frac{1-x}{x^2+2x+1} \cdot \frac{5}{x^2-1} = \frac{5(1-x)}{(x^2+2x+1)(x^2-1)}$$

To simplify the result, factor the numerator and denominator completely. The factor 1 − x in the numerator can be rewritten as −(x − 1), and the common factor (x − 1) in the numerator and denominator can be cancelled:

$$\frac{5(1-x)}{(x^2+2x+1)(x^2-1)} = \frac{-5(x-1)}{(x+1)(x+1)(x+1)(x-1)} = \frac{-5}{(x+1)^3}$$

Note that this expression is equivalent to the original product for all x except x = ±1, since the original expressions are undefined for these values.

Rational expressions are closed under subtraction using closure properties of polynomials.

Rational expressions are closed under subtraction if the difference of any two rational expressions results in a rational expression. Consider two rational expressions $\frac{a(x)}{b(x)}$ and $\frac{c(x)}{d(x)}$, where a(x), b(x), c(x), and d(x) are polynomials. Their difference can be written as follows:

$$\frac{a(x)}{b(x)} - \frac{c(x)}{d(x)} = \frac{a(x) \cdot d(x) - b(x) \cdot c(x)}{b(x) \cdot d(x)}$$

Since polynomials are closed under multiplication, the products in the right side of the equation (including the denominator) are all polynomials. Since polynomials are closed under subtraction, the numerator is also a polynomial. So, the expression is a ratio of polynomials and is therefore a rational expression.

What are the coefficients of the x^2 term, x term, and constant term of the quadratic expression $(2x - 3)(x + 4)$?

To find the coefficients of the x^2 term, x term, and constant term, the quadratic expression must be written in the form $ax^2 + bx + c$. The real numbers a, b, and c are the coefficients. Multiplying the binomials of the factor form gives $2x^2 - 3x + 8x - 12$, and combining like terms $-3x$ and $8x$ yields $2x^2 + 5x - 12$. The coefficient of the x^2 term is 2, the coefficient of the x term is 5, and constant term
is -12.

When does the expression $\frac{-b \pm \sqrt{b^2 - 4ac}}{2a}$ represent a unique number?

The expression $\frac{-b \pm \sqrt{b^2 - 4ac}}{2a}$ gives the solutions to the quadratic equation $ax^2 + bx + c = 0$. The plus or minus symbol, $\pm$, means that one solution is attained by adding the radical term $\sqrt{b^2 - 4ac}$ in the numerator and the other solution is attained by subtracting it. For this reason, if the radical term is equal to zero, the entire expression is equal to the (unique) value $\frac{-b}{2a}$. (The radical term is equal to zero if the radicand is equal to zero, that is if $b^2 = 4ac$.)

Factor the expression $x^2 + 2x + 1 - y^2$ by first recognizing a perfect square trinomial.

The first three terms of the expression, $x^2 + 2x + 1$, represent a perfect square trinomial. This means it factors into two identical binomials. The factorization is $x^2 + 2x + 1 = (x + 1)^2$. Therefore the original expression can be rewritten as $(x + 1)^2 - y^2$, which is a difference of squares. Using the fact $a^2 - b^2 = (a + b)(a - b)$, and setting $a = x + 1$ and $b = y$, the expression $(x + 1)^2 - y^2$ factors as $(x + 1 - y)(x + 1 + y)$.

Find the vertex of the parabola with equation $y = 2x^2 - 4x - 3$.

To find the vertex of the parabola, rewrite the quadratic equation in the form $y = a(x - p)^2 + q$ by completing the square. The point (p, q) is the vertex of the parabola:

$$y = 2x^2 - 4x - 3$$
$$y = 2(x^2 - 2x) - 3$$
$$y = 2(x^2 - 2x + 1) - 3 - 2$$
$$y = 2(x - 1)^2 - 5$$

The vertex of the parabola is $(1, -5)$.

Alternatively, recall the x-coordinate of the vertex is given by $-b/2a$, which in this case is $-(-4)/(2 \cdot 2) = 1$. Substitute this in for x to obtain $y = 2 \cdot 1^2 - 4 \cdot 1 - 3 = -5$. As before, the vertex is at point
$(1, -5)$.

What are the x-intercepts of $y = x^2 - 4x$?

The x-intercepts, or zeros, of the function occur at the values of x that make y = 0, that is, when $x^2 - 4x = 0$. A quadratic function can have 0, 1, or 2 x-intercepts. Factor the given expression to get $x(x - 4) = 0$. Since the product of the two factors is equal to zero, either x = 0 or x - 4 = 0. Therefore the quadratic has two x-intercepts, x = 0 and x = 4.

Solve for b: $6(4)^b = 3(2)^b$.

The variable b appears in the equation as an exponent. Rewrite the equation so that each side has the same base, then equate the exponent expressions:
$6(4)^b = 3(2)^b$
$3 \cdot 2(4)^b = 3(2)^b$
$2(4)^b = 2^b$
$2^1(2^2)^b = 2^b$
$2^{1+2b} = 2^b$
$1 + 2b = b$
$b = -1$

The value of b is –1.

Find the sum $4 + 4(2) + 4(2)^2 + 4(2)^3 + \ldots + 4(2)^8$.

The sum represents a finite geometric series. The common ratio r of the series is 2, and the first term a_1 of the series is 4. Note that the first two terms can be written with exponents as $4(2)^0$ and $4(2)^1$. Use the formula for the sum of the first n terms of a finite geometric series $S_n = \frac{a_1(1-r^n)}{1-r}$, where n is equal to 1 more than the greatest power of r in the series:

$$S_9 = \frac{a_1(1-r^9)}{1-r} = \frac{4(1-(2)^9)}{1-2} = \frac{-2044}{-1} = 2044$$

The sum of the series is 2044.

Prove that polynomials are not closed under division.

Polynomials are additions, subtractions and/or multiplication (but not division by variables) of variable expressions containing only non-negative integer exponents. To prove that polynomials are not closed under division, use a counterexample. Assume that polynomials are closed under division. This means the quotient $(x + 1) \div x = \frac{x+1}{x} = 1 + \frac{1}{x} = 1 + x^{-1}$ would have to be a polynomial. This expression, however, is not a polynomial, because the term x^{-1} contains a negative exponent (or would have to be written as the division by x). All terms of a polynomial must be of the form ax^n, where a is a real number and n is a non-negative integer. Although there are *some* quotients of polynomials that are polynomials, closure requires this to be true for *all* polynomials.

If $p(x)$ is a polynomial and $\frac{p(x)}{x-3}$ leaves a reminder of –6, what is $p(3)$?

By the Remainder Theorem, for a polynomial $p(x)$ and a real number a, the remainder when $p(x)$ is divided by $(x - a)$ is $p(a)$. In the given equation, $p(x)$ is divided by the binomial x – 3,

The diagram at right shows a rectangle inside an equilateral triangle with side length 10 units. One side of the rectangle is part of a side of the triangle. Find the maximum area of the rectangle.

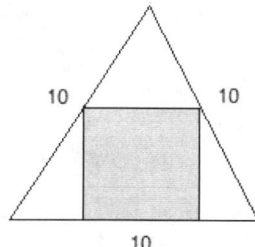

Place the figure on the coordinate plane as shown below. By the Pythagorean Theorem, then, the height of the triangle is $5\sqrt{3}$ units ($10^2 - 5^2 = 75 = \sqrt{75}^2 = \sqrt{25 \cdot 3}^2 = (5\sqrt{3})^2$. The equation of the line that represents the right side of the triangle is $y = -x\sqrt{3} + 5\sqrt{3}$, since the slope is $\frac{\Delta y}{\Delta x} = \frac{0 - 5\sqrt{3}}{5} = -\sqrt{3}$, and the y-intercept is $5\sqrt{3}$. The area of the rectangle is then given by $A = xy = x(-x\sqrt{3} + 5\sqrt{3}) = -x^2\sqrt{3} + 5x\sqrt{3}$. This equation represents a parabola that opens down, with maximum value at the vertex. The x-value of the vertex of a general parabola is given by $-b/2a$, and is therefore $\frac{-5\sqrt{3}}{-2\sqrt{3}} = \frac{5}{2}$, so the maximum area (the value of the area function A at that x-value, is therefore equal to: $-\left(\frac{5}{2}\right)^2 \sqrt{3} + 5\left(\frac{5}{2}\right)\sqrt{3} = \frac{-25\sqrt{3}}{4} + \frac{25\sqrt{3}}{2} = \frac{25\sqrt{3}}{4}$ square units

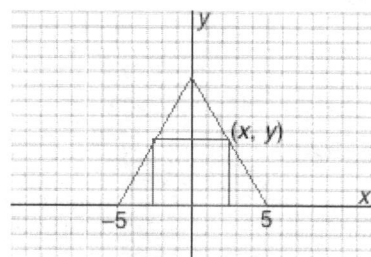

Solve the equation $\frac{1}{R_1} + \frac{1}{R_2} = 2$ for R_1.

To solve a rational equation for which the variable of interest in in the denominator, multiply the equation by the LCD, or least common denominator. The LCD of this equation is $R_1 R_2$. The rest of the algebra is shown here:

$$\frac{1}{R_1} + \frac{1}{R_2} = 2$$
$$R_1 R_2 \left(\frac{1}{R_1} + \frac{1}{R_2}\right) = 2 R_1 R_2$$
$$R_2 + R_1 = 2 R_1 R_2$$
$$R_2 = 2 R_1 R_2 - R_1$$
$$R_2 = R_1 (2 R_2 - 1)$$

$$R_1 = \frac{R_2}{2R_2 - 1}$$

Rearrange the formula $I = P(1+r)^t$ by solving for P.

In the formula $I = P(1+r)^t$, I is equal to the product of the two expressions P and $(1+r)^t$. The exponent t does not apply to the variable P. To solve for P means to isolate P on one side of the equation, with no P appearing on the other side of the equation. To do this, divide each side by $(1+r)^t$:

$$I = P(1+r)^t$$
$$P = \frac{I}{(1+r)^t}$$

Write the linear equation $AX + By = C$ solved for y. State any restrictions.

The equation $AX + By = C$ is the standard form of a linear equation in two variables. To solve for y, isolate y on one side of the equation, and divide the equation by the coefficient of y:

$$Ax + By = C$$
$$By = -Ax + C$$
$$y = -\frac{A}{B}x + \frac{C}{B}$$

The restriction on the transformed equation is that $B \neq 0$. This is because division by zero is undefined.

A farm stand sells vegetables and dairy products. One third of the sales from dairy products plus half of the sales from vegetables should exceed the monthly payment P for the farm. Show variables and write an inequality

Let d represent the sales from dairy products, and v represent the sales from vegetables. One third of the sales from dairy products is given by the expression $\frac{d}{3}$. One half of the sales from vegetables is given by the expression $\frac{v}{2}$. The sum of these expressions should exceed the monthly payment for the farm, represented by P. An inequality expressing this situation is $\frac{d}{3} + \frac{v}{2} > P$.

Sam can write 8 invitations in 20 minutes. With Jane's help, together they can write 30 invitations in 45 minutes. About how many more invitations per hour can Sam write than Jane?

The rate at which Sam can write invitations can be readily expressed in invitations per minute: $\frac{8 \text{ invitations}}{20 \text{ minutes}} = \frac{8}{20} \frac{\text{invitations}}{\text{minute}} = \frac{2}{5} \frac{\text{invitations}}{\text{minute}}$.

Convert this to invitations per hour: $\frac{2}{5} \frac{\text{invitations}}{\text{minute}} \cdot \left(\frac{60 \text{ minutes}}{1 \text{ hour}}\right) = 24 \frac{\text{invitations}}{\text{hour}}$.

Similarly, 30 invitations in 45 minutes is equivalent to 40 invitations per hour. If Jane writes x invitations per hour, then $24 + x = 40$. Subtract 24 from each side to get $x = 16$. Sam can write $24 - 16$ or 8 more invitations per hour than Jane.

Dina will meet her friend at the library in t minutes. She must first bicycle back home 3 miles, leave the bike, and then walk 0.5 miles to the library. Dina can bicycle 3 times as fast as she can walk. If Dina walks w miles per hour, write an equation relating t and w.

The equation $d = rt$ can be rewritten as $t = \frac{d}{r}$. An expression for the time needed to walk is $\frac{0.5}{w}$, where w represents the rate at which Dina walks. Similarly, an expression for the time needed to bicycle is $\frac{3}{3w} = \frac{1}{w}$, where $3w$ represents the rate at which Dina bicycles, which is 3 times her walking rate w. The total time that Dina has to walk and bicycle is t minutes. The sum of the two expressions for time must therefore equal t. An equation relating t and w is $\frac{0.5}{w} + \frac{1}{w} = t$, or $\frac{1.5}{w} = t$.

Write an equation that gives the radius r of a cylinder in terms of its height h and volume V.

The formula for the volume of a cylinder with radius r and height h is $V = \pi r^2 h$. To solve for r, first isolate r^2 by dividing each side of the equation by πh. Then take the square root of each side, so the equation has only r on one side.

$$V = \pi r^2 h$$
$$\frac{V}{\pi h} = r^2$$
$$\sqrt{\frac{V}{\pi h}} = r$$

(The values of r, V, and h are all positive, so a plus-or-minus sign (±) is not needed when taking the square root.)

Construct a viable argument to show the solution to the equation $|1 - x| = |x - 1|$ is all real numbers.

Assuming there is a solution to the equation, there are two possibilities. Either $1 - x = x - 1$, or $1 - x = -(x - 1)$. In other words, the expressions inside absolute value signs are either equal or opposite in value. Assume that $1 - x = x - 1$ has a solution, and that the expressions equal the same real number. Then adding $x + 1$ to each side will give two expressions equal to a new same real number. Doing this results in the equation $2 = 2x$, and dividing by 2 gives $1 = x$. Assume also that $1 - x = -(x - 1)$ has a solution, or equivalently $1 - x = -x + 1$. Adding x to each side gives $1 = 1$, which is always true. Therefore x can equal any real number.

The reciprocal of a number is 0.45 more than the number. Find the number.

Let n represent the unknown number. Then the reciprocal of this number, assuming the number is not zero, is given by the expression $\frac{1}{n}$. This number is 0.45 more than the original number, or $\frac{1}{n} = 0.45 + n$.

$$\frac{1}{n} = 0.45 + n$$

$$n\left(\frac{1}{n}\right) = n(0.45 + n)$$
$$1 = 0.45n + n^2$$

This equation could be solved using the quadratic formula, but also through factoring:

$$100n^2 + 45n - 100 = 0$$
$$20n^2 + 9n - 20 = 0$$
$$(4n + 5)(5n - 4) = 0$$
$$n = -\frac{5}{4} \text{ or } n = \frac{4}{5}$$

There are two possible values of n, $-\frac{5}{4}$ and $\frac{4}{5}$.

Solve the equation 2(3 − (4 − x) − 3x) = 4.

To solve the equation, use the Distributive Property. First, distribute the subtraction that is inside the parentheses:
2(3 − (4 − x) − 3x) = 4

2(3 − 4 + x − 3x) = 4

Next, simplify the expression inside the parentheses by combining like terms:
2(3 − 4 + x − 3x) = 4
2(−1 − 2x) = 4

Distribute one more time, and then isolate x:
2(−1 − 2x) = 4
−2 − 4x = 4
−4x = 6

$$x = -\frac{3}{2}$$

Ron completes the square of the expression 3x² − 10x by writing the equivalent expression 3(x − 5)² − $\frac{25}{3}$. Is Ron correct?

Ron is not correct. This is evident by noting that while the original expression does not have a constant term, Ron's answer will have the constants 75 and $\frac{25}{3}$ in it, which are not opposites so their sum is not zero. This breaks the equality the method of completing the square preserves. Ron should have proceeded as follows:

$$3x^2 - 10x =$$
$$3\left(x^2 - \frac{10}{3}x\right) =$$
$$3\left(x^2 - \frac{10}{3}x + \left(\frac{1}{2} \cdot \frac{10}{3}\right)^2\right) - 3\left(\frac{1}{2} \cdot \frac{10}{3}\right)^2 =$$
$$33\left(x^2 - \frac{10}{3}x + \left(\frac{10}{6}\right)^2\right) - 3\left(\frac{10}{6}\right)^2 = 3\left(x^2 - \frac{10}{3}x + \frac{25}{9}\right) - \frac{25}{3} =$$

$$3\left(x - \frac{5}{3}\right)^2 - \frac{25}{3}$$

Show that the quadratic formula and factoring give the same solution set for the equation $x^2 - 3x + 2 = 0$.

To factor the equation, find two numbers with a product of 2 and a sum of −3. The numbers are −1 and −2, so $x^2 - 3x + 2 = (x - 1)(x - 2)$, and the equation becomes $(x - 1)(x - 2) = 0$, and the solutions are {1, 2}. The quadratic formula, with $a = 1$, $b = -3$, and $c = 2$, gives:

$$x = \frac{-b \pm \sqrt{b^2 - 4ac}}{2a} =$$
$$\frac{3 \pm \sqrt{(-3)^2 - 4(1)(2)}}{2(1)} =$$
$$\frac{3 \pm \sqrt{1}}{2}$$
$$\therefore x = \frac{3+1}{2}, \frac{3-1}{2}$$

The two expressions are equal to 2 and 1, so the solution is the same.

Solve the linear system $\begin{cases} x - y = -3 \\ 2x + 6 = 2y \end{cases}$

The second equation can be simplified by dividing by 2. This gives the equation $x + 3 = y$. The first equation can be rewritten as $x + 3 = y$. Since these are the same equation, there are infinitely many solutions. To verify this, substitute $x + 3$ for y in the first equation to create an equation with only x as a variable:

$$x - y = -3$$
$$x - (x + 3) = -3$$
$$x - x - 3 = -3$$
$$-3 = -3$$

The equation that results is always true. This means that the two equations that make up the system are the same equation. There are therefore infinitely many solutions, and the solution can be written $\{(x, y) \mid x - y = -3\}$. (Graphically, this solution describes a line.)

Solve the system $\begin{cases} x - y^2 = 2 \\ x + y = 4 \end{cases}$

Solve the first equation for x. This gives $x = y^2 + 2$, and the expression $y^2 + 2$ can be substituted into the second equation, which can then be solved for y:

$x + y = 4$
$y^2 + 2 + y = 4$
$y^2 + y - 2 = 0$
$(y + 2)(y - 1) = 0$
$y = -2$ or $y = 1$

If $y = -2$, then $x = 6$. If $y = 1$, then $x = 3$. There are two solutions of the system, $(6, -2)$ and $(3, 1)$. Each solution makes both equations of the system true.

Write the linear system represented by the matrix equation.
$$\begin{bmatrix} 1 & 0 & -1 \\ 0 & 4 & 2 \\ -1 & 3 & 3 \end{bmatrix} \begin{bmatrix} x \\ y \\ z \end{bmatrix} = \begin{bmatrix} 1 \\ -2 \\ 5 \end{bmatrix}$$

By multiplying the matrices on the left, a 3 by 1 matrix is formed. Each entry of this matrix is equal to the corresponding entry in the matrix $\begin{bmatrix} 1 \\ -2 \\ 5 \end{bmatrix}$. Multiplying the first row of $\begin{bmatrix} 1 & 0 & -1 \\ 0 & 4 & 2 \\ -1 & 3 & 3 \end{bmatrix}$ by the column matrix $\begin{bmatrix} x \\ y \\ z \end{bmatrix}$ gives the expression $x - z$. Multiplying the second row of $\begin{bmatrix} 1 & 0 & -1 \\ 0 & 4 & 2 \\ -1 & 3 & 3 \end{bmatrix}$ by the column matrix $\begin{bmatrix} x \\ y \\ z \end{bmatrix}$ gives the expression $4y + 2z$. Multiplying the third row of $\begin{bmatrix} 1 & 0 & -1 \\ 0 & 4 & 2 \\ -1 & 3 & 3 \end{bmatrix}$ by the column matrix $\begin{bmatrix} x \\ y \\ z \end{bmatrix}$ gives the expression $-x + 3y + 3z$. These three equations are equal to 1, -2, and 5, respectively. The linear system is therefore
$$\begin{cases} x - z = 1 \\ 4y + 2z = -2 \\ -x + 3y + 3z = 5 \end{cases}$$

The inverse of the matrix $\begin{bmatrix} a & -4 \\ 7 & -2 \end{bmatrix}$ does not exist. What is the value of a?

In order for the inverse of the matrix $\begin{bmatrix} a & -4 \\ 7 & -2 \end{bmatrix}$ to not exist, its determinant must be zero. The determinant of a 2 by 2 matrix $\begin{bmatrix} a & b \\ c & d \end{bmatrix}$ is given by the expression $ad - bc$. Write an equation that represents this situation:

$-2(a) - 7(-4) = 0$
$-2a = -28$
$a = 14$

The value of a is 14. For any other value of a, the matrix would have an inverse.

Find two exact solutions of $\frac{1}{x^2+1} = 2^x$ using a graphing calculator. Verify the solutions are true.

The solutions can be found by graphing the equations $y = \frac{1}{x^2+1}$ and $y = 2^x$ on a graphing calculator. The intersection points, if there are any, will have x-coordinates that are solutions to the equation. The graphs appear to intersect at the points $(0, 2)$ and $(-1, 0.5)$. Therefore the two solutions of the equation are $x = 0$ and $x = -1$.

Substitute to verify the solutions:

$$\frac{1}{x^2+1} = 2^x \qquad\qquad \frac{1}{(-1)^2+1} = 2^{-1}$$
$$\frac{1}{0^2+1} = 2^0 \qquad\qquad \frac{1}{1+1} = \frac{1}{2}$$
$$1 = 1 \qquad\qquad\qquad \frac{1}{2} = \frac{1}{2}$$

Give an example of a system of two linear inequalities in two variables that has no solution.

A linear inequality in two variables will have a solution described by a half-plane; that is, by the entire region of the plane that is either above or below the line described by the corresponding linear equation. A system of two inequalities will have a solution region that is the intersection of the two half-planes. Therefore, a system that has no solution can be created by choosing lines that are parallel, and choosing the half-planes on opposite sides of the two lines, so there is no intersection. An example is the system

$$\begin{cases} y < 2x + 1 \\ y > 2x + 4 \end{cases}$$

Solve $3x - 2 = -5$ by first assuming the solution exists. Explicitly justify each step.

Assume that the solution exists, and that each side of the equation represents the same real number. In this case, that real number is –5, since the right side of the equation is –5. Adding 2 to each side results in two more equal numbers. So, the equation can be transformed as follows:
$3x - 2 = -5$
$3x - 2 + 2 = -5 + 2$
$3x = -3$

The same approach can be taken with the new equation. Since each side of the equation represents the same real number, divide each side by 3:
$$3x = -3$$
$$\frac{3x}{3} = \frac{-3}{3}$$
$$x = -1$$

The solution of the equation is $x = -1$.

Tom says the equation $3x = 5x$ has no solution. Find his error.

Tom made an error, because the correct (and only) solution is $x = 0$. Tom may have incorrectly thought that 3 times a number can't possibly equal 5 times the same number, or perhaps he divided each side by the variable x. A correct method of solving the equation would be to assume there is a solution, so that each side equals the same real number. Subtract $3x$ from each side, yielding $0 = 2x$, each side of which equals some real number as well, since 3x was a real number. Dividing each side by 2 yields $x = 0$, which is the correct solution.

Find the solution of the equation $x^2 = 36$. Justify your solution method.

One method of solution is to assume there is a solution, so that x^2 and 36 each represent the same real number. Subtract 36 from each side, so that $x^2 - 36 = 0$. The expression on the left side can be factored, and the equation rewritten as $(x + 6)(x - 6) = 0$. If a product of two numbers is equal to zero, then one (or the other) of the numbers must be zero. This leads to the two equations $x + 6 = 0$ and $x - 6 = 0$. Assuming these equations have solutions, add (or subtract) 6 from each side to arrive at the two solutions, $x = -6$ or $x = 6$.

Solve $\frac{6}{x} = \frac{9}{10}$. Determine how each step follows from the equality of numbers.

Assume that the solution exists, and that $\frac{6}{x}$ and $\frac{9}{10}$ equal the same real number. Since $\frac{9}{10}$ is positive, and a positive number divided by a positive number is positive, the value of x must be positive. Multiply each side of the equation by x to get $6 = \frac{9x}{10}$, where each side again represents the same real number. Then multiply each side by $\frac{10}{9}$, to arrive at the solution $\frac{60}{9} = x$.

What isan extraneous solution is, and why they may arise when solving a rational or radical equation.

An extraneous solution is the solution of an equation that arises during the process of solving an equation, which is not a solution of the original equation. When solving a rational equation, each side is often multiplied by x or an expression containing x. Since the value of x is unknown, this may mean multiplying by zero, which will make any equation the true statement $0 = 0$. Similarly, when solving a radical expression, each side of the equation is often squared, or raised to some power. This can also change the sign of unknown expressions. For example, the equation $3 = -3$ is false, but squaring each side gives $9 = 9$, which is true.

Solve the rational equation $\frac{2}{x} - 2 = x - 1$.

To solve the rational equation, multiply each side of the equation by the LCD, which is x. This will transform the rational equation into a quadratic equation that can be solved by factoring:

$$\frac{2}{x} - 2 = x - 1$$
$$x\left(\frac{2}{x} - 2\right) = x(x - 1)$$
$$2 - 2x = x^2 - x$$
$$x^2 + x - 2 = 0$$
$$(x + 2)(x - 1) = 0$$
$$x = -2, x = 1$$

Both $x = -2$ and $x = 1$ check out in the original equation. The solution is $x = \{-2, 1\}$.

Solve the radical equation $\sqrt{x-1} + 3 = x$.

To solve the radical equation, isolate the radical $\sqrt{x-1}$ on one side of the equation. Then square both sides and solve the resulting quadratic equation:

$$\sqrt{x-1} + 3 = x$$
$$\sqrt{x-1} = x - 3$$
$$\left(\sqrt{x-1}\right)^2 = (x-3)^2$$
$$x - 1 = x^2 - 6x + 9$$
$$x^2 - 7x + 10 = 0$$
$$(x-5)(x-2) = 0$$
$$x = 2, x = 5$$

Only $x = 5$ checks out in the original equation; $\sqrt{2-1} + 3 \overset{?}{\Leftrightarrow} 2 \xrightarrow{yields} \sqrt{1} + 3 = 4 \neq 2$!

The solution, then, is just $x = \{5\}$.

Solve $x + 1 = \sqrt{x+1}$. Check for extraneous solutions.

To solve the radical equation, square both sides and solve the resulting quadratic equation by factoring:

$$x + 1 = \sqrt{x+1}$$
$$(x+1)^2 = \left(\sqrt{x+1}\right)^2$$
$$x^2 + 2x + 1 = x + 1$$
$$x^2 + x = 0$$
$$x(x+1) = 0$$
$$x = -1, x = 0$$

To check whether either solution is extraneous, substitute into the original equation:

$x + 1 = \sqrt{x+1}$ $x + 1 = \sqrt{x+1}$
$-1 + 1 = \sqrt{-1+1}$ $0 + 1 = \sqrt{0+1}$
$0 = 0$ $0 = 0$

Both solutions are valid. The solution is $x = \{-1, 0\}$.

Find the solution of the inequality
$-4x + 2 \leq -10$.

To solve the inequality, isolate the variable x on one side. When multiplying or dividing by negative numbers, change the inequality symbol from $\leq$ to $\geq$, or vice versa:
$-4x + 2 \leq -10$
$-4x + 2 - 2 \leq -10 - 2$
$-4x \leq -12$

$$\frac{-4x}{-4} \geq \frac{-12}{-4}$$
$$x \geq 3$$

The solution of the inequality is $x \geq 3$. (Note that when $x = 3$, both sides of the inequality equal -10. Also, when $x = 4$, the inequality is $-14 \leq -10$, which is true. Therefore the solution is correct.)

A softball player's average is the number of hits divided by the number of at-bats. Gene currently has 20 hits in 75 at-bats. If he can get 30 more at-bats, how many hits must he get to have an average of 0.300 or better?

Let h represent the number of additional hits Gene gets in the 30 at-bats. His total number of hits will be $20 + h$, and his total number of at-bats will be $75 + 30 = 105$. The quotient of these two expressions represents Gene's average. Write a greater-than-or-equal-to inequality for this situation:

$$\frac{20 + h}{105} \geq 0.300$$
$$20 + h \geq 31.5$$
$$h \geq 11.5$$

Since there is no such thing as half a hit, Gene needs 12 or more hits in the next 30 at-bats to have an average of 0.300 or better.

A cab company charges $8 to enter the cab, and then $.42 per mile. If the ride cost $19.76, how long was the trip, in miles?

Let m represent the number of miles for a ride in the cab. The total cost is the $8 to enter the cab, plus $.42 per mile. If c represents the total cost for a ride of m miles, an equation for the total cost is
$c = 8 + 0.42m$. Substitute 19.76 for c in the equation and solve for m:

$8 + 0.42m = 19.76$
$0.42m = 11.76$

$$\frac{0.42m}{0.42} = \frac{11.76}{0.42}$$
$$m = 28$$

A ride that cost $19.76 was 28 miles long.

Solve the linear equation $ax + b = c$, where a, b, and c are real numbers. State any restrictions on the values of a, b, and c.

The equation can be solved the same way as if the parameters a, b, and c were real numbers. Isolate x on one side of the equation:

$$ax + b = c$$
$$ax = c - b$$
$$\frac{ax}{a} = \frac{c - b}{a}$$
$$x = \frac{c - b}{a}$$

The solution is $x = \frac{c-b}{a}$. Since division by zero is undefined, the value of a must be nonzero. However, if the value of a were zero, the original equation would not be a one-variable equation, but would simply read $b = c$.

Rewrite $x^2 + 4x = 2$ in the form $(x - p)^2 = q$.

To rewrite $x^2 + 4x = 2$ in the form $(x - p)^2 = q$, complete the square. Begin by adding the square of one half the coefficient of x to each side. In this case, the coefficient is 4, so add $(½ \cdot 4)^2 = 4$ to both sides, and rewrite the trinomial as a squared binomial:

$$x^2 + 4x = 2$$
$$x^2 + 4x + 4 = 2 + 4$$
$$x^2 + 4x + 4 = 6$$
$$(x + 2)^2 = 6$$

This equation is in the form $(x - p)^2 = q$, with $p = -2$ and $q = 6$.

Complete the square in the equation $3x^2 - 5x = 2$.

To complete the square, first divide by 3 so that the leading coefficient (the coefficient of x^2) is 1. Then add the square of one half the coefficient of x to each side of the equation, and rewrite the trinomial as a squared binomial:

$$3x^2 - 5x = 2$$
$$x^2 - \frac{5}{3}x = \frac{2}{3}$$
$$x^2 - \frac{5}{3}x + \left(\frac{5}{6}\right)^2 = 2 + \left(\frac{5}{6}\right)^2$$
$$x^2 - \frac{5}{3}x + \frac{25}{36} = \frac{72}{36} + \frac{25}{36} = \frac{97}{36}$$
$$\left(x + \frac{5}{6}\right)^2 = \frac{97}{36}$$

Derive the quadratic formula by completing the square in the general quadratic equation $ax^2 + bx + c = 0$.

The quadratic formula gives the solutions to the equation $ax^2 + bx + c = 0$ in terms of the parameters a, b, and c. To derive the formula by completing the square:

$a\left(x^2 + \frac{b}{a}x\right) = -c$ Subtract c from each side, and factor out a.

$a\left(x^2 + \frac{b}{a}x + \frac{b^2}{4a^2}\right) = \frac{b^2}{4a} - c$ Complete the square, and add

$\left(\frac{1}{2} \cdot \frac{b}{a}\right)^2 = \frac{b^2}{4a}$ to both sides of the equation.

$\left(x + \frac{b}{2a}\right)^2 = \frac{b^2}{4a^2} - \frac{c}{a}$ Rewrite the trinomial as a perfect square, and divide each side by a.

$x + \frac{b}{2a} = \pm\sqrt{\frac{b^2-4ac}{4a^2}}$ Take the square root of each side, finding the common denominator on the right side.

$$x = -\frac{b}{2a} \pm \frac{\sqrt{b^2-4ac}}{2a}$$

Solve for x and simplify.

$$x = \frac{-b \pm \sqrt{b^2 - 4ac}}{2a}$$

Compare the quadratic forms $a(x - m)(x - n) = 0$ and $(x - p)^2 = q$. What are the solutions of each equation?

The quadratic equation $a(x - m)(x - n) = 0$ is in factored form. Since the right side of the equation is zero, the factors make it easy to find the solutions: the two equations $x - m = 0$ and $x - n = 0$ give the solutions $x = m$ and $x = n$. The equation $(x - p)^2 = q$ has the form of a quadratic after completing the square, which means the left side is a squared binomial. Taking the square root of each side and then adding p to each side of the equation gives the solutions $x = p \pm \sqrt{q}$.

What is the general form of a complex number?

The general form of a complex number is $a + bi$, where a and b are real numbers. The imaginary number i is equal to the square root of -1: $i = \sqrt{-1}$. Therefore the number i itself is a complex number, with $a = 0$ and $b = 1$. Other examples of complex numbers include $-12i$ and $\sqrt{3} + 4i$. Note that all real numbers are also complex numbers: if b = 0, then $a + bi = a + 0i = a$, which is a real number.

Solve $4x^2 = 100$ by inspection.

To solve an equation by inspection means to solve using fairly obvious mental math, without performing calculations on paper or with a calculator. Dividing each side of the equation by 4 gives $x^2 = 25$. The two square roots of 25 are -5 and 5, so the solution of the equation is $x = -5$ or $x = 5$. A check of each solution (by substituting into the original equation) can seem self-evident:

$4x^2 = 100$ $4x^2 = 100$
$4(-5)^2 = 100$ $4(5)^2 = 100$
$4(25) = 100$ $4(25) = 100$
$100 = 100$ $100 = 100$

Write the quadratic formula. Apply it to solve the equation $2x^2 = 5x - 1$.

The quadratic formula is $x = \frac{-b \pm \sqrt{b^2-4ac}}{2a}$. It gives the solution of the quadratic equation $ax^2 + bx + c = 0$. The equation $2x^2 = 5x - 1$ can be written in this form as $2x^2 - 5x + 1 = 0$. Substitute into the quadratic formula with $a = 2$, $b = -5$, and $c = 1$:

$$x = \frac{-b \pm \sqrt{b^2 - 4ac}}{2a}$$

$$x = \frac{-(-5) \pm \sqrt{(-5)^2 - 4(2)(1)}}{2(2)}$$

$$x = \frac{5 \pm \sqrt{17}}{4}$$

The solutions of the equation are $x = \frac{5+\sqrt{17}}{4}$ and $x = \frac{5-\sqrt{17}}{4}$.

Bethany claims the solutions of (x − 2)(x + 3) = −4 are x = −3 and x = 2. Correct her error.

Bethany applied the zero product property to an equation that does not equal zero. Although her values of x make the left side of the equation zero, the right side is −4. To correct her error, she should first multiply the binomials, and then write the equation so that the right side is zero:
(x − 2)(x + 3) = −4
x² − 2x + 3x − 6 = −4
x² + x − 6 = −4
x² + x − 2 = 0
(x + 2)(x − 1) = 0
x = −2 or x = 1
The solution is x = {−2, 1}.

Solve the system $\begin{cases} \frac{x}{2} + \frac{y}{3} = -1 \\ \frac{x}{5} - \frac{y}{3} = 1 \end{cases}$. **Describe your solution method.**

To solve the system, multiply each equation by the least common denominator, or LCD. This will eliminate the fractions, and transform the system into one with integer coefficients.

$$\begin{cases} \left(\frac{x}{2} + \frac{y}{3} = -1\right) 6 \\ \left(\frac{x}{5} - \frac{y}{3} = 1\right) 15 \end{cases}$$

$$\begin{cases} 3x + 2y = -6 \\ 3x - 5y = 15 \end{cases}$$

Subtracting the equations results in the equation 7y = −21, so y = −3. Substitute −3 for y into 3x + 2y = −6 to get 3x = 0, so x = 0. The solution of the system is (0, −3).

Without solving either system, explain why the systems below have the same solution. Then verify this fact.

$\begin{cases} x + y = 4 \\ 2x - y = -1 \end{cases}$ $\begin{cases} x + y = 4 \\ 3x = 3 \end{cases}$

When comparing the two systems, it is clear that the first equation of each system is the same. If an equation of one system is a linear combination of the equations of the other system, then the systems are equivalent and therefore have the same solution. A linear combination is the sum of two equations, with either equation possibly multiplied by a real number. Adding the two equations of the first system results in the equation 3x = 3. This is the 2nd equation of the other system, so the systems are equivalent and have the same solution. The solution is $(x, y) = (1, 3)$ and satisfies both systems.

Show that if (a, b) is the solution to the system on the left below, then it is also the solution to the system on the right. In the system on the right, one equation was replaced with the sum of that equation and a multiple of the first equation.

$$\begin{cases} 3x+8y=2 \\ 2x-5y=-7 \end{cases} \quad \begin{cases} 3x+8y=2 \\ 3x+8y+k(2x-5y)=2-7k \end{cases}$$

The solution of the original system is (a, b). Substituting these values for x and y in the equations gives the following true statements:

$$3a + 8b = 2$$
$$2a - 5b = -7$$

To show that (a, b) is the solution of the system on the right, show that (a, b) makes both equations true. The first equation $3x + 8y = 2$ is true, because it is the same equation as the other system and $3a + 8b = 2$. Substituting a and b for x and y in the second equation gives $3a + 8b + k(2a - 5b) = 2 - 7k$. Using the two true equations above, substitute 2 for $3a + 8b$ and –7 for $2a - 5b$ gives $2 + k(-7) = 2 - 7k$, which is an identity and true for any value of k.

Solve the system $\begin{cases} x - 4y = 3 \\ 2x + y = -3 \end{cases}$

The first equation of the system is $x - 4y = 3$. This equation can easily be solved for x, resulting in the equation $x = 4y + 3$. Substitute this expression for x into the other equation and solve for y:

$2x + y = -3$
$2(4y + 3) + y = -3$
$8y + 6 + y = -3$
$9y = -9$
$y = -1$

Substitute –1 for y in the equation $2x + y = -3$ gives $2x = -2$, and $x = -1$. The solution of the system is therefore $(-1, -1)$.

Use a graph to approximate the solution of the system $\begin{cases} -x + y = 9 \\ 2x + y = 5 \end{cases}$ **to the nearest integer values of x and y.**

The solution to a linear system is the intersection of the graphs of the system. The equations can be sketched by using the x- and y- intercepts of each line. For example, for $-x + y = 9$, the x- and y- intercepts are $(-9, 0)$ and $(0, 9)$, respectively. The intercepts for the other equation are determined similarly.

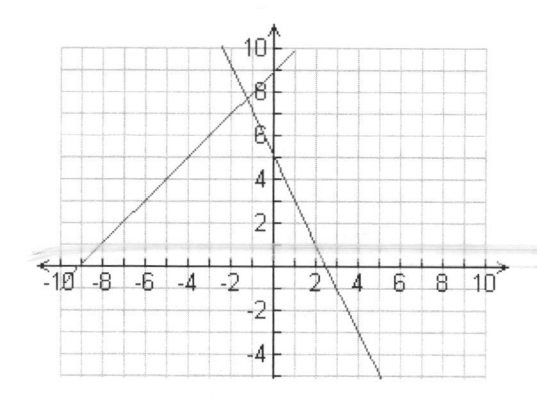

The intersection point is in the second quadrant. To the nearest integer values of x and y, the solution is (−1, 8).

Describe the graph of a linear system with no solution.

If a linear system has no solution, there is no value of x and y that satisfies both equations of the system. Graphically, this means that the lines that represent each equation of the system will never intersect. Lines that never intersect are by definition parallel. Parallel lines have the same slope, so it can often be determined that a system has no solution without graphing or solving algebraically. For example, if the equations of the system are y = −2x + 3 and y = −2x − 5, the system has no solution. The equations represent distinct parallel lines.

At what point or points does the line y = −x + 2 intersect a circle with radius 2 and center at the origin?

The equation of a circle centered at the origin with radius r is $x^2 + y^2 = r^2$. For a radius of 2, this becomes $x^2 + y^2 = 4$. Substitute the expression −x + 2 for y in the equation of the circle, and solve for x:

$x^2 + y^2 = 4$
$x^2 + (-x + 2)^2 = 4$
$x^2 + x^2 - 4x + 4 = 4$
$2x^2 - 4x = 0$
$2x(x - 2) = 0$
$x = 0, x = 2$

If x = 0, then y = −(0) + 2 = 2. If x = 2, the y = −(2) + 2 = 0. The points of intersection, then, are (0, 2) and (2, 0).

Solve the system $\begin{cases} 3x - y = 6 \\ y = 4 - x^2 \end{cases}$**, and find any intersection points.**

The first equation of the system can be rewritten as y = 3x − 6. Substitute the expression 3x − 6 for y in the quadratic equation:

$y = 4 - x^2$
$3x - 6 = 4 - x^2$
$x^2 + 3x - 10 = 0$

$(x + 5)(x - 2) = 0$
$x = -5, x = 2$

If $x = -5$, then $y = 3(-5) - 6 = -21$. If $x = 2$, then $y = 3(2) - 6 = 0$. The points of intersection are $(-5, -21)$ and $(2, 0)$.

A system consists of a linear equation and a quadratic equation. How many solutions are possible? Compare with a linear system.

For a system that consists of a linear equation and a quadratic equation, it is possible to have 0, 1, or 2 solutions. This is different than a linear system, which has 0 solutions, 1 solutions, or infinitely many solutions. When a linear solution has infinitely many solutions, the two equations in the system are equivalent. A line may never intersect a parabola (0 solutions), or may be tangent to the parabola (1 solution), or may intersect the parabola in two points (2 solutions). Since solving a linear/quadratic system leads to a quadratic equation, it is not possible to have more than 2 solutions; that is, no line can intersect a parabola at more than 2 points.

Solve the system $\begin{cases} y = 4 - x^2 \\ y - 3 = 0 \end{cases}$ by graphing.

The equation $y = 4 - x^2$, which can be written as $y = -x^2 + 4$, represents a parabola that opens downward with vertex at $(0, 4)$. The equation $y - 3 = 0$ can be written as $y = 3$, the equation of a horizontal line passing through the point $(0, 3)$. The graph of the equations is shown below.

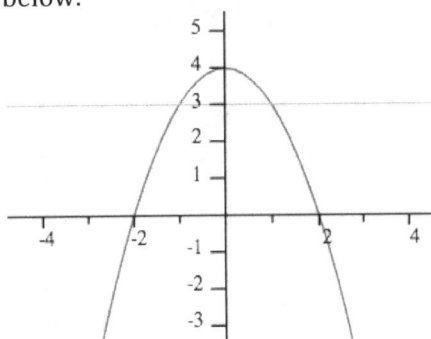

There are two points of intersection of the graphs, $(-1, 3)$ and $(1, 3)$. These are the solutions to the system; both points check out algebraically.

What is a matrix? How can a matrix represent several variables as a vector?

A matrix is a rectangular array of real numbers. These numbers can represent coefficients of a linear system. For example, consider the system $\begin{cases} x + 3y = 1 \\ x - y = 2 \end{cases}$. The coefficients can be represented using the matrix $\begin{bmatrix} 1 & 3 \\ 1 & -1 \end{bmatrix}$. Similarly, a matrix can represent a vector variable, which can represent several non-vector variables. Using the same example, the matrix $\begin{bmatrix} x \\ y \end{bmatrix}$ represents the vector variable $\langle x, y \rangle$, which represents x and y in the linear system.

Represent the system $\begin{cases} 2x - 3y = 11 \\ 6x - y = 20 \end{cases}$ **using a matrix equation.**

To write the system with a matrix equation, first define matrices for the coefficients of the variables, the variables, and the constants.

Coefficient matrix: $\begin{bmatrix} 2 & -3 \\ 6 & -1 \end{bmatrix}$

Variable matrix: $\begin{bmatrix} x \\ y \end{bmatrix}$

Constant matrix: $\begin{bmatrix} 11 \\ 20 \end{bmatrix}$

The product of the coefficient matrix and the variable matrix equals the constant matrix. This can be written as a matrix equation as follows:

$$\begin{bmatrix} 2 & -3 \\ 6 & -1 \end{bmatrix} \begin{bmatrix} x \\ y \end{bmatrix} = \begin{bmatrix} 11 \\ 20 \end{bmatrix}$$

Write the linear system represented by the matrix equation.

$$\begin{bmatrix} 3 & -7 \\ 1 & 5 \end{bmatrix} \begin{bmatrix} x \\ y \end{bmatrix} = \begin{bmatrix} 10 \\ -2 \end{bmatrix}$$

By multiplying the matrices on the left, a 2 by 1 matrix is formed. Each entry of this matrix is equal to the corresponding entry in the matrix $\begin{bmatrix} 10 \\ -2 \end{bmatrix}$. Multiplying the first row of $\begin{bmatrix} 3 & -7 \\ 1 & 5 \end{bmatrix}$ by the column of the matrix $\begin{bmatrix} x \\ y \end{bmatrix}$ gives the expression $3x - 7y$. Multiplying the second row of $\begin{bmatrix} 3 & -7 \\ 1 & 5 \end{bmatrix}$ by the column of the matrix $\begin{bmatrix} x \\ y \end{bmatrix}$ gives the expression $x + 5y$. These two equations are equal to 10 and −2, respectively. The linear system is therefore $\begin{cases} 3x - 7y = 10 \\ x + 5y = -2 \end{cases}$

Represent the system $\begin{cases} 2x - 3z = -1 \\ 6x - y = 2 \\ 2y + z = 4 \end{cases}$ **using a matrix equation.**

The equations describe a three-variable linear system. Since each equation only has two variable terms, the coefficient of the missing term is 0 in each equation. So, for the first row of the coefficient matrix, the entries are 2, 0, and −3, since there is no y-term in the first equation. That is, the first equation could be written as $2x + 0y - 3z = -1$. A matrix equation for the system is shown below:

$$\begin{bmatrix} 2 & 0 & -3 \\ 6 & -1 & 0 \\ 0 & 2 & 1 \end{bmatrix} \begin{bmatrix} x \\ y \\ z \end{bmatrix} = \begin{bmatrix} -1 \\ 2 \\ 4 \end{bmatrix}$$

What is the inverse of a matrix? Which matrices have an inverse?

An inverse of a matrix A is the matrix A^{-1} such that $A(A^{-1}) = I$. The matrix I is the identity matrix, which has the value 1 on the main diagonal, and 0 elsewhere. Only square matrices (same number of rows as columns) have an inverse. Additionally, the determinant of the square matrix must not be zero for the matrix to have an inverse. As example, the inverse of the matrix $\begin{bmatrix} 3 & 1 \\ 5 & 2 \end{bmatrix}$ is $\begin{bmatrix} 2 & -1 \\ -5 & 3 \end{bmatrix}$ as illustrated below:

$$\begin{bmatrix} 3 & 1 \\ 5 & 2 \end{bmatrix}\begin{bmatrix} 2 & -1 \\ -5 & 3 \end{bmatrix} = \begin{bmatrix} 6-5 & -3+3 \\ 10-(-10) & -5+6 \end{bmatrix} = \begin{bmatrix} 1 & 0 \\ 0 & 1 \end{bmatrix}$$

What is the inverse of the matrix $\begin{bmatrix} 5 & 7 \\ 3 & 4 \end{bmatrix}$?

The inverse of a 2 by 2 matrix $A = \begin{bmatrix} a & b \\ c & d \end{bmatrix}$ is given by the following matrix:
$$\frac{1}{\det A}\begin{bmatrix} d & -b \\ -c & a \end{bmatrix}$$

The notation det A represents the determinant of the matrix A. For the 2 by 2 matrix $A = \begin{bmatrix} a & b \\ c & d \end{bmatrix}$, det $A = ad - bc$. Note that since the inverse involves the reciprocal of the determinant, if the determinant is 0, the inverse does not exist. The determinant of $\begin{bmatrix} 5 & 7 \\ 3 & 4 \end{bmatrix}$ is $5(4) - 3(7) = 20 - 21 = -1$, and the inverse is therefore $\frac{1}{-1}\begin{bmatrix} 4 & -7 \\ -3 & 5 \end{bmatrix} = \begin{bmatrix} -4 & 7 \\ 3 & -5 \end{bmatrix}$.

Use a graphing calculator to find the inverse of $\begin{bmatrix} -1 & 2 & 3 \\ 2 & 1 & 1 \\ 3 & 0 & -2 \end{bmatrix}$.

To find the inverse of the matrix, select to edit a 3 by 3 matrix on the calculator. You may have to enter the dimensions first. Then, enter each value for each row of the matrix. Check that the matrix is entered correctly:

```
MATRIX[A]  3 ×3
[ -1      2      3     ]
[  2      1      1     ]
[  3      0     -2     ]




3,3=-2
```

The matrix shown is named A. Next, calculate the inverse, A^{-1}. In the second screen shot on the right, the entries are displayed as fractions.

```
L .4260714266 .0
Ans▶Frac
     [ -2/7   4/7   -1/7 ]
     [  1     -1     1   ]
     [ -3/7   6/7   -5/7 ]

```

Solve the system $\begin{cases} 2x - 3y = -2 \\ x + 4y = 10 \end{cases}$ **by using an inverse matrix.**

To solve the system using an inverse matrix, first write the corresponding matrix equation for the system.

$$\begin{bmatrix} 2 & -3 \\ 1 & 4 \end{bmatrix} \begin{bmatrix} x \\ y \end{bmatrix} = \begin{bmatrix} -2 \\ 10 \end{bmatrix}$$

Multiply each side of the matrix equation from the left by the inverse of the matrix $\begin{bmatrix} 2 & -3 \\ 1 & 4 \end{bmatrix}$, which is $\frac{1}{11}\begin{bmatrix} 4 & 3 \\ -1 & 2 \end{bmatrix} = \begin{bmatrix} \frac{4}{11} & \frac{3}{11} \\ -\frac{1}{11} & \frac{2}{11} \end{bmatrix}$. The result is shown below.

$$\begin{bmatrix} 1 & 0 \\ 0 & 1 \end{bmatrix} \begin{bmatrix} x \\ y \end{bmatrix} = \begin{bmatrix} \frac{4}{11} & \frac{3}{11} \\ -\frac{1}{11} & \frac{2}{11} \end{bmatrix} \begin{bmatrix} -2 \\ 10 \end{bmatrix}$$

$$\begin{bmatrix} x \\ y \end{bmatrix} = \begin{bmatrix} 2 \\ 2 \end{bmatrix}$$

The solution of the system is (2, 2).

How can you show the solutions of the equation x + y = 10 graphically?

The solutions of a two-variable equation are all the ordered pairs that make the equation true. For the equation $x + y = 10$, all of the points (x, y) that satisfy the equation can be shown in the coordinate plane. For example, (3, 7) is a solution of the equation, as is (−2, 12). All of the solutions will fall on a straight line that passes through these two points, given by the equation $y = 10 − x$. The ordered pair (−856, 866) is also a solution, although it may not be visible on the graph of the equation. There are infinitely many solutions, and the line extends in both directions without end.

Must a graph in the coordinate plane have an equation with two variables in it? If not, give an example.

A graph in the coordinate plane is used to show the relationship between two variables. For example, the graph of the equation $y = 2x$ shows all the points such that the y-value is twice the x-value. The equation does not, however, have to have two variables in it. For example, the equation $y = 2$ is a horizontal line that passes through the point (0, 2). For any x-value, the value of y is 2. There is still a relationship, but the value of y does not depend on the value of x.

Describe how to graphically determine the solution of $3x + 4 = x^2$.

A one-variable equation can be solved graphically by considering each side of the equation as the expression for a function of y. By graphing the two equations in the coordinate plane, the x-value of the intersection point(s), if there are any, represent the solution(s) of the equation. The graphs of $y = 3x + 4$ and $y = x^2$ are shown below, and intersect at (−1, 1) and (4, 16). Therefore the solution to the equation is x = {−2, 4}.

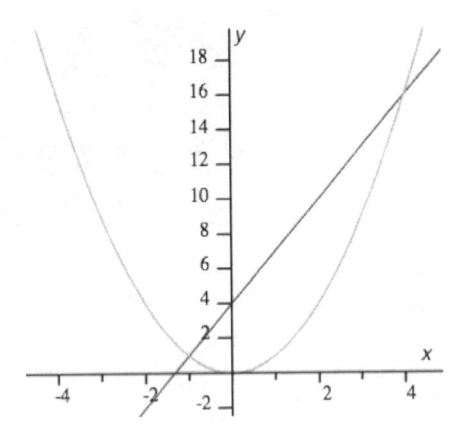

Use a table to determine if $f(x) = 3x^2$ and $g(x) = 8x + 3$ intersect. Use integer values of x from −1 to 5.

Set up a table that shows x, $f(x)$, and $g(x)$. The values for x in the table range from −1 to 5, and the values of $f(x)$ and $g(x)$ are the functions evaluated at the particular value of x.

x	f(x)	g(x)
−1	3	−5
0	0	3
1	3	11
2	12	19
3	27	27
4	48	35
5	75	43

The table reveals that $f(3) = g(3) = 27$. This means that the functions intersect at the point (3, 27). Also, in the interval from $x = -1$ to $x = 0$, $f(x)$ changes from being greater than $g(x)$ to less than $g(x)$. This means that the functions intersect at another x-value between −1 and 0, although the table does not show this value.

Find an approximate solution to $3^x = -(x + 2)$. Use a graphing calculator.

The equation $3^x = -(x + 2)$ cannot be solved for x. An approximate solution can be found by graphing the equations $y = 3^x$ and $y = -(x + 2)$ on a graphing calculator. The intersection points, if there are any, will have an x-coordinate that is a solution to the equation. The graphs intersect at approximately (−2.0996, 0.0996). This is the only intersection point, since the linear function is decreasing and the exponential function is increasing. The approximate solution, then, of the equation is $x = -2.0996$. Another solution is to graph the equation $y = 3^x + x + 2$ and determine where it crosses the x-axis.

What is the process of successive approximations for finding the solution of the equation $f(x) = g(x)$? Use $\ln x = -x^2$ as an example.

The process of successive approximations involves making a guess, or an approximation, for a solution to an equation. Then make another guess that is close to the original guess, and determine whether the result makes each side of the equation closer to being equal. For example, a reasonable first guess for the solution to $\ln x = -x^2$ is $x = 0.5$. This gives −0.6931 and −0.25, and the guess $x = -0.6$ yields −0.5108 and −0.36. Since $x = -0.6$ is better, next guess $x = -0.7$, which yields -0.3567 and -0.49, only a slight improvement. Perhaps guess $x = -0.65$ next, which yields -0.4308 and -0.4225 which are equal to the tenths place. Therefore, $x = -0.65$ is an approximate solution accurate to the tenths place. Further guesses might yield even better approximations.

Sketch the graph of $y \geq -2x + 4$ in the coordinate plane.

To sketch the graph of $y \geq -2x + 4$, begin by graphing the corresponding linear equation $y = -2x + 4$. Draw the line as a solid line, since the greater-than-or-equal-to sign indicates that the line itself is part of the solution. The test point $(0, 0)$, when substituted into the inequality, gives $0 \geq 4$, which is FALSE. Therefore, the half-plane that represents the solution region is the side of the line that does not contain $(0, 0)$. Shade this region, which is above the line, as shown below.

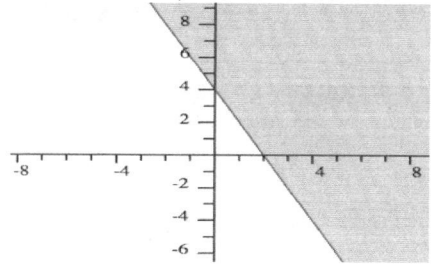

Graph the solution of the system $\begin{cases} x \leq y - 1 \\ 2x \geq y \end{cases}$.

To sketch the graph of the system, graph the equations $y = x + 1$ and $y = 2x$. The lines for $y = 2x$ and $y = x + 1$ should be solid, since the inequality symbols include equality. Shade the half-plane that represents the solution for each inequality. The shaded areas intersect in a triangular region in the first quadrant, as shown in the graph. This represents the solution of the system. Note that the boundary of the solution region is included in the solution.

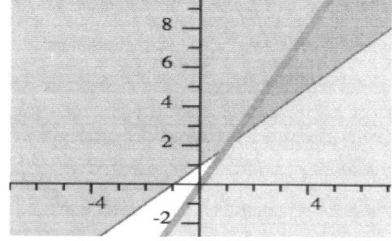

What system of inequalities describes the points in the 3rd quadrant of the coordinate plane?

The coordinate plane is divided into 4 quadrants. The points in each quadrant can be described the signs of the coordinates of the points:
1st quadrant: both coordinates positive
2nd quadrant: y-coordinates positive, x-coordinates negative
3rd quadrant: both coordinates negative
4th quadrant: x-coordinate positive, y-coordinate negative

The x-coordinates are negative, so $x < 0$. Similarly, the y-coordinates are negative, so $y < 0$. A system of inequalities that describes the points is $\begin{cases} x < 0 \\ y < 0 \end{cases}$.

When is the boundary line of the graph of a linear inequality in two variables part of the solution?

The boundary line of a linear inequality in two variables is the line that represents the corresponding equation of the inequality. For example, in both inequalities $y < 3x + 5$ and $y \geq 3x + 5$, the boundary line is given by the equation $y = 3x + 5$. When the inequality has the symbol < or >, the boundary line is not part of the solution. This is indicated by drawing a dashed line for the equation. When the inequality has the symbol $\leq$ or $\geq$, the boundary line is part of the solution. This is indicated by drawing a solid line for the equation.

Example
> Describe what kind of function grows by equal differences over equal intervals, and prove your answer

> A function that grows by equal differences over equal intervals is a *linear function*, a function of the form $f(x) = mx + b$.

> To prove that a linear function meets this criterion, we can consider some arbitrary interval, Δx, and then show that $f(x + \Delta x) - f(x)$ does not depend on x—hence, that when x increases by an interval of Δx, $f(x)$ grows by a constant amount. Substituting in the linear function, we get $f(x + \Delta x) - f(x) = (m(x + \Delta x)) + b - (mx + b) = mx + m\Delta x + b - mx - b = m\Delta x$. As expected, this does not depend on x, proving that the linear function grows by equal differences over equal intervals.

Example
> Describe what kind of function grows by equal factors over equal intervals, and prove your answer

> A function that grows by equal factors over equal intervals is an *exponential function*, a function of the form $f(x) = Ae^{bx}$.

> To prove that an exponential function meets this criterion, we can consider some arbitrary interval, Δx, and then show that $f(x + \Delta x)/f(x)$ does not depend on x—hence, that when x increases by an interval of Δx, $f(x)$ grows by a constant factor. Substituting in the exponential function, we get $f(x + \Delta x)/f(x) = Ae^{b(x+\Delta x)}/Ae^{bx} = Ae^{bx}e^{b\Delta x}/Ae^{bx} = e^{b\Delta x}$. As expected, this does not depend on x, proving that the exponential function grows by equal factors over equal intervals.

Phrases in a word problem indicating quantity changes

If one quantity changes at a constant rate relative to another, this means the two quantities have a linear relationship ($y = mx + b$). There are a number of common phrases in a word problem that might indicate this. Rarely are we told directly that the relationship between two quantities is linear, but there are other ways the relationship could be phrased. Consider the following statement: "For every meter you go deeper underwater, the pressure increases by ten thousand Pascals." This says that one quantity—here the pressure—

increases at a constant rate—ten thousand Pascals per meter—relative to another—the depth.

Another common phrasing that indicates a linear relationship is the statement that one quantity is proportional to another. This can be expressed algebraically as $y = mx$. Note that not all linear relationships are proportional—only those in which the y intercept is zero—but all proportional relationships are linear.

Example
> Describe what kind of equation you would use to model a relationship in which one quantity changes at a constant rate per unit interval relative to another
>
> A relationship in which one quantity changes at a constant rate per unit interval relative to another is necessarily a *linear relationship*, and can be modeled by a linear equation, of the form $f(x) = mx + b$. In this equation, m is equal to the slope of the line, or to the rate at which $f(x)$ changes per unit interval. This rate may be given directly, or it may be possible to derive it from the given information: if, for example, two points in the relationship are given, we can find m by calculating $\frac{f(x_1)-f(x_2)}{x_1-x_2}$. The constant b is the y intercept, or the value $f(0)$; again, this may be given directly, or may be derivable from given information: if you know m and you're given one data point, you can put these known values into the equation $f(x) = mx + b$ and solve for b.

Example
> Suppose you're told an event ticket costs a flat fee of $20 plus $5 per person. Describe how you would write an algebraic expression to describe the total price
>
> To write an expression based on a given situation, the first thing to observe is what quantities we will be concerned with and that will correspond to variables in the expression. In this case, we have a total price that varies by the number of people involved, so we'll be writing $y = f(x)$, where y is the total cost and x is the number of people. Secondly, we can observe exactly how one quantity varies with the other. In this case, the price increases by a fixed amount for each additional person. A situation in which one quantity changes at a constant rate per unit interval relative to the other corresponds to a linear function. In this case, with a flat fee of $20 independent of the number of people, and a fee increase of $5 per person, an appropriate equation is $y = 20 + 5x$.

Phrases in a word problem indicating quantity grows or decays

If one quantity grows or decays by a constant percent rate per unit interval relative to another, this means that the two quantities have an exponential relationship, $y = AB^{Cx}$—or rather, to take into account the percent rate, $y(t) = y_o(1 + P)^{Ct}$, where P is the percent rate. This relationship may be stated directly, but more often it must be partly inferred by other phrases appearing in the problem. For instance, we may be told the number of bacteria in a culture doubles every ten months—"doubles" indicates a percent rate of 100% ($1 + P = 2$, so $P = 1 = 100\%$).

Some common examples of problems involving exponential relationship involve compound interest and radioactive half-lives. In the former, the interest rate is the percent increase, while the coefficient of the exponent depends on how often the interest is compounded—for interest compounded monthly, the exponent would be $t/12$, assuming that t is measured in months. In the latter, the base of the exponent is always $\frac{1}{2}$, and the exponent is $t/t_{1/2}$, where $t_{1/2}$ is the half-life.

Example
> Describe what kind of equation you would use to model a relationship in which one quantity changes by a constant percent rate per unit interval relative to another.
>
> A relationship in which one quantity changes by a constant percent rate per unit interval relative to another is an *exponential relationship*, and can be modeled by an exponential equation, of the form $f(x) = Ae^{bx}$. If the percent rate of change is positive, then b is positive and the equation represents exponential growth; if the percent rate of change is negative, then b is negative and the equation represents exponential decay. Often in such a problem we are given the value of $f(x)$ when $x = 0$; this is simply A, as can be seen as follows: $f(0) = Ae^{b \cdot 0} = Ae^0 = A \cdot 1 = A$. Given this, if we have at least one other data point, we can use it to solve for b.

Example
> Suppose you're told that an item initially sold for $200 and its price has increased by 10% per year. Show how you would write an algebraic expression to describe the price
>
> To write an expression based on a given situation, the first thing to observe is what quantities we will be concerned with and that will correspond to variables in the expression. In this case, we have a price that varies by year, so we'll be writing $y = f(t)$, where y is the total cost and t is the time in years from the item's initial sale. Secondly, we can observe exactly how one quantity varies with the other. In this case, the price increases by a fixed percentage per year. A situation in which one quantity changes at a constant percent rate per unit interval relative to the other corresponds to an exponential function. In this case, with an initial cost of $200 at $t = 0$ and an increase of 10% per year, an appropriate equation is $y = 200 \cdot 1.1^t$.

Example
> Given two points, such as (1,2) and (3,−1), describe how you can find a linear function that includes those points
>
> A linear function is a function of the form $y = mx + b$, where m is the slope of the line and b is its y intercept. Suppose we are given two points, (x_1, y_1) and (x_2, y_2). We can find m by calculating the "rise over run": that is, $m = \frac{y_2 - y_1}{x_2 - x_1}$.

Knowing *m*, we can then put the *x* and *y* values of one of the points into the equation $y = mx + b$ to solve for *b*, the only remaining unknown.

For example, using the sample points (1,2) and (3,–1) we have $m = \frac{-1-2}{3-1} = -\frac{3}{2}$. We can now put that into the linear equation along with the coordinates of the first point, (1,2), to yield $2 = -\frac{3}{2}(1) + b$, which we can solve for *b* to get $b = \frac{7}{2}$. (Had we used the second point instead of the first, we would have arrived at the same answer.) Therefore, the linear function that includes the two given points is $y = -\frac{3}{2}x + \frac{7}{2}$.

Example

Given two points, one of which has an *x* value of zero, such as (0,2) and (3,20), show how you can find an exponential function that includes those points

An exponential function has the form $y = Ae^{bx}$. (We could use a different base for the exponent rather than *e*, but in that case, by the properties of exponents, we'd simply have a different value for *b*; the form of the equation wouldn't change, and neither would the means of solving it.) If one of the given points has an *x* value of zero, then finding *A* is easy: we can just put the *x* and *y* values of this point into the equation, and we'll find that *y* = *A*. For the sample points, using (0,2) we find $2 = Ae^{b \cdot 0} = A$, so *A* = 2.

Knowing *A*, we can now use the *x* and *y* values of the other point to solve for *b*. For the sample points, putting in (3,20) we get $20 = 2e^{b \cdot 3}$. Dividing both sides by 2 yields $10 = e^{3b}$, and now we can take the natural logarithm of both sides, giving $\ln 10 = 3b$, thus $b = \frac{\ln 10}{3}$. Therefore, our final equation is $y = 2e^{\frac{\ln 10}{3}x} = 2(e^{\ln 10})^{x/3} = 2 \cdot 10^{\frac{x}{3}}$.

Example

Given two points with nonzero *x* values, such as (2,4) and (6,60), show how you can find an exponential function that includes both point.

An exponential function has the form $y = Ae^{bx}$. Putting the *x* and *y* values for the given points into this equation yields two equations: in the case of the sample points, $4 = Ae^{2b}$ and $60 = Ae^{6b}$. We have two equations and two unknowns (*A* and *b*), so in principle it should be possible to solve for the unknowns.

There are many ways of doing this. We could, for instance, solve for *A* in one equation and substitute that value into the other. Another relatively simple method is to take the ratio of the two equations, thus canceling *A*: $\frac{60}{4} = \frac{Ae^{6b}}{Ae^{2b}}$, thus $15 = \frac{e^{6b}}{e^{2b}} = e^{6b-2b} = e^{4b}$. Taking the natural logarithm of both sides, $\ln 15 = 4b$, so $b = \frac{\ln 15}{4}$.

Knowing b, we can now use either point to solve for A: using $(2,4)$, we get $4 = Ae^{\frac{\ln 15}{4} \cdot 2} = Ae^{\frac{\ln 15}{2}} = A(e^{\ln 15})^{\frac{1}{2}} = A \cdot 15^{1/2} = \sqrt{15}A$, so $A = \frac{4\sqrt{15}}{15}$. Our full equation is then $y = \frac{4\sqrt{15}}{15} e^{\frac{\ln 15}{4}x} = \frac{4\sqrt{15}}{15}(e^{\ln 15})^{x/4} = \frac{4\sqrt{15}}{15} \cdot 15^{\frac{x}{4}}$.

Example

Given a graph of a linear function, determine how you can construct an algebraic expression for the function

An algebraic expression for a linear function has the form $y = mx + b$. We can find both m and b from the graph of the function. b is simply equal to the y intercept, and can be read from the graph by observing at what point the graph of the linear function intersects the y-axis. To find m, the slope, we can take from the graph any two points that lie on the line, (x_1, y_1) and (x_2, y_2). The slope m is then equal to $m = \frac{y_1 - y_2}{x_1 - x_2}$.

There are two special cases that must be treated differently: horizontal and vertical lines. A horizontal line has a slope of zero; its equation is $y = b$, where b is, again, the y intercept (or the y coordinate of any other point on the line). Conversely, the slope of a vertical line is undefined; its equation is $x = a$, where a is the x intercept (or the x coordinate of any other point on the line).

Example

Given a graph of an exponential function, describe how you can construct an algebraic expression for the function

An algebraic expression for an exponential function has the form $y = Ae^{bx}$. A can be found directly from the graph; it is simply the graph's y intercept. To see this, consider what happens when we evaluate the expression at $x = 0$: $y = Ae^{b \cdot 0} = Ae^0 = A \cdot 1 = A$. Once we know A, we can choose any other point (x_1, y_1) that lies on the graph of the function *except* the y intercept. We can then use this to solve for b: $y_1 = Ae^{bx_1}$, so $\frac{y_1}{A} = e^{bx_1}$, $\ln\left(\frac{y_1}{A}\right) = \ln(e^{bx_1}) = bx_1$, and finally $b = \frac{1}{x_1} \ln\left(\frac{y_1}{A}\right)$. For instance, if the y intercept is $(0, 2)$ and the graph also passes through the point $(5,4)$, then we have $4 = 2e^{b \cdot 5}$, hence $2 = e^{5b}$, $\ln 2 = 5b$, and $b = \frac{\ln 2}{5}$. So an algebraic expression for the function is $y = 2e^{\frac{\ln 2}{5}x}$. This can be simplified: $2e^{\frac{\ln 2}{5}x} = 2(e^{\ln 2})^{\frac{1}{5}x} = 2 \cdot 2^{\frac{1}{5}x} = 2^{\frac{1}{5}x+1}$. So $y = 2 \cdot 2^{\frac{1}{5}x}$ and $y = 2^{\frac{1}{5}x+1}$ are both acceptable ways to write the expression.

Example

Describe how you can write an algebraic expression for an arithmetic sequence given two (not necessarily consecutive) terms of the sequence

An arithmetic sequence is a sequence in which there is a constant difference d between consecutive terms. It can be expressed by the formula $f(n) = a_1 + d(n - 1)$. Suppose we are given two terms of the sequence, $f(n_1)$ and $f(n_2)$. Since the difference between consecutive terms is d, the difference between terms Δn terms apart is simply $\Delta n \cdot d$. In this case, $\Delta n = (n_2 - n_1)$, so $f(n_2) - f(n_1) = (n_2 - n_1)d$, and $d = \frac{f(n_2)-f(n_1)}{n_2-n_1}$. Knowing d, we can use one of the given terms to solve for a_1: $f(n_1) = a_1 + d(n_1 - 1)$, so $a_1 = f(n_1) - d(n_1 - 1)$.

For example, suppose we are told that the third term of an arithmetic sequence is 5 and the seventh term is 17—that is, $f(3) = 5$ and $f(7) = 17$. Then $17 - 5 = (7 - 3)d$, hence $d = \frac{17-5}{7-3} = \frac{12}{4} = 3$. We can now solve for a_1: $5 = a_1 + 3(3 - 1)$, so $a_1 = 5 - 3(3 - 1) = 5 - 3(2) = -1$. So an expression for this arithmetic sequence is $f(n) = -1 + 3(n - 1)$.

Example

Describe how you can write an algebraic expression for a geometric sequence given two (not necessarily consecutive) terms of the sequence

A geometric sequence is a sequence in which there is a constant ratio r between consecutive terms. It can be expressed by the formula $f(n) = a_1 r^{n-1}$. Suppose we are given two terms of the sequence, $f(n_1)$ and $f(n_2)$. Since the ratio of consecutive terms is r, the ratio of terms Δn terms apart is simply $r^{\Delta n}$. In this case, $\Delta n = (n_2 - n_1)$, so $f(n_2)/f(n_1) = r^{n_2-n_1}$, and $r = \bigl(f(n_2)/f(n_1)\bigr)^{1/(n_2-n_1)}$. Knowing r, we can use one of the given terms to solve for a_1: $f(n_1) = a_1 r^{n_1-1}$, so $a_1 = f(n_1)/r^{n_1-1}$.

For example, suppose we are told that the ninth term of an arithmetic sequence is 40 and the fifteenth term is 5—that is, $f(9) = 40$ and $f(15) = 5$. Then $\frac{5}{40} = r^{15-9} = r^6$, hence $r = \left(\frac{5}{40}\right)^{1/6} = \left(\frac{1}{8}\right)^{1/6} = \frac{1}{8^{\frac{1}{6}}} = \frac{1}{\sqrt[6]{8}} = \frac{1}{\sqrt{2}} = \frac{\sqrt{2}}{2}$. We can now solve for a_1: $40 = a_1 \left(\frac{\sqrt{2}}{2}\right)^{9-1} = a_1 \left(\frac{\sqrt{2}}{2}\right)^8 = a_1 \left(\frac{1}{16}\right)$, so $a_1 = 40/(1/16) = 40 \cdot 16 = 640$. So an expression for this arithmetic sequence is $f(n) = 640 \cdot \left(\frac{\sqrt{2}}{2}\right)^{n-1}$.

Exponential functions (with a positive exponent) eventually exceeds any polynomial function

An exponential function has the form $y = Ae^{bx}$. A polynomial function has the form $y = a_n x^n + a_{n-1} x^{n-1} + \cdots + a_1 x + a_0$. The exponential always exceeds the polynomial for sufficiently large x, regardless of the values of A, b, n, and $a_0 \ldots a_n$.

One way to see this is to consider the rate of change. One characteristic of an exponential function is that over a fixed interval it changes by a constant ratio: when x increases by 1, Ae^{bx} increases by e^b. This isn't true of polynomials; for large x, when only the leading term of the polynomial is significant, when x increases by 1 the polynomial increases by a ratio of $\frac{(x+1)^n}{x^n} = \left(\frac{x+1}{x}\right)^n$, which *decreases* as x increases, converging at very large x to 1. Therefore, eventually the rate of change of the polynomial will drop below the rate of change of the exponential, and thereafter at some point the exponential will surpass the polynomial.

Example
The graph below shows a cubic function, an exponential function, a linear function, a logarithmic function, and a quadratic function

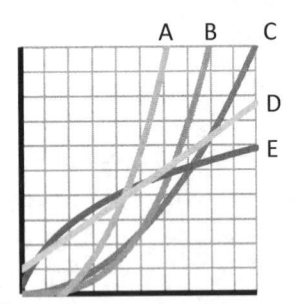

All of these functions tend toward infinity in their right end behavior, but some of them do so more rapidly than others. An exponential equation eventually increases more rapidly than any polynomial, and certainly increases more rapidly than a logarithmic function. The function that, in the end, increases most rapidly must therefore be the exponential, namely A. Conversely, the logarithmic function, the inverse of the exponential, must eventually increase more *slowly* than any polynomial. The logarithmic function must be the one that increases the most slowly in the end, namely E.

This leaves B, C, and D as the cubic, linear, and quadratic. These are all polynomial functions, and in its end behavior a polynomial of a larger order (largest exponent) increases more rapidly than one of a smaller order. This means B must be the cubic (order 3), C the quadratic (order 2), and D the linear (order 1).

Determining how to express the solution of an equation of the form $ab^{ct} = d$ in terms of a logarithm

To express the solution of an equation of the form $ab^{ct} = d$ in terms of a logarithm, we'll have to take the logarithm of both sides of the equation. Before doing that, though, we'd have to isolate the exponential on a side by itself. We can do that by dividing both sides by a: $b^{ct} = d/a$. To cancel an exponential with a base of b, we have to use a logarithm with the base of b: $\log_b b^{ct} = \log_b(d/a)$. Since the logarithm is the inverse of the exponential, the left side, $\log_b b^{ct}$, reduces to just ct. So $ct = \log_b(d/a)$, so $t = \frac{\log_b(d/a)}{c}$. (Using the rule $\log(\alpha/\beta) = \log \alpha - \log \beta$, we can also rewrite this as $t = \frac{\log_b d - \log_b a}{c}$.)

Example
Given an exponential equation such as $20 = 4 \cdot 2^{3x}$, show how you could solve for x

To solve an exponential equation where the variable appears in the exponent, we have to use the fact that the logarithmic function is the inverse of the exponential. First, we rearrange the expression to get the exponential expression on a side by itself. After that, we can cancel the exponential by taking the logarithm of both sides (with the same base as the exponential). From that point on, solving the equation is a matter of simple algebra.

For instance, we can divide by four both sides of our sample equation, $20 = 4 \cdot 2^{3x}$, to get $2^{3x} = \frac{20}{4} = 5$. We can now cancel the exponential with a logarithm: $\log_2 2^{3x} = \log_2 5$, or, simplifying the left hand side, $3x = \log_2 5$. So $x = \frac{1}{3}\log_2 5$.

Using a calculator to evaluate logarithms such as $\log_e 2$, $\log_{10} 7$, and $\log_2 5$

The logarithm base e is also called the natural logarithm, abbreviated *ln*: so $\log_e 2$ is the same thing as ln 2. Scientific calculators generally have an "ln" button, so evaluating natural logarithms is straightforward: to evaluate ln 2 on a TI-84 calculator, for instance, just involves hitting "LN", "2", "ENTER". Similarly, most scientific calculators have a button to calculate logarithms base 10, though it often just says "log" without the base. On a TI-84, $\log_{10} 7$ can be evaluated by hitting "LOG", "7", "ENTER".

Evaluating logarithms with bases other than 10 and e is not quite as straightforward, but still possible using the relation $\log_a b = \frac{\log_c b}{\log_c a}$ (for any base c). Therefore $\log_2 5 =$ ln 5 / ln 2 or $\log_{10} 5 / \log_{10} 2$, either of which is readily evaluable with a calculator.

Example
> In the equation of a linear function, $y = mx + b$, what is the physical significance of the parameters m and b

> The parameter m is the slope of the line. Regarding the relationship between the physical quantities symbolized by x and y, m is the *rate of change* of y with respect to x: specifically, when x increases by 1, y increases by the amount m.

> b is often known as the *y-intercept* of the line: it represents the y coordinate of the point where the line crosses the y-axis. Another way of saying this, and one that makes its physical significance clearer, is that b is the value of y when $x = 0$. When x represents time (as is frequently the case), then b is the *initial value* of y.

Example
> Given an exponential equation such as the compound interest equation $A = P\left(1 + \frac{r}{n}\right)^{nt}$, determine how to interpret its parameters in terms of the context

> While we could memorize the meaning of each parameter in the compound interest equation $A = P\left(1 + \frac{r}{n}\right)^{nt}$, it's also possible to figure out what they mean by examining the exponential equation. The amount of money in an account with compound interest rises exponentially as a function of time. The quantity that rises exponentially in this equation is A, so that must be the total amount of money in the account. The variable in the exponent is t,

so that must be time. (There's also an *n* in the exponent, but that appears elsewhere as well.) *P* is the amount of money in the account when $t = 0$, so that must be the initial amount of money deposited in the account (the *principal*).

Two parameters of compound interest remain: the interest rate and the interval over which it's compounded (monthly, quarterly, etc.) The latter must be *n*, since it affects the exponent: interest compounded monthly would rise exponentially faster than interest compounded quarterly, for instance. That leaves *r* for the interest rate.

Example

Given a logarithmic equation such as the equation for the loudness of a sound in decibels in terms of its intensity, $\beta = 10 \log_{10}\left(\frac{I}{I_0}\right)$, determine how to interpret its parameters in terms of the context

Even if we're not familiar with this equation, we can figure out what its parameters mean by examining the equation. Since the equation is for the loudness of a sound, that must be what the β stands for. This means the intensity, the other quantity mentioned, must be either I or I_0. If the intensity were I_0, that would mean that as the sound intensity increases, the loudness decreases, which seems illogical. It stands to reason, then that I represents the sound intensity. As for I_0, since it doesn't correspond to one of the variables, it must just be a constant factor.

As it happens, I_0 is defined as 10^{-12} watts, but even without knowing that, we can still get useful information from this equation; for instance, we can tell that if a sound's intensity increases by a factor of 100, then its loudness increases by 20 decibels.

Complex Numbers

Problem

Simplify
1. i^{12}
2. $(2i)^8$
3. $(-i)^{25}$

Notice the pattern that emerges when i is raised to consecutive natural number powers:

$$i^1 = i$$
$$i^2 = -1$$
$$i^3 = i^2 i = (-1)(i) = -i$$
$$i^4 = i^2 i^2 = (-1)(-1) = 1$$
$$i^5 = i^4 i = (1)(i) = i$$
$$i^6 = i^4 i^2 = (1)(-1) = -1$$
$$i^7 = i^4 i^3 = (1)(-i) = -i$$
$$i^8 = i^4 i^4 = (-1)(-1) = 1$$

The imaginary number i raised to any whole power n is always $i, -1, -i$, or 1. To find i^n, either continue writing the pattern $i, -1, -i, 1$ to find the nth number in the pattern, or, more simply, use properties of exponents to rewrite and simplify i^n.

1. $i^{12} = (i^4)^3 = (1)^3 = 1$
2. $(2i)^8 = (2^8)(i^4)^2 = (2^4)^2(1)^2 = 16^2 = 256$
3. $(-i)^{25} = (-1)^{25}(i^4)^6(i) = (-1)(1)^6(i) = -i$

Problem

Determine the values of a and b for which $\sqrt{a} \cdot \sqrt{b} \neq \sqrt{ab}$.

$\sqrt{a} \cdot \sqrt{b} = \sqrt{ab}$ when either a or b is positive or when both a and b are positive. For example,
$\sqrt{25} \cdot \sqrt{4} = 5 \cdot 2 = 10$ and $\sqrt{25 \cdot 4} = \sqrt{100} = 10$, so $\sqrt{25} \cdot \sqrt{4} = \sqrt{25 \cdot 4}$;
$\sqrt{-25} \cdot \sqrt{4} = 5i \cdot 2 = 10i$ and $\sqrt{-25 \cdot 4} = \sqrt{-100} = 10i$, so $\sqrt{-25} \cdot \sqrt{4} = \sqrt{-25 \cdot 4}$.
However, $\sqrt{a} \cdot \sqrt{b} \neq \sqrt{ab}$ when both a and b are both negative. For example, $\sqrt{-25} \cdot \sqrt{-4} = 5i \cdot 2i = 10i^2 = -10$ but $\sqrt{-25 \cdot -4} = \sqrt{100} = 10$. Since $10 \neq -10, \sqrt{-25} \cdot \sqrt{-4} \neq \sqrt{-25 \cdot -4}$.

Problem

Simplify $\sqrt{-200}$.

$\sqrt{-200} = \sqrt{-1 \cdot 2 \cdot 2 \cdot 2 \cdot 5 \cdot 5} = \sqrt{-1} \cdot \sqrt{2^2} \cdot \sqrt{2} \cdot \sqrt{5^2} = i \cdot 2 \cdot \sqrt{2} \cdot 5 = 10i\sqrt{2}$.

Problem
   Simplify the following expressions.
   1. $(2 + 3i) + (6 - 2i)$
   2. $(2 + 3i) - (6 - 2i)$
   3. $(2 + 3i)(6 - 2i)$

The commutative, associative, and distributive properties are true for complex numbers. Complex expressions can be simplified just as real variable expressions are simplified. Keep in mind, however, that i is not a variable but is rather the imaginary number, so be sure to simplify i^2 to -1.
1. $(2 + 3i) + (6 - 2i) = 8 + i$
2. $(2 + 3i) - (6 - 2i) = -4 + 5i$
3. $(2 + 3i)(6 - 2i) = 12 - 4i + 18i - 6i^2 = 12 + 14i + 6 = 18 + 14i$

Problem
   Simplify $3i(2 + 4i) - (6 + 2i)^2$.

The commutative, associative, and distributive properties are true for complex numbers. Complex expressions can be simplified just as real, variable expressions are simplified. Keep in mind, however, that i is not a variable but is rather the imaginary number, so be sure to simplify i^2 to -1.

$$3i(2 + 4i) - (6 + 2i)^2$$
$$6i + 12i^2 - (36 + 24i + 4i^2)$$
$$6i + 12i^2 - 36 - 24i - 4i^2$$
$$-18i + 8i^2 - 36$$
$$-18i - 8 - 36$$
$$-44 - 18i$$

Modulus of a complex number

The modulus, or absolute value, of a complex number $z = a + bi$ is the distance from the origin to point z graphed on the complex plane. Since that distance can be represented by the hypotenuse of a right triangle with leg lengths a and b, $|z| = \sqrt{a^2 + b^2}$.

It is **true** that the modulus of a complex number is always a real number and is always positive. Since a and b represent real numbers, their squares are always positive, real numbers. The sum of two positive, real numbers must also be positive and real, so $a^2 + b^2$ is a positive, real quantity. The square root of a positive, real number is also a positive, real number, so $\sqrt{a^2 + b^2}$ must return a number that is both real and positive.

Complex plane

The complex plane is created by the intersection of a real, horizontal axis and an imaginary, vertical axis. For a complex number written in the form $a + bi$, a represents the displacement along the real axis and b along the imaginary axis.

Problem
   Graph these numbers on the complex plane.

1. -4
2. $2i$
3. $3-i$

The number -4 is graphed in its appropriate position on the real number line, while $2i$ is graphed on the imaginary axis since its real number component a is 0. The complex number $3-i$ is represented by a point on the plane which is three units to the right of the origin and one unit down.

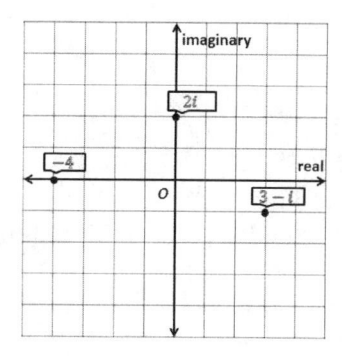

Another way to represent each of these points graphically on the complex plane is to draw a vector from the origin to the point (a, b). For example,

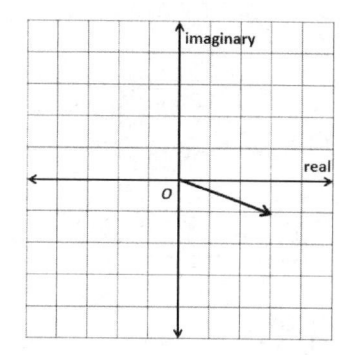

$3 - i$ is graphed below.

Conjugate of a complex number

The conjugate of a complex number $a + bi$ is $a - bi$. It is **true** that the product of a complex number and its conjugate is always real:
$(a + bi)(a - bi) = a^2 - abi + abi - b^2i^2 = a^2 + b^2$. Since a and b are real, and since squares and sums of real numbers are also real, $a^2 + b^2$ is always real.

Problem

Find the modulus and the conjugate of the complex number $4 + 3i$.

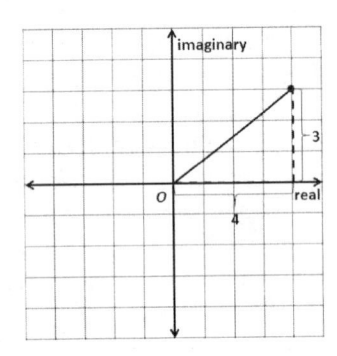

The modulus, or absolute value, of a complex number is the number's distance from the origin when graphed on the complex plane. By graphing $4 + 3i$ on the complex plane, it is easy to see that its distance from the origin is the hypotenuse of a right triangle with leg lengths 4 and 3. Recognize 3-4-5 as a common Pythagorean triple, or evaluate and simply the expression $\sqrt{a^2 + b^2}$, where $a = 4$ and $b = 3$: $\sqrt{4^2 + 3^2} = \sqrt{16 + 9} = \sqrt{25} = 5$. So, the modulus of $4 + 3i$ is 5.

The conjugate of complex number $a + bi$ is defined as $a - bi$, so the conjugate of $4 + 3i$ is $4 - 3i$.

Problem

Write an equation which relates complex number z, its conjugate $\bar{z}$, and its modulus $|z|$.

Let $z = a + bi$. By definition, $\bar{z} = a - bi$, and $|z| = \sqrt{a^2 + b^2}$.
Since $z \cdot \bar{z} = (a + bi)(a - bi) = a^2 - abi + abi - b^2 i^2 = a^2 + b^2$, and since $|z|^2 = \left(\sqrt{a^2 + b^2}\right)^2 = a^2 + b^2$, we have the relationship $\mathbf{z \cdot \bar{z} = |z|^2}$.

Use the property $z \cdot \bar{z} = |z|^2$, where z is a complex number and $\bar{z}$ and $|z|$ are its conjugate and modulus, respectively, to find the modulus of $3 + 4i$.

When $z = 3 + 4i$, $\bar{z} = 3 - 4i$.
$$|z|^2 = z \cdot \bar{z} = (3 + 4i)(3 - 4i) = 9 - 16i^2 = 25$$
$$|z| = 5$$
The modulus is represents the distance of a complex number from zero on the complex plane and can therefore not be negative. So, the modulus of $3 + 4i$ is 5.

Problem

Simplify $\frac{2-4i}{1+3i}$.

To simplify the quotient of two complex numbers, multiply the numerator and denominator by the complex conjugate of the denominator.

$$\frac{2-4i}{1+3i} = \frac{2-4i}{1+3i} \cdot \frac{1-3i}{1-3i} = \frac{2-6i-4i+12i^2}{1-9i^2} = \frac{2-10i-12}{1+9} = \frac{-10-10i}{10}$$
$$= -1 - i$$

Problem

Simplify $\frac{3-i\sqrt{2}}{3+i\sqrt{2}}$.

To simplify the quotient of two complex numbers, multiply the numerator and denominator by the complex conjugate of the denominator.

$$\frac{3-i\sqrt{2}}{3+i\sqrt{2}} = \frac{3-i\sqrt{2}}{3+i\sqrt{2}} \cdot \frac{3-i\sqrt{2}}{3-i\sqrt{2}} = \frac{9-2i\sqrt{2}+2i^2}{9-2i^2} = \frac{9-2i\sqrt{2}-2}{9+2}$$
$$= \frac{7-2i\sqrt{2}}{11} = \frac{7}{11} - \frac{2\sqrt{2}}{11}i$$

Problem

Use the property $\frac{z_1}{z_2} = \frac{z_1 \overline{z_2}}{|z_2|^2}$ to find the quotient of $2 - 4i$ and $1 + 3i$.

$$z_1 = 2 - 4i$$
$$z_2 = 1 + 3i$$
$$\overline{z_2} = 1 - 3i$$
$$|z_2| = \sqrt{1^2 + 3^2} = \sqrt{1+9} = \sqrt{10}$$

So,
$$\frac{2-4i}{1+3i} = \frac{(2-4i)(1-3i)}{\sqrt{10}^2} = \frac{2-6i-4i+12i^2}{10} = \frac{2-10i-12}{10} = \frac{-10-10i}{10}$$
$$= -1 - i$$

Functions and Graphing

A function is a relation between two sets, the *domain* and the *range*, such that each element of the domain is associated with exactly one element of the range.

There are other ways this definition can be phrased. A less technical wording is that a function is a relation that associates each possible value of one variable, *x*, with a unique value of a second variable, *y*.

Note that it is *not* necessarily the case that each element of the *range* is associated with exactly one element of the *domain* (or, under the other definition, that each value of *y* is associated with a unique value of *x*). However, a relation for which this condition does hold is *invertible*—in this case, interchanging the domain and the range of the function gives rise to another function (the original function's *inverse*).

Linear, quadratic, polynomial, and rational functions

A *linear* function is a function the graph of which is a straight line. The expression for a linear function includes *x* (possibly multiplied by some constant coefficient, and possibly added to some other constant), but does not include x^2 or any higher powers of *x*. The following, for example, are all linear functions: $f(x) = x$, $f(x) = 1 - 2x$, $f(x) = \frac{3}{4}x + 3$.

The expression for a *quadratic* function includes a term containing x^2 (again possibly multiplied by some constant coefficient), but no term contains x^3 or any higher powers of *x*. The following, for example, are all quadratic functions: $f(x) = x^2 + x + 1$, $f(x) = 3x^2 - 2$, $f(x) = -\frac{1}{2}x^2$.

The expression for a *polynomial* function is a sum of one or more powers of *x*, possibly multiplied by constant coefficients. (Note that $1 = x^0$ is a power of *x*.) All linear and quadratic functions are polynomials; so are the following: $f(x) = 3x^7$, $f(x) = 2x^3 - 2x^2 + 5x - 6$, $f(x) = x^{2000} - x^{169}$.

A *rational function* is a ratio of polynomials. Examples include $\frac{x^2-1}{x}$, $\frac{1}{3x^3+2x^2+x}$, and $\frac{x^4+3}{x^2-2}$.

Determine how you can tell from looking at a graph whether the graph represents a function

The simplest way to tell by visual inspection whether a graph represents a function is a procedure sometimes known as the "vertical line test". Imagine a vertical line scanning across the graph. If, at any point, the line intersects more than one point on the graph, the graph does *not* represent a function. Otherwise, it does.

For example, consider the following graphs.

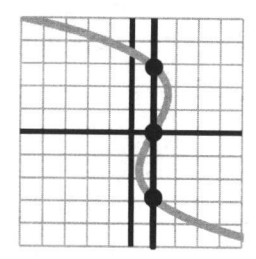

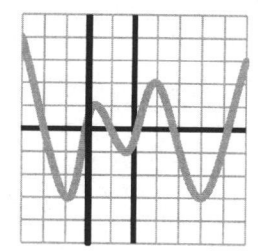

The vertical line in the image on the left intersects the graph in three points. Therefore, the graph on the left does *not* represent a function. On the right, however, no matter where we place the vertical line, it will never intersect more than one point. Therefore, the graph on the right represents a function.

Finding the domain of the function

Given a function expressed in a table like the one below, determine how you can find the domain of the function.

x	0	3	2	1	8	10	6	7
$f(x)$	2	8	6	8	2	3	4	5

The *domain* of a function $f(x)$ is the set of all input values for which the function is defined. For a function expressed in a table like the one in this example, it's simple to find the domain, because every point in the function—that is, every input-output pair—is given explicitly. To find the domain, we just list all the x values: in this case, that would be {0, 3, 2, 1, 8, 10, 6, 7}, or, putting them in ascending order, {0, 1, 2, 3, 6, 7, 8, 10}. (Putting the values in ascending order isn't strictly necessary, but generally makes the set easier to read.)

Note that we don't have to worry about the possibility of an input value being repeated: by definition of a function, no input value can be matched to more than one output value.

Given a function expressed in analytic form such as $f(x) = \sin x$, $g(x) = \sqrt{x+1}$, or $h(x) = \frac{x}{x^2-1}$, explain how you can find the domain of the function.

The *domain* of a function $f(x)$ is the set of all possible input values of the function—that is, of every possible value of x for which the function is defined. Some functions, such as $f(x) = \sin x$, are defined for any real value of x; in this case, the domain of $f(x)$ is $(-\infty, \infty)$, that is, it includes all real numbers. There are functions, however, for which that isn't true. For instance, consider $g(x) = \sqrt{x+1}$. The square root of a negative number is not defined (at least as a real number), so in order for $g(x)$ to be defined we must have $x + 1 \geq 0$, so $x \geq -1$. The domain of $g(x)$ is thus $[-1, \infty)$. Similarly, $h(x) = \frac{x}{x^2-1}$ is not defined when the denominator is zero, which is true when $x = \pm 1$. The domain therefore includes all real numbers *except* 1 and −1, which we can write as $(-\infty, -1) \cup (-1, 1) \cup (1, \infty)$.

Finding the range of a function

Given a function expressed in a table like the one below, determine how you can find the range of the function.

x	-1	4	2	1	0	3	8	6
f(x)	3	0	3	-1	-1	2	4	6

The *range* of a function $f(x)$ is the set of all possible output values of the function—that is, of every possible value of $f(x)$, for any value of x in the function's domain. For a function expressed in a table like the one in this example, it's simple to find the range, because every point in the function—that is, every input-output pair—is given explicitly. To find the range, we just list all the values of $f(x)$; in this case, that would be {3, 0, 3, –1, –1, 2, 4, 6}. Note that some of these values appear more than once. This is entirely permissible for a function; while each value of x must be matched to a unique value of $f(x)$, the converse is not true. We don't need to list each value more than once, so eliminating duplicates, the range is {3, 0, –1, 2, 4, 6}, or, putting them in ascending order, {–1, 0, 2, 3, 4, 6}. (Putting the values in ascending order isn't strictly necessary, but generally makes the set easier to read.)

Given a function expressed in analytic form such as $f(x) = x^3$, $g(x) = x^2 - 2x + 4$, or $h(x) = 1/x$, explain how you can find the range of the function.

For a continuous function, we can find the range by just finding the maximum and minimum values of the function; the range comprises all the points in between. Some functions have no maximum or minimum; this is the case, for instance, with $f(x) = x^3$. At the left, the function decreases indefinitely, and on the right, it increases indefinitely. The range therefore includes all real numbers, $(-\infty, \infty)$. Other functions may have a maximum, but no minimum, or vice versa. The quadratic function $g(x) = x^2 - 2x + 4$ has a minimum at (1,3), but no maximum, so its range is $[3, \infty)$.

For a discontinuous function, we must examine each part separately. $h(x) = 1/x$ has a discontinuity at $x = 0$. On the left side, the function has no minimum, but has an asymptotic maximum of 0 (asymptotic because it approaches 0 but never actually reaches it); the range of this side is $(-\infty, 0)$. Similarly, the right side has a range of $(0, \infty)$. The total range of the function is the union of these two ranges, hence $(-\infty, 0) \cup (0, \infty)$.

<u>Example</u>

Suppose $f(x) = x^2 + 1$ and $g(x) = x - 1$. How would you find each of the following

$f(3)$ $g(3)$ $f(y^2)$ $g(z + 1)$

In function notation, "$f(3)$" can be thought of as a shorthand for "$f(x)$ when $x = 3$". To evaluate the function at this point, just replace the x in the expression for the function with the number. If $f(x) = x^2 + 1$, then to find $f(3)$ we just replace each x in "$x^2 + 1$" with 3. So $f(3) = 3^2 + 1$, which we can simplify to 10. Similarly, $g(3) = 3 - 1 = 2$.

The same principle holds when instead of a number, there is a variable or an expression within the parentheses. To find $f(y^2)$, where $f(x) = x^2 + 1$, we

replace each x in "$x^2 + 1$" with "y^2" (or "(y^2)"—including parentheses may make it easier to keep track of the substitution). This yields $f(y^2) = (y^2)^2 + 1 = y^4 + 1$. Similarly,
$g(z + 1) = (z + 1) - 1 = z$.

Example
Describe in words what a statement such as f(x) = x² + 1 means

This kind of statement defines a particular function; it tells how to match up each point in the domain with a point in the range. The possible values of x comprise the domain—this can usually be assumed to include all real numbers unless specified otherwise, or unless there are some points for which the expression on the right side of the equation is undefined. Each value of x is then matched with a (not necessarily unique) value of $f(x)$ (or y); all the values of $f(x)$ that are matched to values of x comprise the range.

In the case of the statement $f(x) = x^2 + 1$, this defines a function in which each real number x is matched to the number $x^2 + 1$. For instance, $x = 0$ corresponds to $f(0) = 0^2 + 1 = 1$, when $x = 1$ $f(1) = 1^2 + 1 = 2$, and so forth. Note that $f(x)$ in this case can never be less than 1, so the range of this function is $[1, \infty)$.

Real-world situations that can be modeled by statements that use function notation

A statement using function notation can model any situation in which one quantity depends uniquely on one or more other quantities. For example, the area of a rectangle can be expressed as a function of its width and height. The maximum vertical distance a projectile travels can be expressed as a function of its initial vertical speed. An object's position, the amount of money in a bank account, or any other quantity that changes over time can be expressed as a function of time.

A relationship *cannot* be modeled with a function, however, if it involves two quantities neither of which is uniquely determined by the other—that is, if each quantity may have multiple values corresponding to the same value of the other. For example, we could *not* write a function to represent the relationship between peoples' height in inches and their weight in pounds. There are people of the same height with different weights, and people of the same weight but different heights.

Defining a function recursively

To define a function recursively is to give the value of the function for a given input value in terms of the function's values for other input values—for example, to define $f(x)$ in terms of $f(x - 1)$. A function cannot be defined *purely* recursively; it's necessary to define the function absolutely for at least one point to give a starting point for the recursion.

For example, the factorial function, $f(n) = n! = n(n-1)(n-2)\ldots(2)(1)$, can be defined recursively as follows: $f(1) = 1$, otherwise $f(n) = n \cdot f(n-1)$. The domain of this function is the positive integers. (Technically, the factorial function is also defined at $n = 0$, where $0! = 1$, but that's not important for this example.) Then, for example, $f(3) = 3 \cdot f(2) = 3 \cdot 2 \cdot f(1) = 3 \cdot 2 \cdot 1$.

Sequence

A sequence is a function in which the domain is confined to the integers, or some subset of the integers. Very often, the subset in question is the positive integers, in which case the sequence can be thought of as an ordered list of the elements of the range, with $f(n)$ identified directly with the nth element of the sequence. Such sequences are often written in list form; the sequence $f(n) = \frac{n^2+n}{2}$, where $f(1) = 1, f(2) = 3, f(3) = 6$, and so on, can simply be written as 1, 3, 6, 10, 15, ...

Sequences are often defined recursively, with the first few elements of the sequence defined explicitly and with $f(n)$ otherwise defined in terms of $f(n-1)$ or in general of function values for smaller versions of n. Many functions can be equivalently defined explicitly or recursively. For instance, the sequence above, $f(n) = \frac{n^2+n}{2}$, can also be defined as $f(1) = 1$ and $f(n) = f(n-1) + n$.

Fibonacci sequence

The Fibonacci sequence is a sequence in which the first two terms are 1 and each succeeding term is the sum of the preceding two terms: 1, 1, 2, 3, 5, 8, 13, 21... Written algebraically, $f(1) = f(2) = 1$, and thereafter $f(n) = f(n-1) + f(n-2)$. (There are some variations in its definition; sometimes the domain starts at 0 instead of 1, for instance, or the first term may be defined as 0 instead of 1.)

The Fibonacci sequence is the most common and perhaps the simplest sequence that is recursively defined in terms of more than one earlier term in the sequence (rather than each term being only defined in terms of the immediately preceding term). It also arises in many real-world phenomena.

<u>Example</u>
Given a function definition such as $(x) = x^2 - 9$, determine how you would find the function's x and y intercepts

To find the y intercept, simply find $f(0)$. The y intercept is by definition the point where the function crosses the y-axis, which means it's the function's value when $x = 0$. For the example function definition, $f(x) = x^2 - 9$, $f(0) = 0^2 - 9 = -9$. So the y intercept is (0, -9). Since no function can have multiple y values associated with a single value of x, a function cannot have more than one y intercept.

To find the x intercepts, we need to find where the function crosses the x-axis, so we have to find the value(s) of x, if any, for which $f(x) = 0$. There may be more than one such value. In the case of the example function, $f(x) = x^2 - 9$, this means $0 = x^2 - 9$. Solving for x, we get $x^2 = 9$, so $x = \pm 3$. So this function has two x intercepts, (-3, 0) and (3, 0).

All functions do not necessarily have x and y intercepts

No, not all functions necessarily have x and y intercepts. To have a y intercept, a function must be defined at $x = 0$. This is not true of all functions: $f(x) = \sqrt{x-1}$, for instance, does not have a y intercept, because $f(0) = \sqrt{-1}$ is not defined in the real numbers. For a function $f(x)$ to have an x intercept, there must be one or more values of x such that $f(x) = 0$. This, again, is not true of all functions. For instance, for $f(x) = x^2 + 1$, there is no value of x for which $f(x) = 0$, since we cannot find a real value of x that satisfies the equation $x^2 + 1 = 0$. This function has no x intercept.

It is possible for a function to have neither an x nor a y intercept. One simple example is $f(x) = 1/x$. Since $1/0$ is undefined, this function does not have a y intercept. Since there is no finite value of x satisfying $1/x = 0$, this function does not have an x intercept.

"Relative maximum" and "relative minimum" of a function

A "relative maximum" of a function is a point at which the function has a higher value than any other point in its immediate vicinity. More technically, a relative maximum is a point (x, y) such that if we choose a sufficiently small interval around x, $f(x) > f(x')$ for any other point x' within the interval.

A relative minimum is just the opposite: a point at which the function has a *lower* value than any other point in its immediate vicinity, or, more technically, a point (x, y) such that if we choose a sufficiently small interval around x, $f(x) < f(x')$ for any other point x' within the interval.

A function may have multiple relative maxima and relative minima, or it may have none. A linear function such as $y = x$, for instance, has no relative maxima or minima, while $y = \sin(x)$ has infinitely many of each.

Finding a relative maximum or minimum from a graph

At a relative maximum, the graph goes from increasing to decreasing, forming a "peak" on the graph which is generally easy to spot visually. Similarly, at a relative minimum, the graph goes from decreasing to increasing, forming a "trough". On the graph below, for instance, points A and C are relative maxima, and point B is a relative minimum.

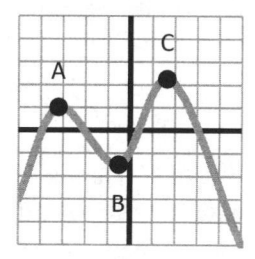

Note that point A is a relative maximum, but not an absolute maximum; the function has a higher value at point C. Similarly, point B is a relative minimum, but not an absolute minimum; the function has a lower value at the left and right ends of the graph than it does at point B. Point C, however, is both a relative and an absolute maximum; nowhere on the graph does the function have a higher value than at point C.

Determining how you can tell over what intervals a function is increasing or decreasing

If the function is presented in graph form, it's easy to tell by inspection where it's increasing and where it's decreasing. Where the slope of the graph is positive—where the graph goes from lower left to upper right—the function is increasing. Where the slope is negative—where the graph goes from upper left to lower right—the function is decreasing. In the graph below, for example, the graph is increasing over the intervals $(-\infty, -3)$ and $(0, 3)$, and decreasing over the intervals $(-3, 0)$ and $(3, \infty)$.

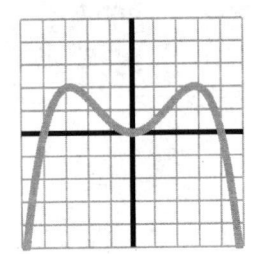

If the function is presented explicitly, such as $f(x) = x^2 - x^4$, we can graph the function and then find the appropriate intervals as above, but we can also, for instance, find the relative maxima and minima; an interval with a minimum on the left and a maximum on the right is increasing, and one with a maximum on the left and minimum on the right is decreasing.

If a function is given symbolically, name some features we can find that may be useful in sketching its graph

Sketching a graph without the aid of technology is facilitated by first determining some key properties of the function. If the function has horizontal asymptotes, we can use these as guidelines for the function's end behavior. If it doesn't have horizontal asymptotes, we can often determine the end behavior by other means. A function's vertical asymptotes likewise indicate its behavior near the corresponding values of x.

Also useful in determining the shape of a function are the relative maxima and minima, and the intervals over which the function is increasing or decreasing. The x and y intercepts provide a few points we know the function passes through. If the function has any symmetries or periodicity, these are also helpful in plotting it. Of course, if all else fails, we can also just pick a few x values at random, solve for $f(x)$ at those points, and plot those points to get a feel for the function's shape.

Periodic **functions**

A function is *periodic* if it comprises successive repetitions of an identical shape. That is, a periodic function is unchanged if displaced by some constant P. This constant—the length of the repeating portion—is called the function's *period*. Periodicity can be defined in a more precise, mathematical form: a function $f(x)$ is periodic if $f(x + P) = f(x)$ for all x. (If this is true for P, it's also true for all multiples of P, but the function's period is defined as the smallest possible value of P for which the relation holds.)

For instance, the function $f(x) = \sin(x)$ is periodic with a period of 2π, since $\sin(x + 2\pi) = \sin(x)$ for all x. (It's also true that, for instance, $\sin(x + 4\pi) = \sin(x)$, and $\sin(x + 6\pi) = \sin(x)$, but there is no positive value of P *smaller* than 2π satisfying $\sin(x + P) = \sin(x)$.

Symmetrical functions

A function is symmetrical if it remains unchanged under certain kinds of transformations. While there are many kinds of transformations and many kinds of symmetries, for functions the type of transformation most often considered is reflection. Particularly important are reflections through the *y*-axis and reflections through the origin.

A function is symmetrical under a reflection through the *y*-axis if it stays the same when "flipped over" around the *y*-axis into its mirror image—mathematically, $f(x) = f(-x)$. Such a function is by definition *even*. A function is symmetrical under a reflection through the origin if it stays the same when each point is reflected to the opposite side of the origin—mathematically, $f(x) = -f(-x)$. Such a function is by definition *odd*.

A periodic function is also symmetrical, not necessarily under reflection, but under an appropriate *translation*. The function is unchanged when translated (moved) horizontally by a distance equal to the function's period.

Function's *end behavior*

A function's *end behavior* refers to its tendency at the extreme right and left sides of the graph—that is, what happens to the function as x tends toward $\pm\infty$. There are essentially three possibilities: either $f(x)$ increases without limit ($f(x)$ goes to ∞), $f(x)$ decreases without limit ($f(x)$ goes to $-\infty$), or $f(x)$ tends toward some finite value (a horizontal asymptote). The behavior may be different at the two sides: while $f(x) = x^2$ goes to ∞ on both sides, $g(x) = x^3$ goes to ∞ on the right side and to $-\infty$ on the left, and $h(x) = e^{-x}$ goes to ∞ on the left and tends toward the horizontal asymptote $y = 0$ on the right.

When writing a function to represent a quantitative relationship given in a word problem, explain how to determine the function's domain

Sometimes the domain is given explicitly; if given the earnings of a company between 1980 and 2000, then if you write this as a function of the company's earnings over time in years, the domain would run from 1980 to 2000.

When not given explicitly, the domain must be deduced by considering logically within what limits the function applies. Often this involves noting that the function and/or its argument must be non-negative. For instance, suppose a word problem says that a builder wishes to use 100 feet of fence to enclose three sides of a rectangle, and asks for the rectangle's length as a function of its width. Such a function could be written as $f(x) = 100 - 2x$, where x is the width and $f(x)$ the length. Clearly, the width cannot be negative, so we must have $x \geq 0$. Nor can the length be negative, so we must have $f(x) \geq 0$, i.e. $100 - 2x \geq 0$, so $x \leq 50$. Therefore, the domain is $0 \leq x \leq 50$.

Determining the domain of a function from its graph

The *domain* of a function is the set of x values for which the function is defined. This can be seen from the graph by observing for what values of x the function is drawn. Essentially, if a vertical line drawn through the graph at a particular value of x intercepts the graph of the function, then the function is defined at that point. If a vertical line intercepts the function no matter where it is drawn, then the domain contains all real numbers.

If this is not the case, then special considerations apply at the endpoints of intervals over which the function is defined. A function is never defined at a vertical asymptote. If $f(x)$ is finite at the endpoint of the interval, however, then the endpoint is drawn either as a filled circle to indicate that it is included in the function, or a hollow circle if not. Of the two graphs below, for instance, the left has a domain of $[-2, \infty)$, and the right of $(-2, \infty)$.

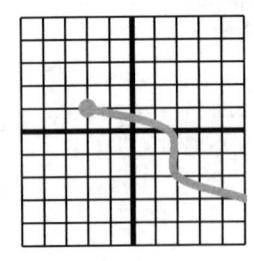

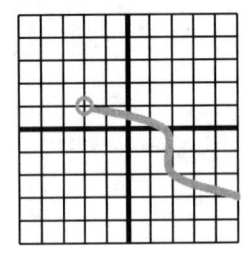

Example
Determine the domains of each of the functions shown below

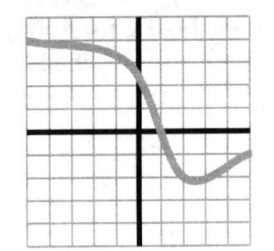

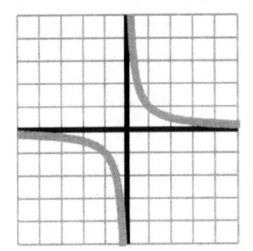

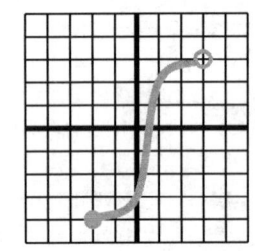

The domain of a function can be seen from its graph by observing what values along the x-axis have part of the function directly above or below them. Often the domain comprises all real numbers, $(-\infty, \infty)$. This is the case for the sample function shown on the left: the function extends unbroken from the left edge of the graph to its right edge; there is no x value for which it is not defined. For a function with a vertical asymptote, the x value corresponding to that asymptote is not part of the domain. The middle example function has a vertical asymptote at $x = 0$, so its domain is $(-\infty, 0) \cup (0, \infty)$.

Other functions are only defined over particular intervals. In this case, a solid circle at the end of the interval means that end point is included in the function's domain, and a hollow circle means it isn't. The example function on the right, then, is defined at $x = -2$ but not at $x = 3$; its domain is $[-2, 3)$.

Example
: Calculating a function's average rate of change over a specific interval when the function is given as a table

x	0	2	4	6	8	10	12	14	16
f(x)	-100	-54	-26	-10	0	10	26	54	100

The function's average rate of change over the interval [x_1, x_2] can be calculated as $\frac{f(x_2)-f(x_1)}{x_2-x_1}$. For the sample table, for instance, if we want to determine the function's rate of change during the entire interval represented in the table, then $x_1 = 0$ and $x_2 = 16$. By reference to the table, $f(x_1) = f(0) = -100$, and $f(x_2) = f(16) = 100$. Thus, the function's rate of change is equal to $\frac{100-(-100)}{16-0} = \frac{200}{16} = 12.5$. If on the other hand we only want to find the rate of change between 0 and 4, then $x_1 = 0$, $x_2 = 4$, $f(x_1) = f(0) = -100$, and $f(x_2) = f(4) = -26$. The rate of change is then $\frac{-26-(-100)}{4-0} = \frac{74}{4} = 18.5$. If we are asked for the rate of change in the interval [6, 10], then $x_1 = 6$, $x_2 = 10$, $f(x_1) = f(6) = -10$, and $f(x_2) = f(10) = 10$. The rate of change is then $\frac{10-(-10)}{10-6} = \frac{20}{4} = 5$.

Example
: Calculating a function's average rate of change over a specific interval when the function is given algebraically, such as $f(x) = x^2 + 1$

The function's average rate of change over the interval [x_1, x_2] can be calculated as $\frac{f(x_2)-f(x_1)}{x_2-x_1}$. For the sample function, for instance, suppose we're asked to find the function's average rate of change between 0 and 10. Then $x_1 = 0$ and $x_2 = 10$. To find $f(x_1)$ and $f(x_2)$, we simply evaluate the function at these two points: $f(x_1) = f(0) = 0^2 + 1 = 1$, and $f(x_2) = f(10) = 10^2 + 1 = 101$. The function's average rate of change in this interval is therefore $\frac{101-1}{10-0} = \frac{100}{10} = 10$.

If we're asked to find the function's average rate of change over the interval [-4, 2], then $x_1 = -4$, $x_2 = 2$, $f(x_1) = f(-4) = (-4)^2 + 1 = 17$, and $f(x_2) = f(2) = 2^2 + 1 = 5$. The average rate of change is therefore $\frac{5-17}{2-(-4)} = \frac{-12}{6} = -2$. If we're asked to find the average rate of change over the interval [-5, 5], then $x_1 = -5$, $x_2 = 5$, $f(x_1) = f(-5) = (-5)^2 + 1 = 26$, and $f(x_2) = f(5) = 5^2 + 1 = 26$. The average rate of change is therefore $\frac{26-26}{5-(-5)} = \frac{0}{10} = 0$.

Estimating a function's average rate of change over a specific interval when the function is given graphically, like the graph below

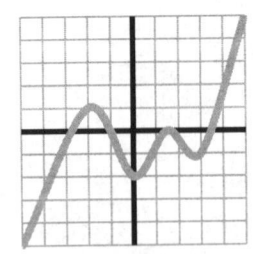

A function's average rate of change over an interval $[a, b]$ contained in the function's domain is the change in the value of $f(x)$ in that interval relative to the change in x. In other words, mathematically, it can be expressed as $\frac{f(b)-f(a)}{b-a}$. To estimate the average rate of change over an interval for a function given graphically, then, we have to estimate the coordinates of the endpoints of the desired interval and then put the appropriate values into that expression and carry out the calculation. For example, consider the sample function over the entire interval shown on the graph, $[-5,5]$. At the left end is passes through the point $(-5, -5)$, and at the right end $(5,5)$; the average rate of change is therefore $\frac{f(5)-f(-5)}{5-(-5)} = \frac{5-(-5)}{10} = \frac{10}{10} = 1$. If we instead consider the interval $[-2,0]$, the left endpoint is about $(-2,1)$ and the right about $(0, -2)$; the average rate of change over the interval $[-2, 0]$ is then $\frac{f(0)-f(-2)}{0-(-2)} = \frac{-2-1}{2} = \frac{-3}{2} = -\frac{3}{2}$. The average rate of change over the interval $[-5, 0]$ is $\frac{f(0)-f(-5)}{0-(-5)} = \frac{-2-(-5)}{5} = \frac{3}{5}$.

Graphing a linear function given in slope-intercept form, such as $f(x) = 3x + 1$

There are several ways to graph a linear function. For a function given in slope-intercept form, like this example, it's usually easiest to use the slope and the y intercept. The slope-intercept form of a linear function takes the form $y = mx + b$, where m is the slope and b the y intercept. (If the x has no coefficient, the slope is 1.) For the sample function $f(x) = 3x + 1$ (i.e. $y = 3x + 1$), the slope is 3 and the y-intercept is 1. Therefore, we can plot the point $(0,1)$, and then draw a line through that point with the appropriate slope: for every 1 unit to the right, the line goes 3 units up. If the slope is negative, then instead of up and to the right, it goes down and to the right (or, equivalently, up and to the left). A graph of the sample function therefore looks as follows:

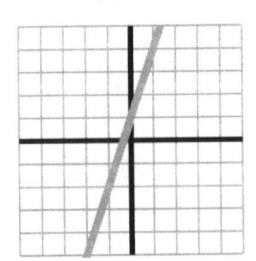

Graphing a linear function given in standard form, such as $2x - 3y = 12$

There are several ways to graph a linear function. If the function is given in standard form, $Ax + By = C$, like this example, then it's usually easiest to use the x and y intercepts. Consider the example equation, $2x - 3y = 12$. When $x = 0$, we get $-3y = 12$, so $y = -4$; this is the y intercept. When $y = 0$, we get $2x = 12$, so $x = 6$; this is the x intercept. We now know the points $(0, -4)$ and $(6, 0)$ are on the graph, so we can plot these two points and draw a straight line through them. A graph of the sample function therefore looks as follows:

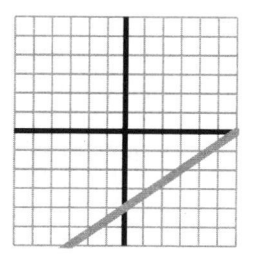

Graphing a quadratic function, such as $f(x) = 2(x - 4)^2 + 3$

If a quadratic function is in *vertex form*, $a(x - h)^2 + k$, we can see at a glance the coordinates of the vertex: they are simply (h, k). In this case, $h = 4$ and $k = 3$, so the vertex is at $(4,3)$. We can use the coefficient a to see the direction of the opening: if $a > 0$, the graph opens upward, while if $a < 0$ it opens downward. Here $a = 2 > 0$, so this graph opens upward. After that, the only remaining feature to distinguish the quadratic function is its width. We can get a feel for this by simply plotting a few other points. The x intercepts are good choices, but some quadratic functions have no x intercepts, like this one: the equation $0 = 2(x - 4)^2 + 3$ has no real solutions. However, we can still choose other values to plot: $f(3) = 2(3 - 4)^2 + 3 = 5$ and $f(5) = 2(5 - 4)^2 + 3 = 5$, so we can plot the points $(3,5)$ and $(5,5)$. Our final graph in this case looks like this:

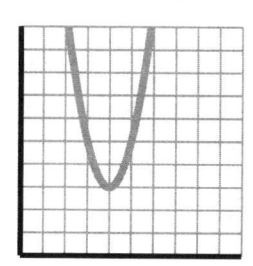

Piecewise-defined function

A *piecewise-defined function* is a function that has different definitions on two or more different intervals. The following, for instance, is one example of a piecewise-defined function:

$$f(x) = \begin{cases} x^2, & x < 0 \\ x, & 0 \leq x \leq 2 \\ (x - 2)^2, & x > 2 \end{cases}$$

To graph this function, we'd simply graph each part separately in the appropriate domain. Our final graph would look like this:

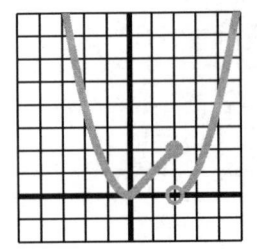

Note the filled and hollow dots at the discontinuity at $x = 2$. This is important to show which side of the graph that point corresponds to. Because $f(x) = x$ on the closed interval $0 \leq x \leq 2$, $f(2) = 2$. The point $(2,2)$ is therefore marked with a filled circle, and the point $(2,0)$, which is the endpoint of the rightmost $(x - 2)^2$ part of the graph but *not actually part of the function*, is marked with a hollow dot to indicate this.

Graphing a square root function, such as $f(x) = -2\sqrt{4x + 4}$

All square root functions have a characteristic shape (essentially, the shape of half a quadratic function rotated ninety degrees). They vary, however, in their dimensions and displacement. If we rewrite the given function as $f(x) = -2\sqrt{4(x + 1)}$, we can see by inspection how it differs from the "plain" square root function $f(x) = \sqrt{x}$: it is shifted one unit to the left (because of the $x + 1$), flipped over vertically (because of the sign of the coefficient -2), stretched vertically by a factor of 2, and squashed horizontally by a factor of 4. Alternately, we can just plot a few points to get a feel for the graph's shape: for instance, $f(-1) = -2\sqrt{-4 + 4} = 0$, $f(0) = -2\sqrt{0 + 4} = -4$, and $f(1) = -2\sqrt{4 + 4} = -4\sqrt{2} \approx -5.66$. Our final graph looks like this:

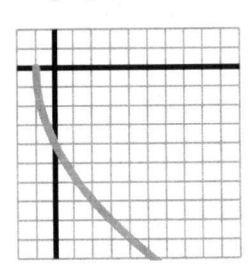

Graphing a cube root function such as $f(x) = 3\sqrt[3]{x} - 2$

All cube root functions have a characteristic shape (somewhat like a stretched-out S—note that unlike that of the square root, the domain of the cube root function encompasses all real numbers). They vary, however, in their dimensions and displacement. In the case of the given function, $3\sqrt[3]{x} - 2$, we can see by inspection how it differs from the "plain" cube root function $f(x) = \sqrt[3]{x}$: it is stretched vertically by a factor of 3 (because of the coefficient 3), and shifted two units downward (because of the -2). We can just draw a cube root function modified accordingly. Alternately, we can just plot a few points to get a feel for the graph's shape: for instance, $f(0) = 3\sqrt[3]{0} - 2 = -2$, $f(1) = 3\sqrt[3]{1} - 2 = 1$, $f(8) = 3\sqrt[3]{8} - 2 = 4$, and so on.

Our final graph looks like this:

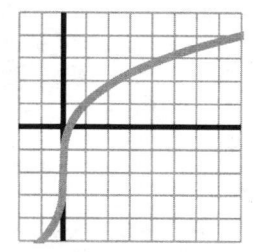

Graphing an absolute value function such as $f(x) = 2|x + 1| - 3$

The key to graphing an absolute value function is to recognize that its behavior depends on whether the expression within the absolute value sign is positive or negative, and to graph these parts separately. In the case of the function $f(x) = 2|x + 1| - 3$, the point at which the behavior changes is when $x + 1 = 0$, i.e. when $x = -1$. When $x \geq -1$, $|x + 1| = x + 1$, and the function reduces to the linear function $f_+(x) = 2(x + 1) - 3 = 2x - 1$. When $x \leq -1$, $|x + 1| = -(x + 1)$, and the function reduces to $f_-(x) = 2(-(x + 1)) - 3 = -2x - 5$. So we can graph $y = -2x - 5$ to the left of $x = -1$ and $y = 2x - 1$ to the right, yielding the following graph:

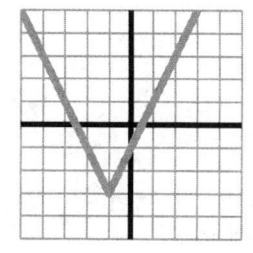

Graphing a step function such as $f(x) = 2 \left[\!\left[\frac{1}{3}(x - 1) \right]\!\right]$

The double brackets indicate a step function. For a step function, all values inside the double brackets are rounded down to the nearest integer. The graph of the function $f_0(x) = [\![x]\!]$ appears as shown on the graph on the left below. In this case, we can see by inspection how the given $f(x) = 2 \left[\!\left[\frac{1}{3}(x - 1) \right]\!\right]$ differs from $f_0(x)$. The coefficient of 2 shows that it's stretched vertically by a factor of 2 (so there's a vertical distance of 2 units between successive "steps"). The coefficient of $\frac{1}{3}$ in front of the x shows that it's stretched horizontally by a factor of 3 (so each "step" is three units long), and the $x - 1$ shows that it's displaced one unit to the right. The final graph, then, is on the right below.

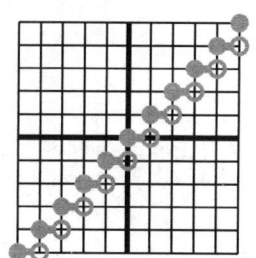

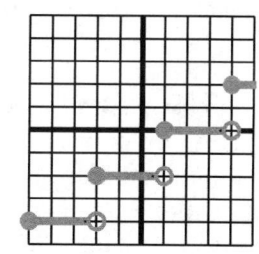

Determining the end behavior of a polynomial function

The "end behavior" of a function is what happens to the function when $|x|$ is very large. For a polynomial function, there are only two possibilities: either the function continues increasing indefinitely (it "goes to infinity"), or the function continues *de*creasing indefinitely (it "goes to negative infinity").

To see which is true, we need only look at the largest-order term of the polynomial, that is, the term with the largest exponent. To find the behavior of the function as $x \to \infty$ (at the right end), we just look at the coefficient of that term: if it's positive, the function goes to infinity; if it's negative, the function goes to negative infinity. The behavior of the function as $x \to -\infty$ (at the left end) is only slightly more complicated. If the exponent is even, the same rule holds as for the right end. If the exponent is odd, they're reversed: if the coefficient is positive, the function goes to negative infinity, and if it's negative, the function goes to positive infinity.

Graphing a polynomial such as $\frac{1}{4}x^4 - \frac{9}{4}x^2$

To graph a polynomial, like most other functions, there are a few key characteristics we can observe. First, we can observe the end behavior, which depends only on the largest order term. To find the y intercept, we evaluate the function at $x = 0$. To find the x intercepts, the points where the polynomial equals zero, is a little harder, but often we can factor the function and set each factor equal to zero. Depending on the polynomial, there may be other characteristics we can find, such as the local maxima and minima.

For the given example, since the highest order term has an even order and a positive coefficient, the polynomial goes to positive infinity at both ends. The y intercept is at $\frac{1}{4}(0^4) - \frac{9}{4}(0^2) = 0$. We can factor the polynomial as $\frac{1}{4}x^4 - \frac{9}{4}x^2 = \frac{1}{4}x^2(x^2 - 9) = \frac{1}{4}x^2(x + 3)(x - 3)$, so it has x intercepts at $x = 0, 3,$ and -3. Its graph looks like this:

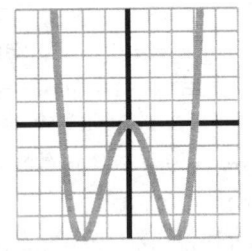

Example
Identifying the zeroes of a polynomial such as $x^3 - 3x^2 - 4x$ or $x^3 + 2x^2 - 2x - 4$

We can find the zeroes of a polynomial by factoring it. Cubics and higher polynomials can be difficult to factor, but there are special cases that can be readily factored. In the first sample polynomial here, for instance, $x^3 - 3x^2 - 4x$, it's clear that every term of the polynomial is divisible by x. We can therefore factor out the x to get $x(x^2 - 3x - 4)$. This now leaves a quadratic factor, which can be further factored to yield $x(x + 1)(x - 4)$. The zeroes of the polynomial are therefore 0, -1, and 4.

In the second polynomial, $x^3 + 2x^2 - 2x - 4$, there's no such divisor that goes into every term. If we compare the first two terms with the last two, however, we note that both *pairs* of terms are divisible by $x + 2$. We can then write the polynomial as $x^2(x + 2) - 2(x + 2)$, or $(x^2 - 2)(x + 2)$, and further factoring the first term, $(x + \sqrt{2})(x - \sqrt{2})(x + 2)$. The zeroes of this polynomial are -2 and $\pm\sqrt{2}$.

Finding the horizontal asymptote of a rational function

A rational function is a ratio of polynomials, and the horizontal asymptote is a horizontal line that the rational function tends toward as x approaches $\pm\infty$. To find the horizontal asymptote, first compare the orders of the numerator and the denominator—that is, the largest exponents appearing in them. If the numerator has a larger order than the denominator (as in $\frac{x^2-1}{x}$ or $\frac{x^4+x+2}{x^2-x}$), then the function has no horizontal asymptote. If the numerator has a smaller order the denominator (as in $\frac{x}{x^2-1}$ or $\frac{x^2+x+1}{x^5}$), then the function has a horizontal asymptote at $y = 0$.

If the orders of the numerator and denominator are equal (as in $\frac{2x^2+2}{x^2+2x+1}$ or $\frac{3x-4}{4x-3}$), then the horizontal asymptote is $y = y_0$, where y_0 is the ratio of the coefficients of the highest-order terms. For instance, the rational function $\frac{2x^2+2}{x^2+2x+1}$ has a horizontal asymptote at $y = \frac{2}{1} = 2$; $\frac{3x-4}{4x-3}$ has a horizontal asymptote at $y = \frac{3}{4}$.

Determining whether a rational function has a horizontal asymptote, a slant asymptote, or neither

To determine the end behavior of a rational function, it is only necessary to compare the orders of the numerator and the denominator—that is, the largest exponents appearing in them. If the order of the numerator is less than or equal to the order of the denominator, then the function has a horizontal asymptote. If the order of the numerator is one more than the order of the denominator, then the function has a slant asymptote. If the order of the numerator exceeds the order of the denominator by two or more, then the function has neither a horizontal nor a slant asymptote.

For instance, consider the rational function $\frac{3x^3+4x^2-2}{5x^7-5}$. The order of the numerator is 3; the order of the denominator is 7. Since $3 \leq 7$, this function has a horizontal asymptote (at $y = 0$). In the rational function $\frac{2x^4-x^2+3}{x^3-x}$, the order of the numerator is 4 and the order of the denominator is 3. Since $4 = 3 + 1$, this function has a slant asymptote.

Finding the vertical asymptotes of a rational function

Generally, a rational function has a vertical asymptote where the denominator is equal to zero, making the function undefined at that point (since the result of dividing by zero is undefined). For instance, consider the function $\frac{x^2+4x+4}{x^3-1}$. $1^3 - 1 = 0$, so this function has a vertical asymptote at $x = 1$.

There is one important exception to the above rule, however. If there is a common term to the numerator and denominator of the rational function, then it has vertical asymptotes only where the denominator is zero *after canceling common terms*. For instance, the function $f(x) = \frac{x^2-2x+1}{x^2+x-2}$ is undefined at $x = 1$, since $1^2 + 1 - 2 = 0$. However, $\frac{x^2-2x+1}{x^2+x-2} = \frac{(x-1)(x-1)}{(x-1)(x+2)}$; canceling the common term yields $\frac{x-1}{x+2}$. So $f(x)$ has a vertical asymptote at $x = -2$, but *not* at $x = 1$. (This doesn't change the fact that $f(x)$ is undefined at $x = 1$, but it can be undefined there without having a vertical asymptote.)

Determining the end behavior of a rational function such as $f(x) = \frac{3x^2+2x-3}{6x^3-2x^2+1}$ or $g(x) = \frac{-7x^7+1}{2x^2-x+3}$

To determine the end behavior of a rational function, it's only necessary to consider the leading terms of the numerator and denominator—the terms with the largest exponents. If the leading term of the denominator has a larger exponent, then $f(x)$ goes to zero as x goes to $\pm\infty$. We can then take the ratio of these leading terms, which will result in a single term of which the end behavior should be clear. For example, consider the first example, $f(x) = \frac{3x^2+2x-3}{6x^3-2x^2+1}$. The leading term of the numerator is $3x^2$, and the leading term of the denominator is $6x^3$. The latter has a larger exponent, so this function goes to zero as x goes to $\pm\infty$. In the second function, $g(x) = \frac{-7x^7+1}{2x^2-x+3}$, the leading term of the numerator is $-7x^7$, and the leading term of the numerator is $2x^2$. The ratio is $\frac{-7x^7}{2x^2} = -\frac{7}{2}x^5$, which goes to ∞ as x goes to $-\infty$ and $-\infty$ as x goes to ∞.

Finding the zeroes of a rational function such as $f(x) = \frac{x^2+3x+2}{x^3+x+1}$ or $g(x) = \frac{x^4-x^2}{x^3-2x^2+1}$.

A rational function $R(x)$ is a ratio of two polynomials, which we can write as $\frac{P(x)}{Q(x)}$. The rational function has a zero at any point $x = x_0$ for which the numerator $P(x_0)$ is equal to zero and the denominator $Q(x_0)$ is *not* equal to zero. If $Q(x_0) = 0$, then $R(x_0)$ is undefined.

In the first sample function, $f(x) = \frac{x^2+3x+2}{x^3+x+1}$, the numerator $P(x) = x^2 + 3x + 2$ has zeroes at $x = -1$ and $x = -2$. Neither of these is a zero of the denominator $Q(x) = x^3 + x + 1$: $Q(-1) = -1$, and $Q(-2) = -9$. So both of these are zeroes of $f(x)$.

In the second sample function, $g(x) = \frac{x^4-x^2}{x^3-2x^2+1}$, the numerator $P(x) = x^4 - x^2 = x^2(x^2 - 1)$ has zeroes at $x = 0$ and $x = \pm 1$. Before concluding that these are zeroes of $g(x)$, though, we have to check whether they're zeroes of the denominator $Q(x) = x^3 - 2x^2 + 1$. $Q(-1) = -2$, $Q(0) = 1$, and $Q(1) = 0$. This means $x = 1$ is *not* a zero of $g(x)$, so the zeroes of $g(x)$ are $x = -1$ and $x = 0$.

Example
Given a trigonometric function of the form $f(x) = A\sin(Bx + C) + D$ (such as $f(x) = 2 + \frac{3}{2}\sin\left(\pi x + \frac{\pi}{2}\right)$), determine how you would find the function's period, amplitude, and midline and use them to graph the function

In the function $f(x) = A\sin(Bx + C) + D$, the amplitude is simply equal to A, and the midline is $y = D$. The period is only a little more complicated; the period is equal to $2\pi/B$. For instance, consider the example function $f(x) = 2 + \frac{3}{2}\sin\left(\pi x + \frac{\pi}{2}\right)$. Here $A = \frac{3}{2}$, $B = \pi$, $C = \frac{\pi}{2}$, and $D = 2$, so the midline is at $y = 2$, the amplitude is $\frac{3}{2}$, and the period is $2\pi/\pi = 2$.

To graph this equation, we center the sine wave on the midline and extend it to a height above and below the midline equal to the amplitude—so this graph would have a minimum value of $2 - \frac{3}{2} = \frac{1}{2}$ and a maximum of $2 + \frac{3}{2} = \frac{7}{2}$. The period (here equal to 2) is the distance between successive peaks or troughs. As for the last value, C, this is related to the *phase shift*, which is equal to $-\frac{C}{B}$ (in this case $-\frac{1}{2}$) and can be thought of as a starting point where $f(x) = D$ (the midline) and increasing. So the function above would be graphed as follows:

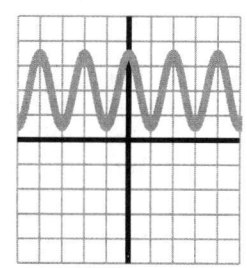

Example

Find the x and y intercepts, if any, of an exponential function of the form $f(x) = Ae^{bx} + C$

To find the y intercept, we just evaluate the function at $x = 0$. This gives $f(0) = Ae^{b \cdot 0} + C = Ae^0 + C = A(1) + C = A + C$. For instance, if $f(x) = \frac{1}{2}e^{3x} - 4$, $f(0) = \frac{1}{2}e^{3 \cdot 0} - 4 = \frac{1}{2}(1) - 4 = -\frac{7}{2}$. This function has a y intercept at $(0, -\frac{7}{2})$.

To find the x intercept, we have to find a value of x for which $f(x) = 0$. Thus, $Ae^{bx} + C = 0$, so $Ae^{bx} = -C$, and $e^{bx} = -\frac{C}{A}$. From here, we have to take the logarithm of both sides, so $bx = \ln\left(-\frac{C}{A}\right)$, and $x = \frac{1}{b}\ln\left(-\frac{C}{A}\right)$. (Note that the logarithm of a negative number is undefined, so this has a solution only if $-\frac{C}{A} > 0$, i.e. $\frac{C}{A} < 0$. Otherwise, there is no x intercept.) If $f(x) = \frac{1}{2}e^{3x} - 4$, then to find the x intercept we use $\frac{1}{2}e^{3x} - 4 = 0$, so $\frac{1}{2}e^{3x} = 4$, $e^{3x} = 8$, and hence $3x = \ln 8$ and $x = \frac{\ln 8}{3} \approx 0.693$.

Example

Determine the end behavior of an exponential function such as $f(x) = 2e^{2x}$ or $g(x) = -e^{-x}$

The exponential function $y = e^x$ goes to zero as x goes to $-\infty$ and goes to ∞ as x goes to ∞. Multiplying either the exponent or the full exponential by a positive coefficient doesn't change this behavior, so this is the end behavior of $f(x) = 2e^{2x}$: it goes to zero on the left and goes to ∞ on the right.

Negative coefficients, on the other hand, do make a difference. A negative coefficient in the exponent interchanges the left and right side behavior, while a negative coefficient in front of the entire function makes the function go to negative infinity on the right instead of positive infinity. The function $g(x) = -e^{-x}$ has negative coefficients in *both* places, so it goes to $-\infty$ as x goes to $-\infty$, and goes to zero as x goes to ∞.

Example

Determine the end behavior of a logarithmic function such as $f(x) = \ln(-x)$ or $g(x) = -\frac{1}{2}\log_{10}(x+2)$

Regardless of the base, the logarithmic function $y = \log(x)$ goes to ∞ as x goes to ∞. The domain of $y = \log(x)$ is $(0, \infty)$, so we don't need to consider what happens as x goes to $-\infty$, but as x approaches the vertical asymptote at $x = 0$, $\log(x)$ goes to $-\infty$.

The function $f(x) = \ln(-x)$ has a negative coefficient in front of the x, which means the function is reflected from left to right. This function, therefore, goes to ∞ as x goes to $-\infty$, and on the right $f(x)$ goes to $-\infty$ as x approaches the vertical asymptote at $x = 0$.

The $x + 2$ in the function $g(x) = -\frac{1}{2}\log_{10}(x+2)$ means the function is shifted two units to the left—which means, in particular, that the vertical asymptote is shifted two units to the left. The negative coefficient in front of the function means the entire graph is flipped vertically. Therefore, $g(x)$ goes to $-\infty$ as x goes to ∞, and goes to ∞ as x approaches the vertical asymptote at $x = -2$.

Example

Given a tangent function such as $f(x) = 2\tan(3x - 4) + 1$, determine how you would find the function's period and midline and use them to graph the function

In the function $f(x) = A\tan(Bx + C) + D$, the midline is $y = D$, and the period is π/B. Larger values of A stretch the tangent vertically, but since the range of the tangent includes all real numbers, the tangent doesn't have an amplitude in the same sense as the sine and cosine do. If A is negative, the function is flipped vertically. C is related to the *phase shift*, ϕ, which is equal to $-C/B$, and is the amount by which the function is displaced horizontally.

For instance, consider the example function $f(x) = 2\tan(3x - 4) + 1$. Here $A = 2$, $B = 3$, $C = -4$, and $D = 1$, so the midline is at $y = 1$, the period is $\pi/3 \approx 1.05$, and the phase shift is $-(-4/3) = 4/3$. To graph this equation, we start at the point (ϕ, D)—in this case, $(4/3, 1)$—and we draw the tangent shape centered on this point, with a width equal to the period. We then repeat this shape to both sides at regular intervals. The result is as follows:

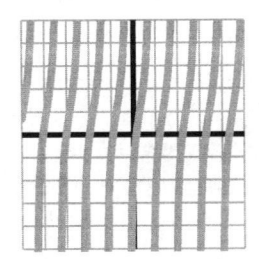

What it means to "complete the square" of a quadratic function, and what purpose it serves

A quadratic function in the "vertex form" $f(x) = a(x - h)^2 + k$ readily shows the coordinates of the vertex, (h, k). However, quadratic functions are often given in "standard form", $f(x) = ax^2 + bx + c$, which doesn't show the coordinates of the vertex directly. Completing the square is one way to convert the function from standard form to vertex form.

To complete the square, we first factor out the a from the first two terms: $f(x) = a\left(x^2 + \frac{b}{a}x\right) + c$. Now, we have to find a linear expression which, squared, yields a quadratic the first two terms of which match the terms in parentheses. This is probably most easily shown with an example: if $f(x) = 2x^2 + 8x + 6 = 2(x^2 + 4x) + 6$, then a suitable linear expression is $x + 2$, because $(x + 2)^2 = x^2 + 4x + 4$. Therefore, we have $f(x) = 2(x + 2)^2 + h$. All we have to do now is find a value for h that matches the original equation. Expanding, we have $f(x) = 2x^2 + 8x + 8 + h$, so we require $8 + h = 6$, thus $h = -2$, and $f(x) = 2(x + 2)^2 - 2$.

Factoring a quadratic function such as $f(x) = x^2 + x - 6$, $g(x) = x^2 - 16$, or $h(x) = 2x^2 + 3x - 7$

Factoring a quadratic function of the form $ax^2 + bx + c$ means finding two factors $(px + q)$ and $(rx + s)$ such that $(px + q)(rx + s) = ax^2 + bx + c$. Since $(px + q)(rx + s) = prx^2 + (ps + qr)x + qs$, we're looking specifically for p, q, r, s such that $pr = a$, $ps + qr = b$, and $qs = c$. The matter is much simpler if $a = 1$; then we need only find q and s such that $q + s = b$ and $qs = c$. For instance, for the first example, $f(x) = x^2 + x - 6$, $b = 1$ and $c = -6$, so we need to find two numbers that add to 1 and multiply to -6. -2 and 3 qualify, so $f(x)$ can be factored to $(x - 2)(x + 3)$. When the quadratic function has the form $x^2 - c$, we don't even need to do that much work; we know the function's factors are $(x + \sqrt{c})$ and $(x - \sqrt{c})$. So $g(x) = x^2 - 16$ factorizes to $(x + \sqrt{16})(x - \sqrt{16}) = (x + 4)(x - 4)$.

Sometimes a quadratic function can't readily be factored by any of these systems. In this case, one can resort to the *quadratic formula*: $x = \frac{-b \pm \sqrt{b^2 - 4ac}}{2a}$. Note that when you use the quadratic formula to solve the equation $0 = ax^2 + bx + c$ what you are really solving is $0 = x^2 + \frac{b}{a}x + \frac{c}{a}$; therefore, when using the quadratic formula to find the factors of $ax^2 + bx + c$ you must include the coefficient a as one of your factors. In the case of our third sample function, $h(x) = 2x^2 + 3x - 7$, this gives us $x = \frac{-3 \pm \sqrt{3^2 - 4(2)(-7)}}{2 \cdot 2} = \frac{-3 \pm \sqrt{65}}{4} = -\frac{3}{4} \pm \frac{\sqrt{65}}{4}$, and the factorization is $2\left(x + \frac{3}{4} - \frac{\sqrt{65}}{4}\right)\left(x + \frac{3}{4} + \frac{\sqrt{65}}{4}\right)$.

Finding the extreme values of a quadratic function such as $f(x) = x^2 - 6x + 3$

A quadratic function of the form $ax^2 + bx + c$ has only a single extreme value, at its vertex. Whether this is a maximum or a minimum depends on whether the graph opens upward or downward. This in turn depends on the sign of the coefficient a: if a is positive, then the graph opens upward and the vertex is a minimum, while if a is negative, the graph opens downward and the vertex is a maximum.

In the case of the sample function $f(x) = x^2 - 6x + 3$, the coefficient $a = 1 > 0$, so the vertex is a minimum. To find the coordinates of the vertex, we can put the function in *vertex form*, $f(x) = a(x - h)^2 + k$. We can do this by completing the square: $(x - 3)^2 = x^2 - 6x + 9$, so $f(x) = (x - 3)^2 - 6$. The vertex is at the coordinates (h, k)—in this case, $(3, -6)$.

Symmetry of a quadratic function such as $f(x) = 3(x - 2)^2 + 5$

Any quadratic function is symmetrical through a vertical line passing through the vertex. When the quadratic function is in vertex form, $f(x) = a(x - h)^2 + k$, the coordinates of the vertex can be readily seen from the equation; they are simply (h, k). The axis of symmetry is then $x = h$; the function is unchanged when reflected through this line. If $h = 0$, then the axis of symmetry is the line $x = 0$, which is the y axis; the function is then symmetrical with respect to reflections through the y axis, which means it is an even function. Quadratic functions with $h \neq 0$ are neither even nor odd.

In the case of the sample function given here, $f(x) = 3(x - 2)^2 + 5$, $h = 2$ and $k = 5$. This function, therefore, is symmetrical with respect to reflections through the line $x = 2$.

<u>Example</u>
> Given an exponential equation such as $f(x) = 200 \cdot (1.2)^{3x}$, show how you can determine whether it represents exponential growth or exponential decay
>
> If the coefficient of the exponent is positive (as it is in the sample function given), then the function represents exponential growth if the base of the exponent is greater than 1, and exponential decay if the exponent is less than 1. The sample function therefore represents exponential growth, since the base, 1.2, is greater than 1. An example of a function that would represent exponential decay would be $g(x) = 13 \cdot (0.9)^{2.5x}$, since here the base, 0.9, is less than one.
>
> If the coefficient in the exponent is negative, then this rule of thumb is reversed. Thus, for instance,
> $h(x) = 10 \cdot (1.1)^{-2x}$ represents exponential decay, since the coefficient (−2) is negative, and the base (1.1) is greater than 1; $k(x) = 7 \cdot (0.8)^{-1.5x}$ is exponential growth, since the exponent (−1.5) is negative, and the base (0.8) is less than 1.

Example
Finding the percent rate of change of an exponential function such as
$f(t) = 70 \cdot (1.4)^{1.05t}$

The percent rate of change is the amount by which a function changes per unit of time, expressed as a percentage. This can be calculated as $\frac{f(t+1)-f(t)}{f(t)}$. For the sample function, $f(t) = 70 \cdot (1.4)^{1.05t}$, this calculation gives $\frac{70 \cdot (1.4)^{1.05(t+1)} - 70 \cdot (1.4)^{1.05t}}{70 \cdot (1.4)^{1.05t}} = \frac{70 \cdot (1.4)^{1.05(t+1)}}{70 \cdot (1.4)^{1.05t}} - 1 = (1.4)^{(1.05(t+1)-1.05t)} - 1 = 1.4^{1.05} - 1 \approx 0.424 = 42.4\%$ per unit of time. Note that the time, t, cancels from the calculation, and therefore the rate of change does not depend on t. This is a characteristic of exponential functions; they have a constant percent rate of change.

The answer we obtained for the sample function can be generalized: in general, the percent rate of change of an exponential function $f(t) = a \cdot b^{ct}$ is equal to $b^c - 1$. Note that if $b^c < 1$, then the percent rate of change is negative. For instance, consider $g(t) = 2 \cdot \left(\frac{1}{2}\right)^t$. The percent rate of change is $\left(\frac{1}{2}\right)^1 - 1 = -\frac{1}{2} = -50\%$. This makes sense, because if $b^c < 1$ then the function represents exponential decay; the function is decreasing, so the percent rate of change is indeed negative.

Important properties of exponents, and explain how they could be used in a problem

One important property of exponents is the property that $x^a x^b = x^{a+b}$. This could come into play in a problem in which we have a product of two exponentials, and it simplifies the problem to combine them into one. Conversely, we can use it to simplify an expression with a sum in the exponent, such as $3 \cdot 2^{x+4}$; this simplifies to $3 \cdot 2^x 2^4 = 3 \cdot 2^x \cdot 16 = 48 \cdot 2^x$.

Often given separately is the property $x^a / x^b = x^{a-b}$, but this is really a special case of the previous property where $b < 0$, and applies under similar circumstances.

Another important property of exponents is the property that $(x^a)^b = x^{ab}$. This can be used to simplify expressions in which an exponential is raised to a power, or to simplify an expression with a product in the exponent into a single exponent: for example, $3^{3x} = (3^3)^x = 27^x$.

Given two functions, one represented algebraically and one graphically, determine how you can find which has the larger maximum

One way to compare the features of two functions represented in different ways is to convert them both to the same manner of representation. If one function is represented algebraically and the other graphically, we can graph the first function on the same axis as the second, enabling us to compare their maxima visually by just observing which one extends farther in the positive y direction.

It's also possible to compare their maxima without converting them to the same representation, by simply finding the maximum of each function and comparing them. If the function expressed algebraically is one for which we can find the maximum analytically (for example, a quadratic function), we can compare that value directly with the maximum estimated from the graphed function by observing the y coordinate of its highest peak.

Given two functions, one of which is given algebraically and the other in a verbal description, determine how you could find which has the larger maximum

When given two functions in different formats, one way to compare their properties is to convert both functions to the same format. If one of the functions is given in the form of a verbal description, we can write an algebraic expression to represent the described relationship. For instance, if we're told that a function represents the area of a rectangular field for which the total distance around three sides is 40 meters (implying that, if we write l as the length and w as the width, $l + 2w = 40$), we can write the relationship between the area and the width algebraically as $A = l \cdot w = (40 - 2w)w$. Or, using the more familiar f and x, $f(x) = (40 - 2x)x = -2x^2 + 40x$. Completing the square gives us $f(x) = -2(x - 10)^2 + 200$. This function has a maximum when $x = 10$, at which point $f(x) = 200$. We can likewise find the maximum of the other function given algebraically, and we can now compare the maxima directly.

Given two functions, one of which is given graphically and one in a table, determine how you can find which has the larger y intercept

When given two functions in different formats, one way to compare their properties is to convert both functions to the same format. If one of the functions is given as a table, we can graph that function and then compare it to the graph directly. Conversely, we could determine the values of the graphed function at the x values given in the table and therefore express both functions in tabular format.

It's also sometimes possible to compare properties of the functions even without converting them to the same format, and in the case of finding the y intercept this isn't difficult (assuming that the y intercept of the second function is actually given in the table). We can find the y intercept of the graphed function by seeing where the graph crosses the y-axis, find the y intercept of the table function by seeing what value of the function corresponds to an x value of 0, and compare these values directly.

<u>Example</u>
>Given a description of a relationship, such as a statement that the population of a particular area is 2000 in the year 1980 and doubles every 10 years thereafter, determine how you can write an explicit expression to describe that relationship
>
>The first step in writing an expression to describe a relationship is to pinpoint the variables involved in the expression. In the sample case, the statement describes how the population changes over time, we will write the population P as a function of time, t.
>
>Next, we look for telltale signs that tell us what kind of function we are dealing with. Here, the population increases by a fixed proportion over a specific unit of time, a hallmark of an exponential relationship. Therefore, the expression will take the form $P(t) = P_0 A^{ct}$. More specifically, since we're

given the population at 1980 as a starting point, we can simplify matters by setting the exponent proportional to the number of years since 1980: $P(t) = P_{1980}A^{c(t-1980)}$.

Finally, we use the given data to put in numbers. When $t = 1980$, $P(t) = 2000$, so $P_{1980} = 2000$. Incorporating the other information gives us $P(t) = 2000 \cdot 2^{(t-1980)/10}$.

Determine what kinds of relationships lend themselves to being written as recursively defined functions

A recursively defined function is generally a *sequence*; that is, its domain consists of a subset of the integers (usually, though not always, the positive integers). Furthermore, the value of the function for a given value of x must be defined in terms of its value for smaller values of x. Often this means $f(x)$ is defined in terms of $f(x-1)$, though it may also be defined in terms of even smaller values. Finally, we need to have $f(x_0)$ explicitly defined for the smallest value or values of x_0 to give us a starting point.

For example, consider the following relationship: A pile of stones starts with three stones, and then every day its size is doubled and then one stone is removed. On day one, then, the size of the pile is $f(1) = 3$. On day x thereafter, we have the relationship $f(x) = 2f(x-1) - 1$. This is a valid recursive definition.

Example

Suppose $f(x) = x^2 - 1$ and $g(x) = x - 1$. How would you find each of the following

$(f+g)(x) \quad (f-g)(x) \quad (f \cdot g)(x) \quad (f/g)(x)$

To combine functions using arithmetic operations, we need only apply the appropriate arithmetic operation to the function's expression. So $(f+g)(x) = f(x) + g(x) = (x^2 - 1) + (x - 1) = x^2 + x - 2$. $(f-g)(x) = (x^2 - 1) - (x - 1) = x^2 - x$. $(f \cdot g)(x) = (x^2 - 1)(x - 1) = x^3 - x^2 - x + 1$.

Finally, $(f/g)(x) = (x^2 - 1)/(x - 1)$. Here we have to be a little more careful. $(x^2 - 1) = (x+1)(x-1)$, so it's tempting to cancel out the $(x-1)$ terms and state simply that $(f/g)(x) = \frac{(x+1)(x-1)}{x-1} = x + 1$. However, this doesn't hold when $x = 1$: $(f/g)(1) = (1^2 - 1)/(1 - 1) = 0/0$, which is undefined, and *not* equal to $1 + 1$. It's more accurate, therefore, to state that $(f/g)(x) = x + 1$ when $x \neq 1$, but is undefined when $x = 1$.

Example

Determine under what circumstances a relationship might be modeled by an arithmetic operation of two functions

A relationship might be modeled by an arithmetic operation of two functions if it represents a sum, product, difference, or quotient of two processes each modeled by a different function. For example, consider the following: A man has $1000 in one bank account that generates 4% interest, compounded annually, and $2000 in another bank account that generates 3% annual interest, continually compounded. We want to find the total amount of money he has in the bank after t years.

Applying the compound interest formula, $A = P\left(1 + \frac{r}{n}\right)^{nt}$, we find that the amount of money he has in the first account is equal to $f(t) = 1000(1.04)^t$. For continually compounded interest, the formula is $A = Pe^{rt}$, so the amount he has in the second account is equal to $g(t) = 2000e^{0.03t}$. The *total* amount of money he has in the bank is then simply the arithmetic sum of these two: $h(t) = f(t) + g(t) = 1000(1.04)^t + 2000e^{0.03t}$.

Example

Given two functions $f(x)$ and $g(x)$, show how you would determine the domain of each of the following

$$(f + g)(x) \quad (f - g)(x) \quad (f \cdot g)(x) \quad (f/g)(x)$$

In order for an arithmetic operation of two functions to be defined for a given x, each of the two functions themselves must also be defined at that x. In other words, in order to be in the domain of $(f + g)(x)$, $(f - g)(x)$, $(f \cdot g)(x)$, or $(f/g)(x)$, a particular number must be in the domain of both $f(x)$ and $g(x)$. For instance, if $f(x) = \ln(x + 1)$ and $g(x) = \sqrt{2 - x}$, since the domain of $f(x)$ is $(-1, \infty)$ and the domain of $g(x)$ is $(-\infty, 2]$, the domain of $(f + g)(x)$ is the intersection of those two domains, namely $(-1, 2]$.

For $(f/g)(x)$, we also have to take into account the fact that we can't divide by zero. Therefore, any values x for which $g(x) = 0$ are excluded from the domain of $(f/g)(x)$. For the sample $f(x)$ and $g(x)$ given above, for instance, the domain of $(f/g)(x)$ would be not $(-1, 2]$ but $(-1, 2)$, since $g(2) = 0$.

Function composition

Function composition is a process in which the "output" of one function is used as the "input" of another. The composition of two functions $f(x)$ and $g(x)$ can be written as $(f \circ g)(x)$ or as $f(g(x))$.

How to evaluate the composition of two functions
This means we find the value of $f(x')$ at $x' = g(x)$. In other words, to evaluate the function composition $(f \circ g)(x)$ at $x = x_0$, we first find $y_0 = g(x_0)$ and then find $f(y_0)$, which is our final answer. For example, if $f(x) = x^2 + 1$ and $g(x) = x - 1$, then to find $(f \circ g)(3)$, we first find $g(3) = 2$, and then find $f(2) = 5$. So $(f \circ g)(3) = 5$. We can also rewrite the composition of two functions explicitly as a single function by substituting the expression for one function into the other. For instance, for the above functions, $(f \circ g)(x) = f(x - 1) = (x - 1)^2 + 1 = x^2 - 2x + 2$.

Example

Suppose $f(x) = x^2 - x$ and $g(x) = \frac{x}{x+1}$. How you would find each of the following

$(f \circ g)(3)$ $\qquad$ $g(f(-1))$ $\qquad$ $(f \circ f)(2)$
$f\big(g(f(1))\big)$

All of these expressions indicate function composition, though they use different notations: the notation $(f \circ g)(x)$, for instance, is equivalent to $f(g(x))$. To evaluate a function composition, we can first evaluate the "inner" function expression, and then put that in as the input to the "outer" function. For instance, to evaluate $(f \circ g)(3)$, we first evaluate $g(3) = \frac{3}{3+1} = \frac{3}{4}$, and then $f(g(3)) = f\left(\frac{3}{4}\right) = \left(\frac{3}{4}\right)^2 - \frac{3}{4} = \frac{9}{16} - \frac{12}{16} = -3/16$. Similarly, $g(f(-1)) = g((-1)^2 - (-1)) = g(1+1) = g(2) = \frac{2}{2+1} = 2/3$, and $f(f(2)) = f(2^2 - 2) = f(2) = 2^2 - 2 = 2$.

The last expression here can be evaluated similarly; it only takes an extra step: $f\big(g(f(1))\big) = f(g(1^2 - 1)) = f(g(0)) = f\left(\frac{0}{0+1}\right) = f(0) = 0^2 - 0 = 0$. In principle, we could apply the same procedure to a composition of any number of functions, such as $(f \circ g \circ g \circ f \circ g)(4)$.

Example
Suppose $f(x) = x^2 + 1$ and $g(x) = x - 1$. How would you write each of the following as a single function?

$f(g(x))$ $\qquad$ $(g \circ f)(x)$ $\qquad$ $(g \circ g)(x)$
$g\big(f(g(x))\big)$

All of these expressions indicate function composition, though they use different notations: the notation $(g \circ f)(x)$, for instance, is equivalent to $g(f(x))$. To rewrite a function composition as a single expression, we substitute the expression for one function in for x in the expression for the other. To find $f(g(x))$, for instance, we replace each x in the expression for $f(x)$—that is, $x^2 + 1$—with the expression for $g(x)$ —$(x - 1)$. This gives us $f(g(x)) = f(x-1) = (x-1)^2 + 1 = x^2 - 2x + 1 + 1 = x^2 - 2x + 2$. Similarly, $(g \circ f)(x) = g(f(x)) = (x^2 + 1) - 1 = x^2$, and $(g \circ g)(x) = g(g(x)) = (x-1) - 1 = x - 2$.

The final expression, $g\big(f(g(x))\big)$, looks complex but requires the same procedure, just done in two steps. We've already found $f(g(x)) = x^2 - 2x + 2$. To find $g\big(f(g(x))\big)$, then, we just substitute this into the expression for $g(x)$: $g\big(f(g(x))\big) = g(x^2 - 2x + 2) = (x^2 - 2x + 2) - 1 = x^2 - 2x + 1$.

Under what circumstances a relationship might be modeled by a composition of two functions

A relationship might be modeled by a composition of two functions if it represents a process that depends on the output of another process. For example, consider the following: The population of a town increases exponentially according to the formula $P(t) = 1500e^{0.2t}$, where t is the time in years from a fixed starting year. On average, each person in the town eats 800 kilograms of food per year. We want to find the total amount of food eaten by the entire population of the town in year t.

The relationship between the total amount of food eaten in a year and the population of the town is straightforward: $f(x) = 800x$, where x equals the population. However, x is itself a function: specifically, it's $P(t)$, as given above. Therefore, the total amount of food, as a function of t, is $f(P(t)) = f(1500e^{0.2t}) = 800 \cdot 1500e^{0.2t} = 1200000e^{0.2t}$.

Example

Given two functions $f(x)$ and $g(x)$, show how you would determine the domain and range of $(f \circ g)(x)$

The notation $(f \circ g)(x)$ indicates function composition; this can also be written as $f(g(x))$. $(f \circ g)(x)$ can be evaluated at a point $x = x_0$ by first finding $g(x_0)$ and then putting that as the "input" for $f(x)$. In order for a value x_0 to be in the domain of $(f \circ g)(x)$, then, it's necessary first that x_0 be in the domain of $g(x)$ and second that $g(x_0)$ be in the domain of $f(x)$. For instance, if $f(x) = \sqrt{x}$ and $g(x) = x - 2$, then $x = 1$ is not in the domain of $(f \circ g)(x)$, even though it *is* in the domain of $f(x)$ and $g(x)$, since $g(1) = -1$ is not in the domain of $f(x)$.

Similarly, for a value $y = y_0$ to be in the range of $(f \circ g)(x)$, it's necessary not only that y_0 is in the range of $f(x)$, but that there is at least one value y' in the range of $g(x)$ such that $f(y') = y_0$.

Example

Given an arithmetic sequence expressed recursively, such as $a_1 = 2$, $a_n = a_{n-1} + 3$, explain how to write this sequence in an explicit (nonrecursive) form

An arithmetic sequence is one with a constant difference between consecutive terms: each term is equal to the preceding term plus (or minus) some constant number. An arithmetic sequence can be uniquely characterized by two specific numbers: the first element of the sequence a_1, and the sequence's common difference d. The latter is the difference between two consecutive terms of the sequence; d is positive if the sequence is increasing and negative if the sequence is decreasing.

An arithmetic sequence can be defined recursively by specifying a_1 and then giving the relationship between consecutive terms, $a_n = a_{n-1} + d$. It can also be defined explicitly with the expression $a_n = a_1 + d(n-1)$ (or, equivalently, $a_n = (a_1 - d) + dn$).

Here, we have a recursive definition; by inspecting it, we see that $a_1 = 2$ and $d = 3$. We can simply put those values into the explicit expression to get $a_n = 2 + 3(n - 1)$ (or, equivalently, $a_n = -1 + 3n$).

Example

Given a geometric sequence expressed recursively, such as $a_1 = 3$, $a_n = 2a_{n-1}$, determine how to write this sequence in an explicit (nonrecursive) form

A geometric sequence is one with a constant ratio between consecutive terms: each term is equal to the preceding term multiplied (or divided) by some constant number. A geometric sequence can be uniquely characterized by two specific numbers: the first element of the sequence a_1, and the sequence's common ratio r. The latter is the ratio between two consecutive terms of the sequence; r is greater than one if the sequence is increasing and less than one if the sequence is decreasing. (If r is negative, the terms of the sequence alternate between positive and negative.)

A geometric sequence can be defined recursively by specifying a_1 and then giving the relationship between consecutive terms, $a_n = r \cdot a_{n-1}$. It can also be defined explicitly with the expression $a_n = a_1 \cdot r^{n-1}$ (or, equivalently, $a_n = (a_1/r) \cdot r^n$).

Here, we have a recursive definition; by inspecting it, we see that $a_1 = 3$ and $r = 2$. We can simply put those values into the explicit expression to get $a_n = 3 \cdot 2^{n-1}$ (or, equivalently, $a_n = \frac{3}{2} \cdot 2^n$).

Example

Given an arithmetic sequence defined explicitly, such as $a_n = 3 + 4n$, determine how you can write this sequence in a recursive form

An arithmetic sequence is a sequence in which each term differs from the previous amount by a fixed amount. An arithmetic sequence can be uniquely specified by this fixed difference, d, and the first term, a_1. The sequence can be expressed either explicitly, in the form $a_n = a_1 + d(n-1)$, or recursively, in the form $a_n = a_{n-1} + d$ (after specifying the first term).

In this case, being given the sequence in explicit form, we can find a_1 and d by inspection: $a_n = 3 + 4n = 3 + 4(1 + n - 1) = 3 + 4 + 4(n - 1) = 7 + 4(n - 1)$. So, comparing this to the general equation $a_n = a_1 + d(n - 1)$, we find $a_1 = 7$ and $d = 4$. We can therefore write the sequence recursively as follows: $a_1 = 7$, $a_n = a_{n-1} + 4$.

Example

Given a geometric sequence defined explicitly, such as $a_n = 3\left(\frac{2}{3}\right)^n$, determine how you can write this sequence in a recursive form

A geometric sequence is a sequence in which each term differs from the previous amount by a fixed ratio. A geometric sequence can be uniquely specified by this fixed ratio, r, and the first term, a_1. The sequence can be expressed either explicitly, in the form $a_n = a_1 r^{n-1}$, or recursively, in the form $a_n = r \cdot a_{n-1}$ (after specifying the first term).

In this case, being given the sequence in explicit form, we can find a_1 and r by inspection: $a_n = 3\left(\frac{2}{3}\right)^n = 3\left(\frac{2}{3}\right)^{1+n-1} = 3\left(\frac{2}{3}\right)\left(\frac{2}{3}\right)^{n-1} = 2\left(\frac{2}{3}\right)^{n-1}$. So, comparing this to the general equation $a_n = a_1 r^{n-1}$, we find $a_1 = 2$ and $r = \frac{2}{3}$. We can therefore write the sequence recursively as follows: $a_1 = 2, a_n = \frac{2}{3}a_{n-1}$.

Situations modeled by arithmetic sequences

An arithmetic sequence is a good model for any situation that involves a quantity that increases at equal intervals by a constant difference. That is, if the quantity is only defined relative to the positive integers (or technically at any other discrete, evenly spaced intervals), and the difference between the quantity corresponding to any two consecutive integers is the same, then it can be modeled by an arithmetic sequence.

Consider, for instance, the following situation: a large jar initially contains five marbles, and every day three more marbles are added to it. This fits the criteria described above: the quantity is defined relative to the positive integers (number of days), and the difference between the quantity corresponding to consecutive integers (the number of marbles on consecutive days) is constant (three). We can model this situation by the arithmetic sequence
$f(n) = 5 + 3(n - 1)$.

Situations modeled by geometric sequences

A geometric sequence is a good model for any situation that involves a quantity that increases at fixed intervals by a fixed ratio. That is, if the quantity is only defined relative to the positive integers (or technically at any other discrete, evenly spaced intervals), and the ratio of the quantity corresponding to any two consecutive integers is the same, then it can be modeled by a geometric sequence.

Consider, for instance, the following situation: the score for completing level one of a video game is 100, and the score for completing each level afterward is double the score for the previous level. This fits the criteria described above: the quantity is defined relative to the positive integers (levels), and the ratio between the quantity corresponding to consecutive integers (the scores for completing two consecutive levels) is constant (two). We can model this situation by the geometric sequence $f(n) = 100 \cdot 2^{n-1}$.

Example
> Graphing of a function $f(x)$ compares with the graph of $f(x) + k$ for some constant k. What about the graph of $f(x + k)$
>
> If we replace $f(x)$ by $(x) + k$, this means the y coordinate of each point on the graph increases by k. This means the graph will be displaced vertically by a value of k: for instance, the graph of $y = x^2 + 1$ will be one unit higher than the graph of $y = x^2$. If k is negative, then the graph will be lowered.
>
> Replacing $f(x)$ by $f(x + k)$ effectively means the x coordinate of each point on the graph *decreases* by k. (Consider that $f((x - k) + k) = f(x)$, so evaluating $f(x)$ at $x = x_0$ yields the same value as evaluating $f(x + k)$ at

$x = x_0 - k$.) This means the graph will be displaced horizontally to the left by a value of k: for instance, the graph of $y = (x + 1)^2$ will be one unit to the left of the graph of $y = x^2$. If k is negative, the graph will be displaced to the right.

Example

Graphing of a function $f(x)$ compares with the graph of $kf(x)$ for some constant k. What about the graph of $f(kx)$

If we replace $f(x)$ by $kf(x)$, this means the y coordinate of each point on the graph is multiplied k. This means the graph will be stretched vertically by a factor of k: for instance, the graph of $y = 2x^2$ will be stretched by a factor of 2 in the vertical direction relative to the graph of $y = x^2$. If k is less than one, then the graph will be compressed; if k is negative, it will be inverted vertically (in addition to the stretch or compression).

Replacing $f(x)$ by $f(kx)$ effectively means the x coordinate of each point on the graph is *divided* by a factor of k. This means the graph will be compressed horizontally by a factor of k (or, if $k < 1$, stretched horizontally by a factor of $1/k$): for instance, the graph of $y = (2x)^2$ will be compressed horizontally by a factor of two relative to the graph of $y = x^2$. If k is negative, the graph will be inverted horizontally (in addition to the stretch or compression).

Determining from inspection of a graph whether the graph represents an odd or even function

An *odd function* is one for which $f(-x) = -f(x)$. This means that when the x coordinate is inverted, so is the y coordinate. The left half of the graph (to the left of the y-axis) will therefore be an inverted version of the right half (to the right of the y-axis). Rotating the graph by 180° inverts both the x and the y coordinates, so an odd function is symmetrical with respect to 180° rotations around the origin.

An *even function* is one for which $f(-x) = f(x)$. This means that when the x coordinate is inverted, the y coordinate does not change. The left half of the graph is therefore a mirror image of the right half. Reflecting the graph through the y-axis inverts the x coordinate without changing the y coordinate, so an even function is symmetrical with respect to reflections through the y-axis.

A graph that exhibits neither symmetry is neither even nor odd.

Determining whether a function given algebraically is even or odd

A function $f(x)$ is *even* if it is unchanged when x is replaced by $-x$. It is *odd* if the sign of the function is changed when x is replaced by $-x$. In other words, for an even function, $f(-x) = f(x)$; for an odd function, $f(-x) = -f(x)$. We can therefore check whether a function is even or odd by evaluating $f(-x)$ and checking whether (perhaps after some suitable algebraic manipulation) it is equal to $f(x)$ or $-f(x)$.

For instance, consider the function $f(x) = x^2 + 1$. $f(-x) = (-x)^2 + 1 = x^2 + 1 = f(x)$. $f(-x) = f(x)$, so this function is even. Now consider $g(x) = x^3 + \frac{1}{x}$. $g(-x) = (-x)^3 + \frac{1}{-x} = -x^3 - \frac{1}{x} = -\left(x^3 + \frac{1}{x}\right) = -g(x)$. $g(-x) = -g(x)$, so this function is odd. Finally, consider $h(x) = x - 1$. $h(-x) = -x - 1 = -(x + 1)$. This is equal to neither $h(x)$ nor $-h(x)$, so this function is neither even nor odd.

Example

Given an expression for a function such as $f(x) = x^3 + 1$ or $g(x) = \frac{x}{x-1}$, determine how to find the function's inverse

One algorithm for finding the inverse of the function is as follows: Solve the equation of the function for x—that is, manipulate the equation to get x by itself on one side of the equation. This equation now shows the inverse function of $f(x)$; to write it explicitly as an inverse, change the x to $f^{-1}(x)$ and change each instance of $f(x)$ on the other side of the equation to x.

For instance, we can rewrite our first equation, $f(x) = x^3 + 1$, as $x^3 = f(x) - 1$, so $x = \sqrt[3]{f(x) - 1}$. Writing this explicitly as an inverse function, we can change the x to $f^{-1}(x)$ and the $f(x)$ to x to get $f^{-1}(x) = \sqrt[3]{x - 1}$. Our second example, $g(x) = \frac{x}{x-1}$, takes a little more work: multiplying both sides by $x - 1$ gives $(x - 1)g(x) = x$, which we can rearrange to $xg(x) - x = g(x)$, and finally to $x = \frac{g(x)}{g(x)-1}$. Replacing the x by $g^{-1}(x)$ and the $g(x)$ by x yields $g^{-1}(x) = \frac{x}{x-1}$: this function is its own inverse.

Example

Given a function such as $f(x) = 3x^3 - 4$, determine how you could solve an equation such as $f(x) = 20$

To solve an equation such as $f(x) = 20$, we're not asked to evaluate the function. Rather, we're asked to find a value for x at which the function evaluates to a given value. While in some cases it may be possible to solve such an equation through trial and error, a more reliable method is to use inverse functions (if $f(x)$ is invertible, which is the case here). If we find the inverse $f^{-1}(x)$ of $f(x)$, then we can apply that inverse function to both sides, yielding $f^{-1}(f(x)) = f^{-1}(20)$, which is to say $x = f^{-1}(20)$.

For our sample equation, $f(x) = 3x^3 - 4$, we can find the inverse algebraically. If $y = 3x^3 - 4$, then $3x^3 = y + 4$, $x^3 = \frac{y+4}{3}$, and finally $x = \sqrt[3]{(y + 4)/3}$. So $f^{-1}(x) = \sqrt[3]{(x + 4)/3}$. We can now find $f^{-1}(20)$: $f^{-1}(20) = \sqrt[3]{(20 + 4)/3} = \sqrt[3]{24/3} = \sqrt[3]{8} = 2$.

Under what circumstances an equation of the form $f(x) = C$ will have a unique solution

An equation of the form $f(x) = C$ may have one solution, multiple solutions, or no solution. For example, $x + 1 = 1$ has one solution; $x^2 = 1$ has two solutions; $\sin x = 1$ has infinitely many solutions; and $e^x + 2 = 1$ has no solutions.

In order for $f(x) = C$ to have any solutions at all, C must be in the range of $f(x)$. (Note that 1 is not in the range of $f(x) = e^x + 2$.) However, this doesn't guarantee that the solution is unique. If the function $f(x)$ is invertible, then $f(x) = C$ is guaranteed to have a unique solution for all values of C in the range of $f(x)$. If not, then for at least some values of C the solution of $f(x) = C$ will not be unique. For instance, if $f(x) = x^3 - x$, then $f(x) = 0$ has three solutions, since $f(0) = f(1) = f(-1) = 0$, but $f(x) = 6$ has the unique solution $x = 2$.

Example
> Given two functions expressed algebraically, explain how to determine whether they are inverses

> The simplest way to determine algebraically whether two functions are inverses is to evaluate their composition. If $(f \circ g)(x) = x$ and $(g \circ f)(x) = x$, then $g(x) = f^{-1}(x)$ and vice versa; these two functions are inverses.

> For example, consider $f(x) = x^3 + 1$ and $g(x) = \sqrt[3]{x-1}$. $(f \circ g)(x) = f(\sqrt[3]{x-1}) = (\sqrt[3]{x-1})^3 + 1 = (x-1) + 1 = x$, and $(g \circ f)(x) = g(x^3 + 1) = \sqrt[3]{(x^3+1) - 1} = \sqrt[3]{x^3} = x$.. These two functions, therefore, are inverses. Some functions are their own inverses. Consider $h(x) = \frac{x}{x-1}$: $(h \circ h)(x) = h\left(\frac{x}{x-1}\right) = \frac{x/(x-1)}{x/(x-1) - 1} = \frac{x}{x - (x-1)} = \frac{x}{1} = x$. So $h^{-1}(x) = h(x)$.

Example
> If $f(g(x)) = x$ for all x in the domain of $g(x)$, and $g(f(x)) = x$ for all x in the domain of $f(x)$, what does this imply about the relationship between $f(x)$ and $g(x)$

> If $f(g(x)) = x$ and $g(f(x)) = x$ for all x in the appropriate domains, then this means that $f(x)$ and $g(x)$ are inverse functions, i.e. $f^{-1}(x) = g(x)$ and $g^{-1}(x) = f(x)$. This means that if $f(x_0) = y_0$, then $g(y_0) = x_0$, and vice versa.

> Inverse functions are useful because they can be used to solve equations of the form $f(x) = C$. We can get the solution by simply taking the inverse function of both sides: $f^{-1}(f(x)) = f^{-1}(C)$, but $f^{-1}(f(x)) = x$, so $x = f^{-1}(C)$. For example, the exponential function e^x and the logarithm $\ln x$ are inverses, so we can use the exponential to solve logarithmic functions, and vice versa: if $e^x = 3$, then $\ln e^x = \ln 3$, so $x = \ln 3$.

Example
> Given a function represented by a table like the one below, determine how you can find the function's inverse

x	0	1	2	3	4	5	6	7
$f(x)$	4	5	0	2	7	1	6	3

> To change a function into its inverse, essentially all we need to do is to interchange its domain and range. Therefore, when the function is given in table form, we can just switch the two rows, as follows:

x	4	5	0	2	7	1	6	3
$f^{-1}(x)$	0	1	2	3	4	5	6	7

Putting the domain in ascending order (which isn't technically necessary, but makes the table easier to refer to) gives:

X	0	1	2	3	4	5	6	7
$f^{-1}(x)$	2	5	3	7	0	1	6	4

So, for instance, $f^{-1}(0) = 2$, and $f^{-1}(1) = 5$ —as we would expect, since $f(2) = 0$ and $f(5) = 1$.

Describe how the graph of a function compares to the graph of its inverse

To convert an invertible function $f(x)$ into its inverse, we interchange the domain and range. This means that the point (x, y) in $f(x)$ maps into the point (y, x) in $f^{-1}(x)$. On a graph, this is equivalent to reflecting the point through the line $y = x$, i.e. flipping it over diagonally, from upper left to lower right. Since this transformation applies to each point, it also applies to the function as a whole: we can get the graph of $f^{-1}(x)$ from the graph of $f(x)$ by just flipping the whole graph over through the diagonal line $y = x$. For example, if the graph of $f(x)$ is the graph shown on the left below, then flipping it over diagonally yields the graph on the right, which is the graph of $f^{-1}(x)$.

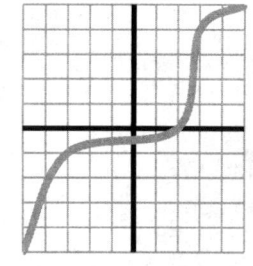

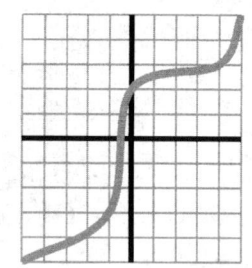

Example
Given a graph of an invertible function $f(x)$ and a value x_0, determine how you can read the value $f^{-1}(x_0)$ from the graph

While it's possible to turn the graph of $f(x)$ into a graph of $f^{-1}(x)$ by simply flipping it over diagonally through the line $y = x$, it's also possible to read values of $f^{-1}(x)$ off the graph of $f(x)$ directly. Just as we can read the value of $f(x_0)$ from a graph by finding the point where the graph intersects the line $x = x_0$ and observing the y coordinate of that point, so we can read the value of $f^{-1}(x_0)$ by the inverse process: We can find the point where the graph intersects the line $y = x_0$, and then read off the point's x-coordinate. The diagram below illustrates this procedure:

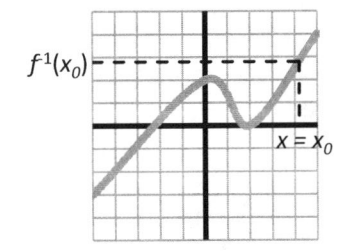

Determine how you can tell from the graph of a function whether the function has an inverse

A function has an inverse if and only if each point in the range corresponds to a unique point in the domain. This is similar to the definition of a function itself—in a function, each point in the domain corresponds to a unique point in the range. Therefore, we can use similar guidelines to identify invertible functions. One simple way to tell whether a graph represents a function is the "vertical line test"; we observe whether there exists any vertical line that intersects the graph in more than one point. Similarly, we can check whether a function is invertible from its graph by using a sort of "horizontal line test": we check whether there exists any *horizontal* line that intersects the function in more than one point. If so, then the y coordinate corresponding to that line is matched up with more than one x coordinate, which means that the function is *not* invertible. If no such horizontal line exists, then the function is invertible.

Example

Given a non-invertible function such as $f(x) = x^2 + 1$ or $g(x) = x^3 - x$, determine how you could produce an invertible function by restricting the domain

What makes these functions non-invertible is that there are certain y values that correspond to more than one x value. For instance, $f(1) = f(-1) = 2$, and $g(-1) = g(0) = g(1) = 0$. However, this only occurs because the graph is increasing in some parts of the domain and decreasing in others. If we restrict the domain to regions where the function is only increasing or decreasing, within these regions each y corresponds to a unique x, so this restricted function is invertible.

Our first example, $f(x) = x^2 + 1$, decreases from $-\infty$ to 0, and increases from 0 to ∞. Restricting the domain to either the interval $(-\infty, 0]$ or $[0, \infty)$ produces an invertible function. Finding exactly where $g(x) = x^3 - x$ transitions between increasing and decreasing is difficult without calculus, but we don't need to know the precise transition points; we can choose a smaller interval over which it's clearly increasing or decreasing. For instance, if we graph $g(x)$, we can see it's clearly increasing for all $x > 1$, so we can get an invertible function by restricting its domain to $[1, \infty)$.

Example

Why is it incorrect (or at least incomplete) to say that the functions $f(x) = x^2$ and $g(x) = \sqrt{x}$ are inverses

At first, it might seem obvious that $f(x) = x^2$ and $g(x) = \sqrt{x}$ are inverses. After all, if we take the function composition $f(g(x))$, we find $f(g(x)) = f(\sqrt{x}) = (\sqrt{x})^2 = x$. However, one characteristic of inverse functions is that the domain of the inverse function is the same as the range of the original function, and vice versa. In this case, the range of $f(x)$ is indeed equal to the domain of $g(x)$: $[0, \infty)$. But the domain of $f(x)$ is not equal to the range of $g(x)$: the former is $(-\infty, \infty)$ but the latter only $[0, \infty)$. And, indeed, while $f(g(x)) = x$, we can find points for which $g(f(x)) \neq x$. For example, $g(f(-1)) = g((-1)^2) = g(1) = \sqrt{1} = 1$.

The root of the problem is that the function $f(x)$ is not invertible. There are elements in the range that match up to multiple points in the domain, such as $f(1) = f(-1) = 1$. If we make a new function $f_+(x)$ by restricting the domain of $f(x)$ to the interval $[0, \infty)$, then indeed $g(x) = f_+^{-1}(x)$.

Example

Is it possible that $f(g(x)) = x$ for all x in the domain of $g(x)$, but $g(f(x)) \neq x$ for some x in the domain of $f(x)$

Yes, it's possible that $f(g(x)) = x$ for all x in the domain of $g(x)$ without the same being true for $g(f(x))$. A simple example is $f(x) = x^2$ and $g(x) = \sqrt{x}$. For all x in the domain of $g(x)$, $f(g(x)) = f(\sqrt{x}) = (\sqrt{x})^2 = x$. However, this isn't true for $g(f(x))$: consider $g(f(-1)) = g((-1)^2) = g(1) = \sqrt{1} = 1 \neq -1$.

The reason that occurs is because in this case $f(x)$ is not an invertible function; there are multiple values of x that correspond to the same value of $f(x)$. Accordingly, there can be no function for which $f(g(x)) = x$ and $g(f(x)) = x$, because then the functions would be inverses. If we restrict $f(x)$ to the interval $[0, \infty)$, to produce a new function $f_2(x)$, then $f_2(x)$ is invertible, $f_2(g(x)) = x$, and $g(f_2(x)) = x$.

Example

Given a logarithmic equation such as $3 \log_2 2x = 15$, determine how you could solve for x.

To solve a logarithmic equation where the variable appears in the argument of the logarithm, we have to use the fact that the exponential function is the inverse of the logarithmic. First, we rearrange the expression to get the logarithmic expression on a side by itself. After that, we can cancel the logarithm by taking the exponential function of both sides (with the same base as the logarithm). From that point on, solving the equation is a matter of simple algebra.

For instance, we can divide by three both sides of our sample equation, $3 \log_2 2x = 15$, to get $\log_2 2x = \frac{15}{3} = 5$. We can now cancel the logarithm with an exponential: $2^{\log_2 2x} = 2^5$, or, simplifying the left hand side, $2x = 2^5$. So $x = \frac{2^5}{2} = \frac{32}{2} = 16$.

Relationship between exponential functions and logarithms

Exponential functions and logarithms are inverse functions. More specifically, an exponential function of a particular base is the inverse of a logarithmic function of the same base. For instance, e^x and $\ln x$ are inverse functions. 10^x and $\log_{10} x$ are inverse functions. And, in general, a^x and $\log_a x$ are inverse functions.

<u>How we can use this relationship to solve problems</u>
This relationship is often useful for solving problems, because we can use it to cancel an exponential or logarithmic function on one side of an equation. For example, given an equation of the form $a^x = C$, we can solve for x by taking the logarithm of both sides: $\log_a(a^x) = \log_a C$, which, since a^x and $\log_a x$ are inverse functions, reduces to $x = \log_a C$. Conversely, given an equation of the form $\log_a x = C$, we can solve for x by taking the exponential of both sides: $a^{\log_a x} = a^C$, which reduces to $x = a^C$.

Describe under what circumstances you would use a logarithmic function to solve a problem

The logarithm is the inverse of the exponential, and so can be used to cancel an exponential function. This is useful if a problem involves an exponential equation in which the variable to be solved for is in the exponent; we can then use the logarithmic equation to get the variable out of the exponent. For instance, we can solve the equation $10^x = 20$ by simply taking the logarithm, base 10, of both sides: $\log_{10}(10^x) = \log_{10}(20)$, thus $x = \log_{10} 20$.

More complex equations may require some algebraic manipulation: from $2e^{3x+5} + 6 = 20$, we get $2e^{3x+5} = 14$, then $e^{3x+5} = 7$. We can now take the logarithm of both sides: $\ln(e^{3x+5}) = \ln 7$, hence $3x + 5 = \ln 7$ and finally $x = (\ln 7 - 5)/3$.

Practice Test

Practice Questions

1. Which of the following represents the product of $(4x^3 - 2x + 4)(x - 8)$?
   - Ⓐ $4x^4 - 32x^3 + 18x - 32$
   - Ⓑ $4x^4 - 32x^3 - 18x^2 - 2x - 12$
   - Ⓒ $4x^4 - 32x^3 - 2x^2 + 20x - 32$
   - Ⓓ $4x^4 - 28x^3 - 2x^2 + 16x - 4$

2. The polynomial, $x^3 - 2x^2 - 40x - 64$, has a zero at $x = -4$. Which of the following represents the other zeros of the polynomial?
   - Ⓐ $x = -8$ and $x = 2$
   - Ⓑ $x = 6$ and $x = -4$
   - Ⓒ $x = -6$ and $x = -2$
   - Ⓓ $x = 8$ and $x = -2$

3. Which of the following represents the sum of $\frac{3}{x+2} + \frac{x}{x^2+10x+16}$?
   - Ⓐ $\frac{3}{x+2}$
   - Ⓑ $\frac{x+6}{x+8}$
   - Ⓒ $\frac{2(x+6)}{(x+2)(x+8)}$
   - Ⓓ $\frac{4(x+6)}{(x+8)(x+2)}$

4. What is the solution to the equation, $\frac{x}{x-6} + \frac{1}{2} = \frac{6}{x-6}$?
   - Ⓐ $x = 3$
   - Ⓑ $x = 6$
   - Ⓒ $x = 9$
   - Ⓓ No solution

5. Which of the following expressions is equivalent to the expression, $\frac{x-3}{x^3-6x^2-9x+54}$?
   - Ⓐ $\frac{x-3}{x-6}$
   - Ⓑ $\frac{1}{(x+3)(x-6)}$
   - Ⓒ $\frac{1}{x-6}$
   - Ⓓ $\frac{x-3}{(x+3)(x-6)}$

6. The polynomial, $x^3 + 4x + 7$, is divided by the factor, $x - 2$. Which of the following represents the remainder?

   Ⓐ 17

   Ⓑ 19

   Ⓒ 21

   Ⓓ 23

7. Given the equation, $\frac{2}{x+4} = \frac{3}{x}$, what is the value of x?

   Ⓐ 10

   Ⓑ 12

   Ⓒ −12

   Ⓓ −14

8. Which of the following represents the difference of $(3x^3 - 9x^2 + 6x) - (8x^3 + 4x^2 - 3x)$?

   Ⓐ $-5x^3 - 13x^2 + 9x$

   Ⓑ $11x^3 - 13x^2 + 3x$

   Ⓒ $-5x^3 - 5x^2 + 3x$

   Ⓓ $5x^3 + 13x^2 + 9x$

9. How many terms are included in the expression, $2x^2 + 12x - 8 + 10x$?

   Ⓐ 3

   Ⓑ 4

   Ⓒ 5

   Ⓓ 6

10. Which of the following represents the factors of the expression, $x^2 - 3x - 40$?

    Ⓐ $(x - 8)(x + 5)$

    Ⓑ $(x - 7)(x + 4)$

    Ⓒ $(x + 10)(x - 4)$

    Ⓓ $(x + 6)(x - 9)$

11. Which of the following represents the zeros of the expression, $x^2 - 2x - 24$?

    Ⓐ $x = 4$ and $x = 6$

    Ⓑ $x = -4$ and $x = 6$

    Ⓒ $x = 4$ and $x = -6$

    Ⓓ $x = -4$ and $x = -6$

12. Given the expression, $6x^2 - 9(x - 4) + 2$, which of the following represents a coefficient?

    Ⓐ 6

    Ⓑ 9

    Ⓒ −4

    Ⓓ 2

13. Which of the following is a rational number?

    Ⓐ $3\sqrt{121} + 7$

    Ⓑ $4 + \sqrt[3]{150}$

    Ⓒ $7\sqrt{30}$

    Ⓓ $(8)^{2/3} + (8)^{1/5}$

14. Simplify: $(3 - 6i)(5 + 4i)$

    Ⓐ $39 - 18i$

    Ⓑ $15 - 24i$

    Ⓒ $-9 - 18i$

    Ⓓ $-18i^2$

15. Simplify: $3(6 + 2i) - 4(1 + i)$

    Ⓐ $14 + 3i$

    Ⓑ $14 + 2i$

    Ⓒ $22 + 10i$

    Ⓓ $13 + i$

16. Solve: $\dfrac{(3+4i)}{(5-2i)}$

    Ⓐ $\dfrac{3}{5} - 2i$

    Ⓑ $\dfrac{7+26i}{29}$

    Ⓒ $\dfrac{17+26i}{25}$

    Ⓓ $\dfrac{23+26i}{21}$

17. Compute the modulus of $6 + 8i$.

    Ⓐ -10

    Ⓑ -28

    Ⓒ 10

    Ⓓ 28

18. Which of the following is the correct graphical representation of 3 + 2i?

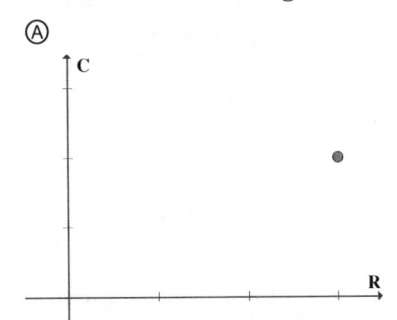

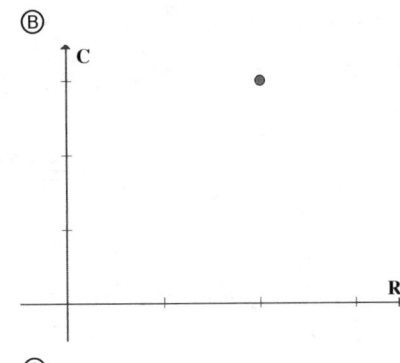

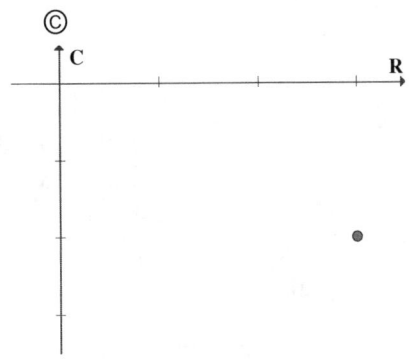

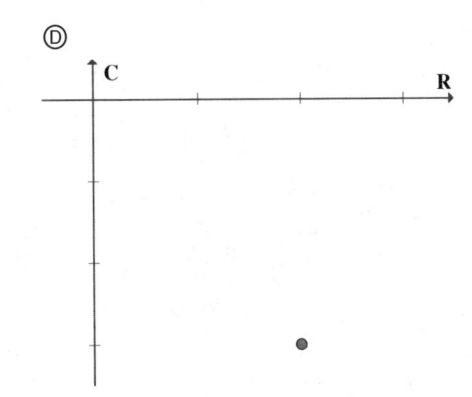

Ⓐ

Ⓑ

Ⓒ

Ⓓ

19. Convert from rectangular to polar form: $z = 12 + 5i$.

   Ⓐ $z = 12(cos5° + isin5°)$

   Ⓑ $z = 13(cos67° + isin67°)$

   Ⓒ $z = 17(cos60° + isin60°)$

   Ⓓ $z = 13(cos23° + isin23°)$

20. Usain Bolt set a world record of 9.58 seconds for the 100 meter dash. White-tailed deer can run at 48 kilometers per hour for short periods. If Mr. Bolt and a white-tailed deer run a 100 meter dash at these speeds, who would win, and by how much?

   Ⓐ Mr. Bolt wins by 3.75 seconds

   Ⓑ Mr. Bolt wins by 2.08 seconds

   Ⓒ Deer wins by 3.75 seconds

   Ⓓ Deer wins by 2.08 seconds

21. After getting his wisdom teeth pulled, Matt was prescribed 60 mg of Codeine to be taken every 4 hours for 5 days. The pharmacy has 30 mg pills. How many pills should Matt receive when filling the prescription?

   Ⓐ 72

   Ⓑ 60

   Ⓒ 30

   Ⓓ 24

22. What are the zeros of a quadratic expression, represented by the factors, $(x + 6)$ and $(x - 7)$?

   Ⓐ $x = 6$ and $x = 7$

   Ⓑ $x = 6$ and $x = -7$

   Ⓒ $x = -6$ and $x = 7$

   Ⓓ $x = -6$ and $x = -7$

23. Which of the following expressions is equivalent to $(x - 3)^2$?

   Ⓐ $x^2 - 3x + 9$

   Ⓑ $x^2 - 6x - 9$

   Ⓒ $x^2 - 6x + 9$

   Ⓓ $x^2 + 3x - 9$

24. Which of the following equations represents the relationship between x and y, shown in the table below?

x	y
−3	−21
−1	−3
0	6
2	24
5	51

Ⓐ $y = 9x + 6$

Ⓑ $y = 7x$

Ⓒ $y = 3x + 18$

Ⓓ $y = 12x + 6$

25. The formula for finding the volume of a cone is $V = \frac{1}{3}\pi r^2 h$. Which of the following equations is correctly solved for r?

Ⓐ $r = \frac{1}{3}\pi h$

Ⓑ $r = \sqrt{\frac{3V}{\pi h}}$

Ⓒ $r = \frac{V}{\frac{1}{3}\pi h}$

Ⓓ $r = V - \frac{1}{3}\pi h$

26. Given the equation, $2^x = 64$, what is the value of x?

Ⓐ 4

Ⓑ 5

Ⓒ 6

Ⓓ 7

27. What is the solution to the equation, $4\sqrt{x} + 8 = 24$?

Ⓐ $x = 2$

Ⓑ $x = 4$

Ⓒ $x = 12$

Ⓓ $x = 16$

28. Given the equation, $ax + b = c$, what is the value of x?

Ⓐ $\frac{c+b}{a}$

Ⓑ $\frac{ca}{b}$

Ⓒ $c - ba$

Ⓓ $\frac{c-b}{a}$

29. What is the solution to the inequality, $3x + 18 > 6$?

   Ⓐ $x > -4$

   Ⓑ $x < -4$

   Ⓒ $x > -8$

   Ⓓ $x < -8$

30. What are the zeros of the quadratic equation, $4x^2 - 6x = 8$?

   Ⓐ $2 \pm \sqrt{41}$

   Ⓑ $3 \pm \frac{\sqrt{41}}{2}$

   Ⓒ $3 \pm \frac{\sqrt{41}}{4}$

   Ⓓ $\frac{3 \pm \sqrt{41}}{4}$

31. Which of the following represents the solution of the equation, $6x^2 - 8x = -8$?

   Ⓐ $\frac{2(1 \pm i\sqrt{2})}{3}$

   Ⓑ $2 \pm i\sqrt{2}$

   Ⓒ $\frac{2(2 \pm i\sqrt{2})}{3}$

   Ⓓ $\frac{1}{4} \pm i\sqrt{2}$

32. When solving the equation, $12x^2 + 24x = 48$, by completing the square, which of the following equations may be used to find the solution?

   Ⓐ $(x + 2)^2 = 6$

   Ⓑ $(x + 1)^2 = 7$

   Ⓒ $(x + 1)^2 = 5$

   Ⓓ $(x + 2)^2 = 8$

33. Given the system of equations, $\begin{array}{l} 3x + 6y = 36 \\ 2x + 9y = 34 \end{array}$, which of the following equations may be added to produce the correct y-value solution?

   Ⓐ $\begin{array}{l} 6x + 15y = 72 \\ -6x - 36y = -102 \end{array}$

   Ⓑ $\begin{array}{l} 6x + 12y = 72 \\ -6x - 27y = -102 \end{array}$

   Ⓒ $\begin{array}{l} 6x + 12y = 108 \\ -6x - 27y = -102 \end{array}$

   Ⓓ $\begin{array}{l} 6x + 15y = 108 \\ -6x - 36y = -72 \end{array}$

34. Given the equation, $4x - 9 = 7$, what property is used when writing the next step as $4x = 7 + 9$?

Ⓐ Associative property of addition

Ⓑ Commutative property of addition

Ⓒ Addition property of equality

Ⓓ Additive inverse property

35. Given the equation, $2x + 6y = 18$, what property is used when writing the next step as $x + 3y = 9$?

Ⓐ Subtraction property of equality

Ⓑ Multiplicative identity property

Ⓒ Division property of equality

Ⓓ Multiplicative inverse property

36. The system of equations, $\begin{array}{l} y = x^2 + 4x \\ y = x \end{array}$, has a solution of (0, 0). Which of the following represents another solution of the system?

Ⓐ (−3, −3)

Ⓑ (3, 3)

Ⓒ (2, 2)

Ⓓ (−2, −2)

37. Which of the following represents the points of intersection of the line, $x + y = -6$ and a circle, given by the equation, $(x - 2)^2 + (y + 4)^2 = 16$?

Ⓐ (2, −6) and (−2, 4)

Ⓑ (−2, −4) and (2, −8)

Ⓒ (2, 4) and (−2, 8)

Ⓓ (−2, −6) and (2, −12)

38. Which of the following graphs represents the solutions of the equation, $9x - 3y = 15$?

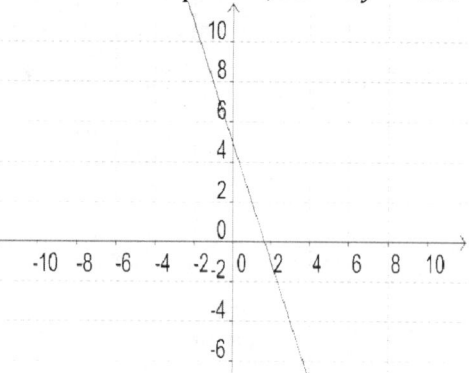

Ⓐ

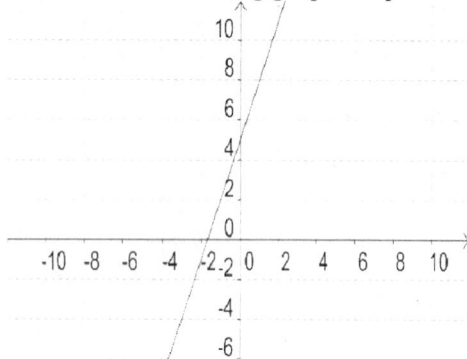

Ⓑ

Ⓒ

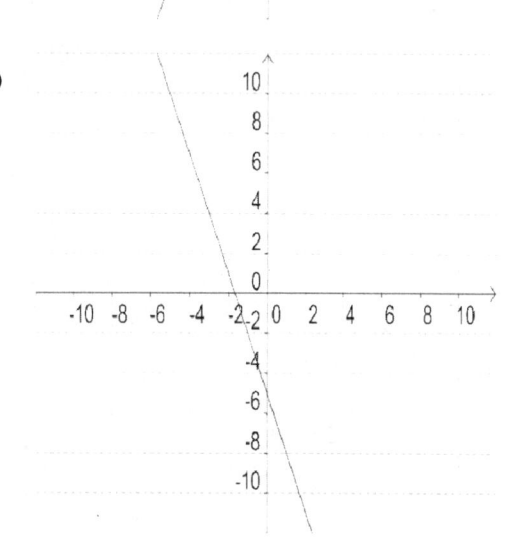

Ⓓ

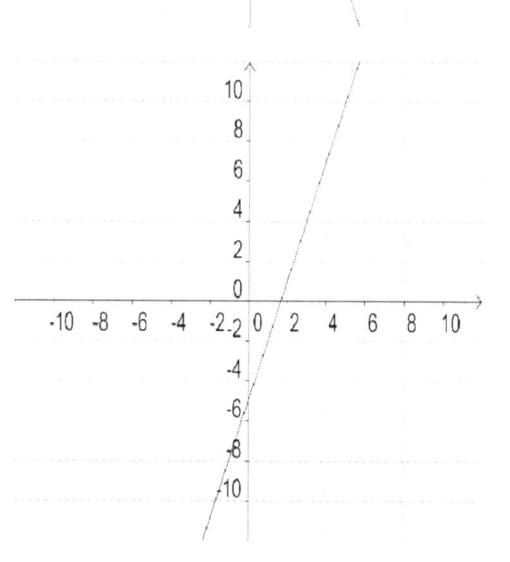

39. Given the functions, $f(x) = 3x + 6$ and $g(x) = 2x - 8$, what is the solution of the equation, $f(x) = g(x)$?

Ⓐ $x = -12$

Ⓑ $x = -8$

Ⓒ $x = -14$

Ⓓ $x = -10$

40. Which of the following systems of inequalities has a solution set, represented by the graph shown below?

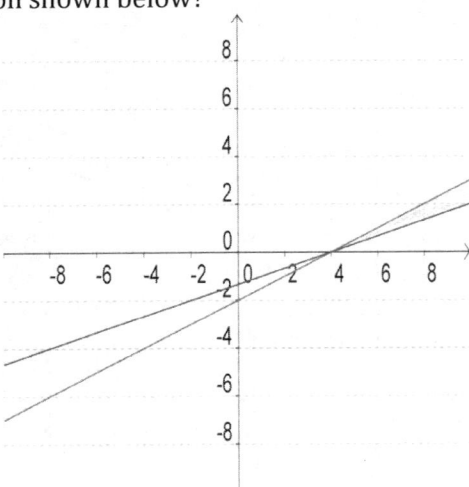

Ⓐ $2x - 4y \geq 8$
    $3x - 9y \leq 12$

Ⓑ $2x - 4y \leq 8$
    $3x - 9y \geq 12$

Ⓒ $6x - 2y \geq 12$
    $-9x + 4y \leq 15$

Ⓓ $6x - 2y \leq 12$
    $-9x + 4y \geq 15$

41. The function *f* is defined as $f(x) = \sqrt{x-3}$. Its domain is $x \geq 3$, and its range is $f(x) \geq 0$. Which of the following is true of *f*?

Ⓐ If $x \geq 3$, then $f(x) \geq 0$.

Ⓑ It assigns exactly one value to every positive value of *x*.

Ⓒ The range of the function is *f*(3).

Ⓓ The value of *f*(3) is undefined.

42. John puts his money into a bank account that pays monthly interest. His monthly balance (in dollars) after *t* months is given by the exponential function $b(t) = 315(1.05)^t$. How much money did John initially put into the account?

Ⓐ $5

Ⓑ $105

Ⓒ $300

Ⓓ $315

43. Solve the exponential equation $3e^{2t} = 12$ for t.
    ⓐ $t = \frac{\ln 4}{2}$
    ⓑ $t = \frac{\ln 12}{6}$
    ⓒ $t = \ln 2$
    ⓓ $t = 2\ln 4$

44. A librarian makes time-and-a-half for each hour that he works over 40 hours per week. The linear function $s(h) = 27h + 720$ represents his weekly salary (in dollars) if he works h hours more than 40 hours that week. For example, his weekly salary is $s(10) = 990$ dollars if he works 50 hours in one week (because 10 + 40 = 50). What is his hourly salary after he has already worked the initial 40 hours in one week?
    ⓐ $7.20 per hour
    ⓑ $18.00 per hour
    ⓒ $27.00 per hour
    ⓓ $72.00 per hour

45. A linear function can be used to convert a temperature from Fahrenheit to Celsius. For example, you can use it to convert 32°F to 0°C and 68°F to 20°C. Use this information to convert 104°F to Celsius.
    ⓐ 25°C
    ⓑ 30°C
    ⓒ 40°C
    ⓓ 50°C

46. Which of the following would be an appropriate domain for the function $t(n)$, the average temperature (in °F) during the nth month of the year in Washington, DC?
    ⓐ $0 \leq n \leq 12$
    ⓑ $1 \leq n \leq 12$
    ⓒ $10 \leq n \leq 90$
    ⓓ $40 \leq n \leq 60$

47. A theater will sell 500 tickets to a play if it charges $10 per ticket. Furthermore, every time it raises the price by one dollar, it will sell 50 fewer tickets because some people will think it too expensive. Which of the following functions $t(d)$ represents the number of tickets the theater will sell if it charges d dollars per ticket?
    ⓐ $t(d) = -50d + 10$
    ⓑ $t(d) = -50d + 1000$
    ⓒ $t(d) = 50d$
    ⓓ $t(d) = 50d + 10$

48. Calculate the fifth term of the sequence defined as $f(0) = 2, f(n + 1) = 2f(n) - 1$ for $n \geq 1$.

Ⓐ 9

Ⓑ 17

Ⓒ 32

Ⓓ 33

49. Kevin saves 2 dollars during the month of January. Each month, he plans to save twice the amount saved during the previous month. With this plan, how much will he have saved after 18 months?

Ⓐ $218,174

Ⓑ $262,144

Ⓒ $478,195

Ⓓ $524,286

50. Dr. Thompson creates a pattern with drawings, containing 4 red dots, 12 red dots, 36 red dots, and 108 red dots. If this pattern continues, how many red dots will he have drawn in the first 20 drawings?

Ⓐ 4,649,045,868

Ⓑ 896,321,650

Ⓒ 7,283,441,275

Ⓓ 6,973,568,800

51. Bob's Bakery sells cupcakes for $1.25 each and cups of coffee for $2.75 each. His daily sales total $227.50. He sold 110 cupcakes and cups of coffee. How many cupcakes and how many cups of coffee did he sell?

Ⓐ 40 cupcakes and 70 cups of coffee

Ⓑ 50 cupcakes and 60 cups of coffee

Ⓒ 40 cups of coffee and 70 cupcakes

Ⓓ 50 cups of coffee and 60 cupcakes

52. Which of the following represents the solution of the following system of linear equations: $\begin{array}{l} 5x + 9y = -7 \\ 2x - 4y = 20 \end{array}$?

Ⓐ $x = 3, y = 2$

Ⓑ $x = 4, y = 3$

Ⓒ $x = 4, y = -3$

Ⓓ $x = 3, y = -2$

53. Which of the following graphs represents the solution of the system of linear equations shown below?

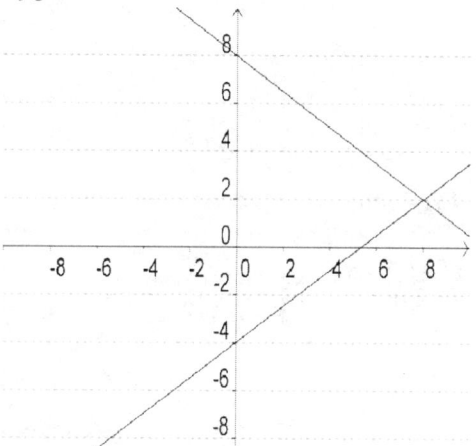

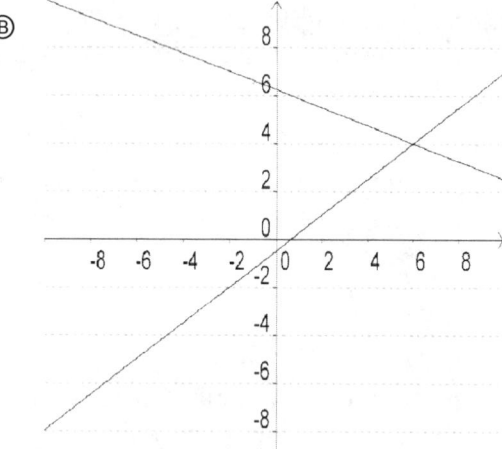

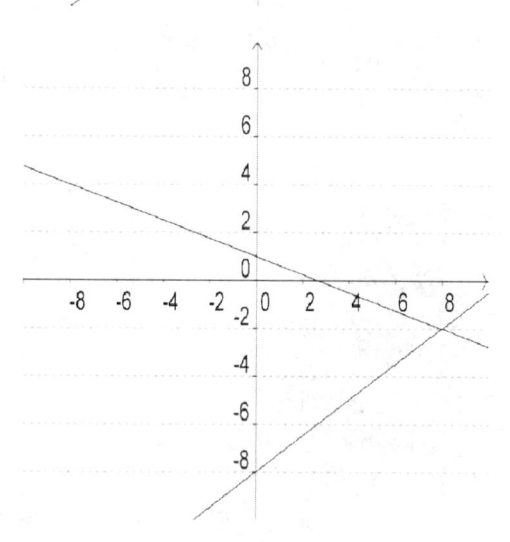

$$3x + 8y = 8$$
$$-9x + 12y = -96$$

Ⓐ

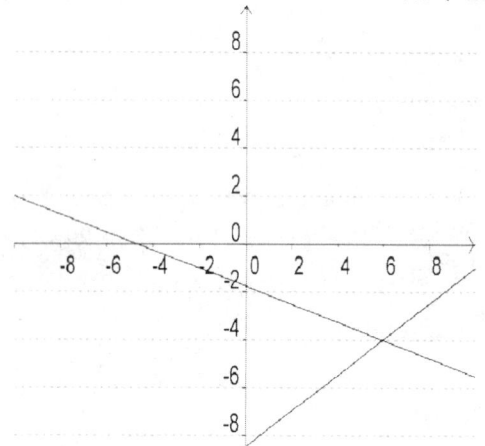

Ⓑ

Ⓒ

Ⓓ

54. Which of the following matrix equations may be used to represent the system of equations, $\begin{array}{l}2x+4y-3z=26\\2z-6y=-3x-23\\-4z+6x=-9y+49\end{array}$?

Ⓐ $\begin{bmatrix}2&4&-3\\3&-6&2\\6&9&-4\end{bmatrix}\begin{bmatrix}x\\y\\z\end{bmatrix}=\begin{bmatrix}26\\-23\\49\end{bmatrix}$

Ⓑ $\begin{bmatrix}2&4&-3\\2&-6&-3\\-4&6&-9\end{bmatrix}\begin{bmatrix}x\\y\\z\end{bmatrix}=\begin{bmatrix}26\\-23\\49\end{bmatrix}$

Ⓒ $\begin{bmatrix}2&4&3\\2&-6&-3\\4&6&-9\end{bmatrix}\begin{bmatrix}x\\y\\z\end{bmatrix}=\begin{bmatrix}26\\23\\49\end{bmatrix}$

Ⓓ $\begin{bmatrix}2&4&-3\\-3&-6&2\\6&-9&-4\end{bmatrix}\begin{bmatrix}x\\y\\z\end{bmatrix}=\begin{bmatrix}26\\23\\49\end{bmatrix}$

55. Which of the following products represents the solution to the system of equations, $\begin{array}{l}2x+3y=-5\\-4x-2y=-2\end{array}$?

Ⓐ $\begin{bmatrix}\frac{1}{4}&-\frac{1}{2}\\\frac{1}{2}&-\frac{3}{8}\end{bmatrix}\cdot\begin{bmatrix}-5\\-2\end{bmatrix}$

Ⓑ $\begin{bmatrix}2&-\frac{3}{8}\\\frac{1}{4}&\frac{1}{2}\end{bmatrix}\cdot\begin{bmatrix}5\\2\end{bmatrix}$

Ⓒ $\begin{bmatrix}-\frac{1}{4}&-\frac{3}{8}\\\frac{1}{2}&\frac{1}{4}\end{bmatrix}\cdot\begin{bmatrix}-5\\-2\end{bmatrix}$

Ⓓ $\begin{bmatrix}-2&-3\\4&2\end{bmatrix}\cdot\begin{bmatrix}-5\\-2\end{bmatrix}$

56. Kim is given $21 to buy gallons of milk and cartons of eggs. Each gallon of milk costs $3.50, and each carton of eggs costs $1.75. Which of the following graphs represents the possible combinations of gallons of milk and cartons of eggs she may purchase?

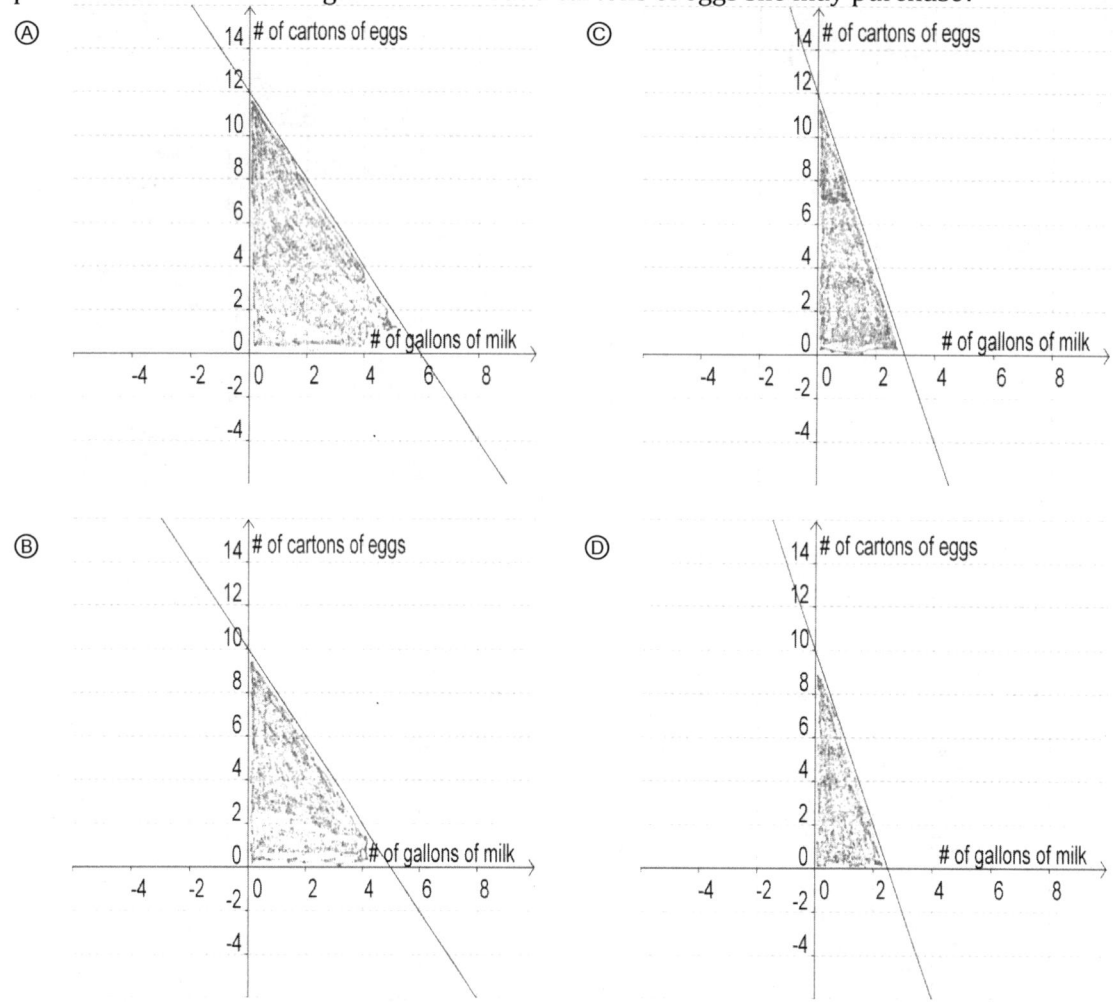

57. Ana opens a savings account with $100. She plans to deposit $25 dollars each month. Which of the following graphs represents the amount of money she will have in her savings account, after x months?

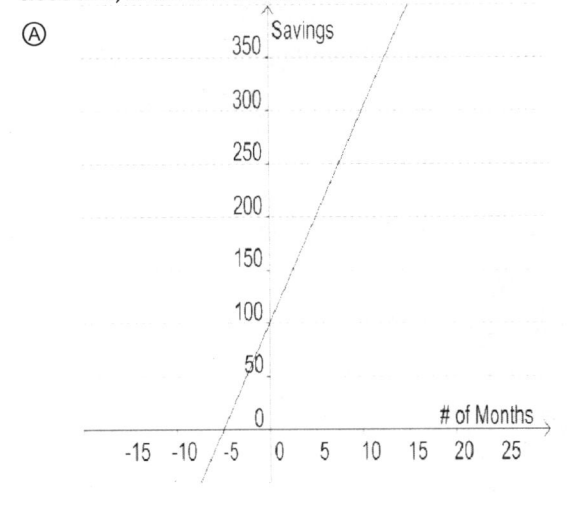

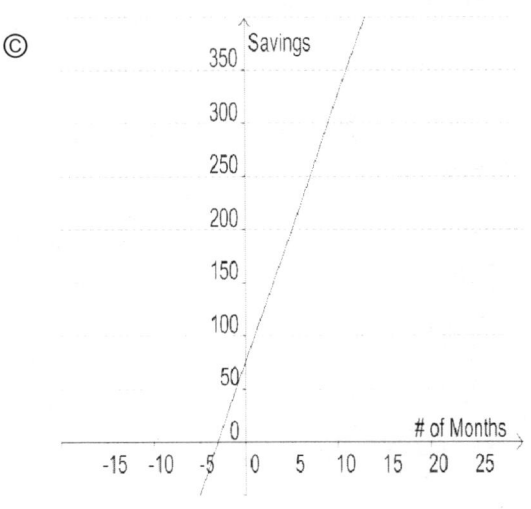

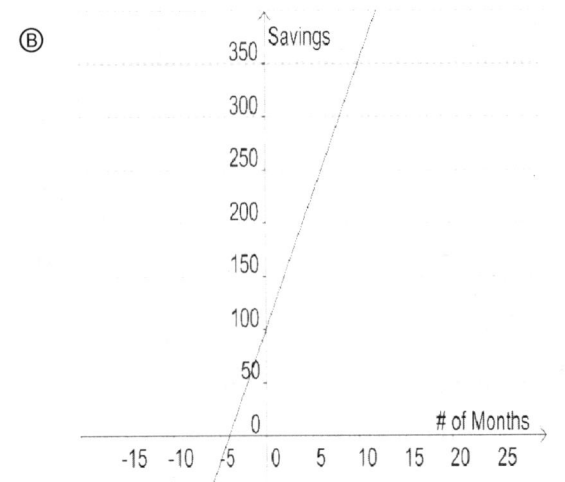

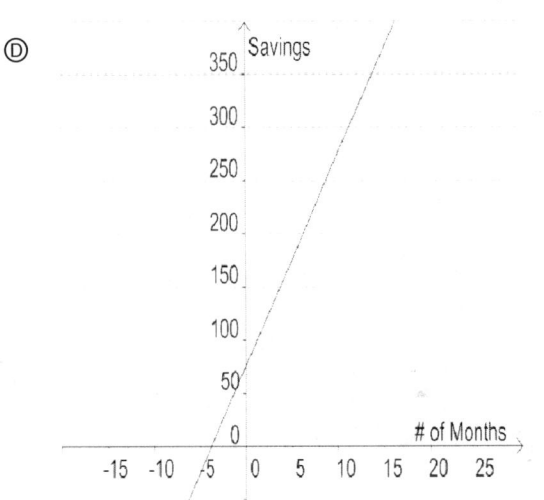

Ⓐ [graph]

Ⓑ [graph]

Ⓒ [graph]

Ⓓ [graph]

58. Find the complex roots: $y = x^2 - 2x + 10$.

   Ⓐ $1 + 3i, 1 - 3i$

   Ⓑ $1 + 6i, 1 - 6i$

   Ⓒ $1 + i\sqrt{22}, 1 - i\sqrt{22}$

   Ⓓ $2 + i\sqrt{22}, 2 - i\sqrt{22}$

59. Factor: $4x^2 + 25$.

   Ⓐ $(4x - 5i)(x + 5i)$

   Ⓑ $(4x + 5i)(x - 5i)$

   Ⓒ $(2x - 5)(2x + 5)$

   Ⓓ $(2x + 5i)(2x - 5i)$

60. Factor: $9x^2 + 42ix - 49$.
   Ⓐ $(3x + 7i)^2$
   Ⓑ $(3x - 7i)^2$
   Ⓒ $(3x + 7i)(3x - 7i)$
   Ⓓ $i(3x + 7)^2$

61. Find the distance, rounded to the nearest integer, between $-30 + 15i$ and $12 - 3i$.
   Ⓐ 22
   Ⓑ 44
   Ⓒ 46
   Ⓓ 51

62. Find the midpoint between $-30 + 15i$ and $12 - 3i$.
   Ⓐ $9 + 6i$
   Ⓑ $-9 + 6i$
   Ⓒ $-21 + 9i$
   Ⓓ $-24 + 13.5i$

63. The table below displays the value of the linear function $g(x)$ for five different values of x.

x	-2	-1	0	1	2
g(x)	10	7	4	1	-2

Write an explicit formula for $g(x)$.
   Ⓐ $g(x) = -4x + 3$
   Ⓑ $g(x) = -4x + 4$
   Ⓒ $g(x) = -3x + 3$
   Ⓓ $g(x) = -3x + 4$

64. The exponential function $h(x)$ is graphed below.

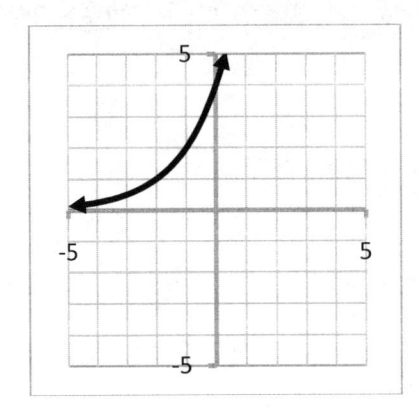

Write an explicit formula for $h(x)$.

Ⓐ $h(x) = 2^x$

Ⓑ $h(x) = 4 \cdot 2^x$

Ⓒ $h(x) = 4^x$

Ⓓ $h(x) = 2 \cdot 4^x$

65. Graph the function $f(x) = 2x - 4$. Show its x- and y-intercepts.

Ⓐ

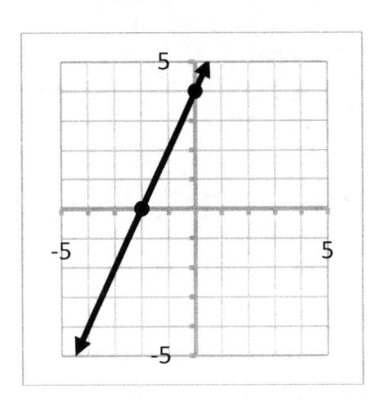

Ⓑ

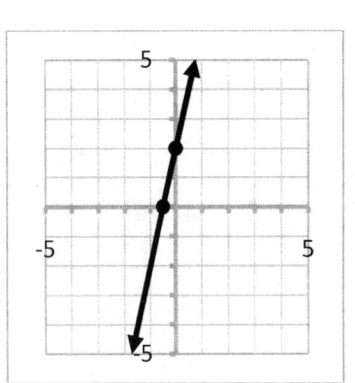

Ⓒ

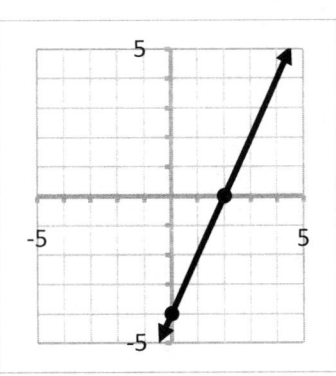

Ⓓ

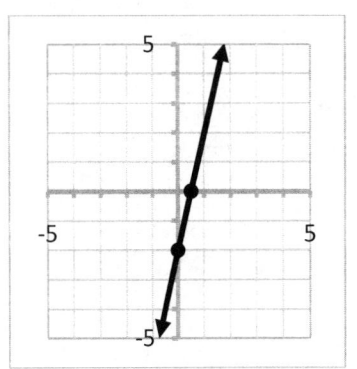

66. The dollar-value V of a particular interest-earning investment after t years is modeled by the exponential function $V = 200(1.04)^t$. What is the yearly interest of the investment?

Ⓐ 2%

Ⓑ 4%

Ⓒ 104%

Ⓓ 200%

67. The growth of bacteria can be modeled with an exponential function. If you start with 160 bacteria in a Petri dish, in two days, there will be 360 bacteria. And in three days, there will be 540 bacteria. If this continues, how many bacteria will there be in the Petri dish in five days?

Ⓐ 740 bacteria

Ⓑ 810 bacteria

Ⓒ 900 bacteria

Ⓓ 1215 bacteria

68. Exponential functions grow by equal factors over equal intervals. By what factor does the exponential function $f(x) = 3 \cdot 2^x$ grow by over every interval whose length is 3?

Ⓐ By a factor of 6

Ⓑ By a factor of 8

Ⓒ By a factor of 18

Ⓓ By a factor of 24

69. Graph the function $g(x) = x^2 - 2x - 3$. Show its minimum.

Ⓐ

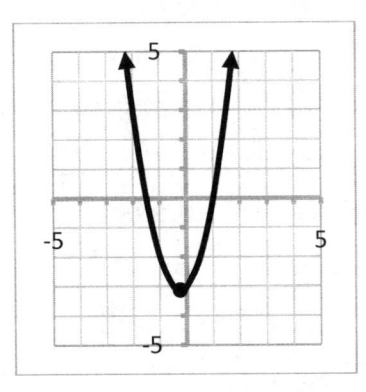

Ⓑ

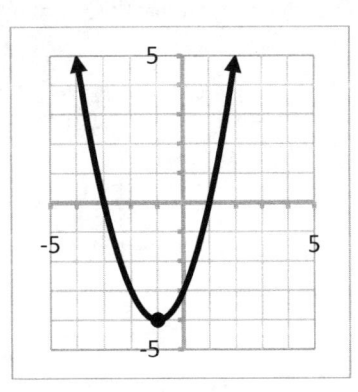

Ⓒ

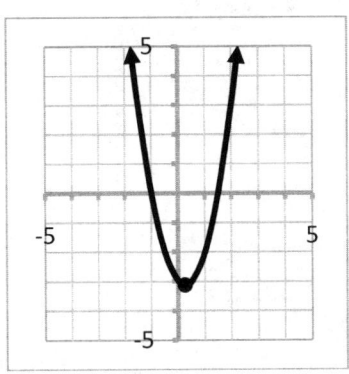

Ⓓ

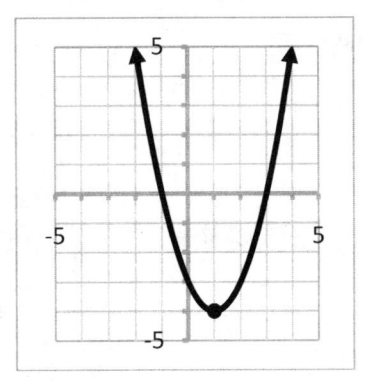

70. A metal ball is thrown up in the air. Its height above the ground (in feet) t seconds after it is thrown is given by the function $h(t)$. The equation $y = h(t)$ is graphed below.

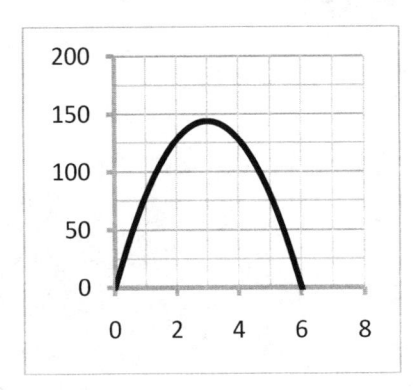

How many seconds after it is thrown does the metal ball reach its highest point?

Ⓐ 3 seconds

Ⓑ 6 seconds

Ⓒ 50 seconds

Ⓓ 144 seconds

71. Graph the function $f(x) = x^3 + x^2 - 4x - 4$. Show the function's zeroes.

Ⓐ

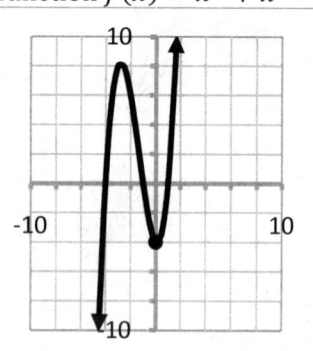

Ⓑ

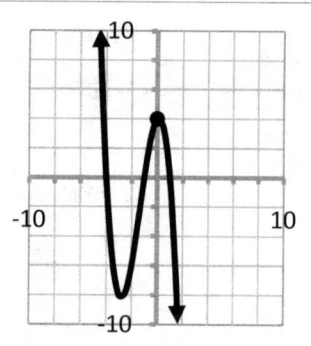

Ⓒ

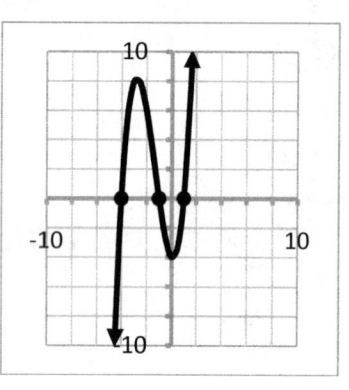

Ⓓ

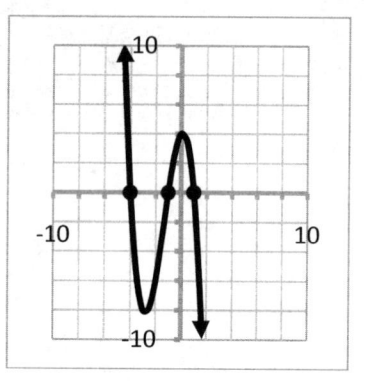

72. Graph the piecewise-defined function $h(x) = \begin{cases} \frac{1}{2}x, & x < 2 \\ 4 - x, & x \geq 2 \end{cases}$.

Ⓐ

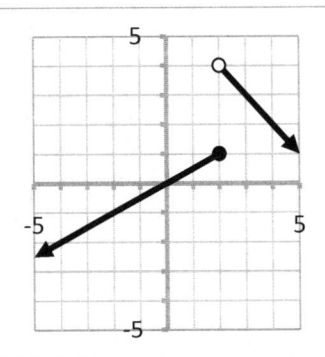

Ⓑ

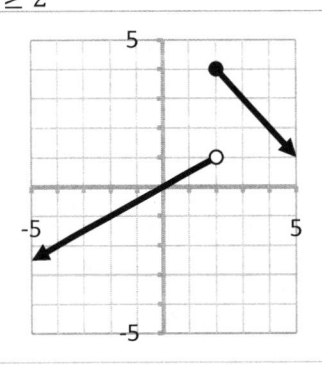

Ⓒ

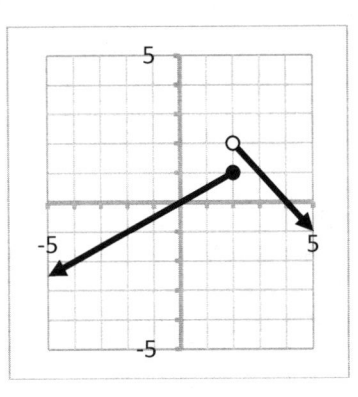

Ⓓ

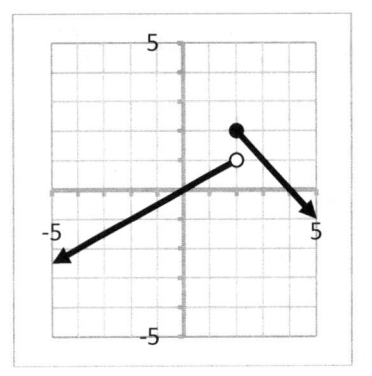

73. Four functions are graphed below.

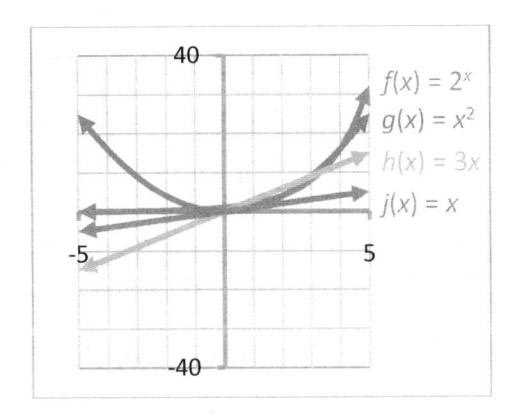

$f(x) = 2^x$
$g(x) = x^2$
$h(x) = 3x$
$j(x) = x$

Which function eventually exceeds the other three as x increases?

Ⓐ $f(x) = 2^x$

Ⓑ $g(x) = x^2$

Ⓒ $h(x) = 3x$

Ⓓ $j(x) = x$

74. Which function has the same x-intercept as the function graphed below?

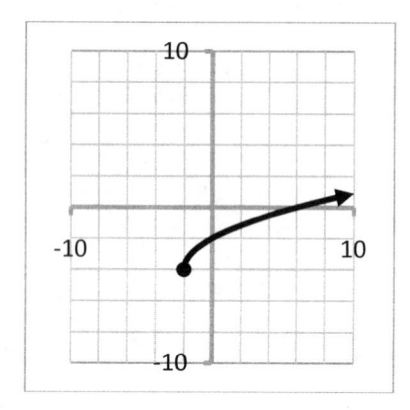

Ⓐ $g(x) = -4x - 12$
Ⓑ $g(x) = x^2 - 12x + 36$
Ⓒ $g(x) = x^3 + 6x^2 - 2x - 2$
Ⓓ $g(x) = \frac{6}{x-3}$

75. A taxi ride costs $4.25 for the first mile and $0.70 for each mile after the first. Which of the following functions $c(d)$ gives the total cost (in dollars) of traveling d miles (assuming that $d \geq 1$)?

Ⓐ $c(d) = 3.55 + 0.70d$
Ⓑ $c(d) = 3.55 + 0.70(d - 1)$
Ⓒ $c(d) = 4.25 + 0.70d$
Ⓓ $c(d) = 4.25 + 0.70(d - 1)$

76. A pump fills a cylindrical tank with water at a constant rate. The function $L(g) = 0.3g$ represents the water level of the tank (in feet) after g gallons are pumped into the tank. The function $w(t) = 1.2t$ represents the number of gallons that can be pumped into the tank in t minutes. Write a function $L(t)$ for the water level of the tank after t minutes.

Ⓐ $L(t) = 0.25t$
Ⓑ $L(t) = 0.36t$
Ⓒ $L(t) = 0.9t$
Ⓓ $L(t) = 3.6t$

77. Grains of wheat are placed on the squares of a chessboard so that one grain is placed on the first square, two on the second, four are on the third, and so on, continuing so that twice as many grains are placed on each subsequent square. Write a formula for the number of wheat grains that are placed on the *n*th square.

Ⓐ $g(n) = 2(n-1)$

Ⓑ $g(n) = 2n$

Ⓒ $g(n) = n^2$

Ⓓ $g(n) = 2^{n-1}$

78. Graph the function $g(x) = \frac{3}{2x-4}$. Show its zeroes and asymptotes if there are any.

Ⓐ

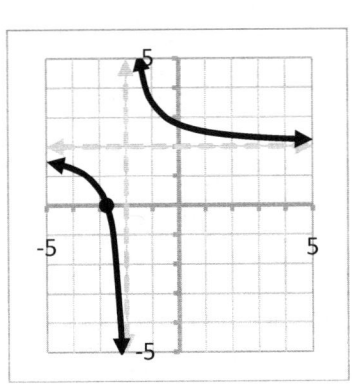

Ⓑ

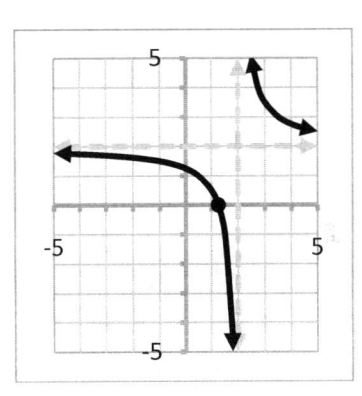

Ⓒ

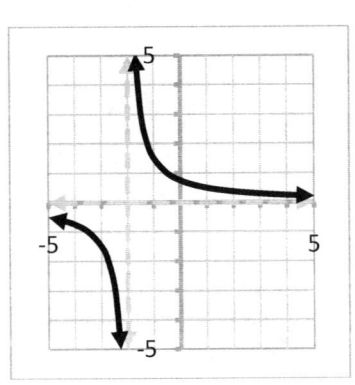

Ⓓ

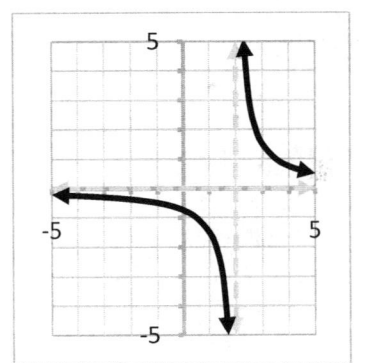

79. Graph the function $h(x) = \log_2 2(x+3)$. Show its x- and y-intercepts if there are any.

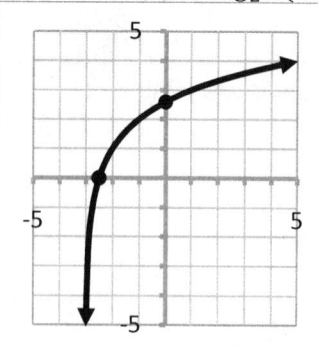

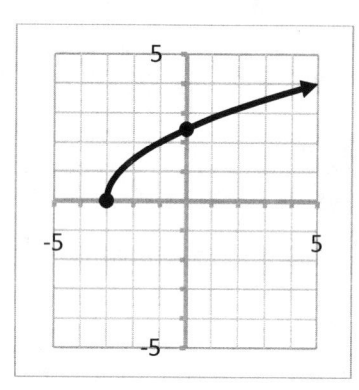

Ⓐ   Ⓑ

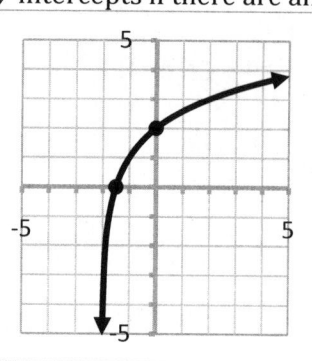

Ⓒ   Ⓓ

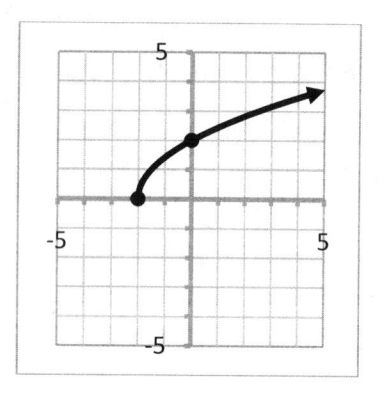

80. Use factoring to identify the zeroes of the function $f(x) = x^2 + 5x - 24$.
Ⓐ −24
Ⓑ −8 and 3
Ⓒ −6 and 4
Ⓓ 24

81. Compare the graphs of $f(x) = 3^x$ and $g(x) = 3^{x+1}$.
Ⓐ The graph of g is the graph of f shifted one unit down.
Ⓑ The graph of g is the graph of f shifted one unit up.
Ⓒ The graph of g is the graph of f shifted one unit to the left.
Ⓓ The graph of g is the graph of f shifted one unit to the right.

82. Compare the graphs of $f(x) = \sqrt{x}$ and $g(x) = 5\sqrt{x}$.
Ⓐ The graph of g is the graph of f shifted five units to the right.
Ⓑ The graph of g is the graph of f shifted five units up.
Ⓒ The graph of g is the graph of f stretched horizontally
Ⓓ The graph of g is the graph of f stretched vertically.

83. What is the inverse of the function $f(x) = \frac{3-x}{2}$?
    Ⓐ $f^{-1}(x) = \frac{1}{2}x + 3$
    Ⓑ $f^{-1}(x) = 2x + 3$
    Ⓒ $f^{-1}(x) = 3 - \frac{1}{2}x$
    Ⓓ $f^{-1}(x) = 3 - 2x$

84. What is the inverse of the function $f(x) = x^3 + 8$?
    Ⓐ $f^{-1}(x) = \sqrt[3]{x-2}$
    Ⓑ $f^{-1}(x) = \sqrt[3]{x} - 2$
    Ⓒ $f^{-1}(x) = \sqrt[3]{x-8}$
    Ⓓ $f^{-1}(x) = \sqrt[3]{x} - 8$

85. The equation $y = g(x)$ is graphed below.

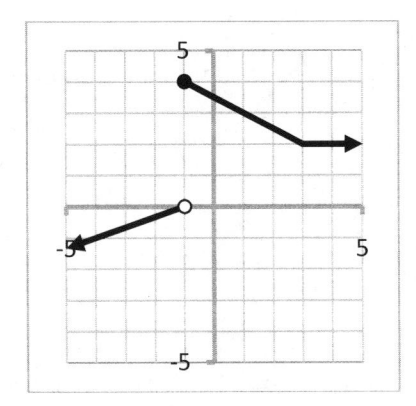

    What is the value of $g^{-1}(3)$?
    Ⓐ $g^{-1}(3) = -1$
    Ⓑ $g^{-1}(3) = 1$
    Ⓒ $g^{-1}(3) = 2$
    Ⓓ $g^{-1}(3) = 3$

86. The height of a weight suspended from a spring can be modeled with a cosine function. The weight is initially at its lowest point of 5 inches, and it takes 0.5 seconds for the weight to go from that point to its highest height of 25 inches, and then it takes 0.5 seconds to go back again. Write a function $h(t)$ that represents the height of the weight (in inches) after t seconds.
    Ⓐ $h(t) = 10\cos(2t) + 5$
    Ⓑ $h(t) = -10\cos(2t) + 15$
    Ⓒ $h(t) = -10\cos(2\pi t) + 5$
    Ⓓ $h(t) = -10\cos(2\pi t) + 15$

87. John is sitting in a car on the London Eye, the tallest Ferris wheel in Europe. The trigonometric function $h(t) = -60 \cos\left(\frac{\pi t}{15}\right) + 70$ represents his height above the ground (in meters) t minutes after he starts moving. Use an inverse function to determine when he is 90 m above the ground for the first time. Round your answer to the nearest minute.

Ⓐ After about 6 minutes

Ⓑ After about 9 minutes

Ⓒ After about 18 minutes

Ⓓ After about 29 minutes

88. If $g(x) = 3x + x + 5$, evaluate $g(2)$.

Ⓐ $g(2) = 8$

Ⓑ $g(2) = 9$

Ⓒ $g(2) = 13$

Ⓓ $g(2) = 17$

89. The function $S(r) = 4\pi r^2$ gives the surface area of a sphere of radius r. What is the surface area of a sphere of radius 4?

Ⓐ 8π

Ⓑ 16π

Ⓒ 32π

Ⓓ 64π

90. Calculate the average rate of change of the function $f(x) = -3x + 1$, over the range from $x = 1$ to $x = 5$.

Ⓐ −4

Ⓑ −3

Ⓒ 3

Ⓓ 4

91. The table below displays the value of $h(x)$ for nine different values of x.

x	−4	−3	−2	−1	0	1	2	3	4
h(x)	−16	−8	−4	−2	−1	−1	0	2	6

What is the value of $h^{-1}(-2)$?

Ⓐ $h^{-1}(-2) = -4$

Ⓑ $h^{-1}(-2) = -1$

Ⓒ $h^{-1}(-2) = 0$

Ⓓ $h^{-1}(-2) = 3$

92. The function $f(x) = x^2 - 4x + 3$ is not invertible if the domain is all real numbers. Which domain makes the function invertible?

Ⓐ $x \geq -1$

Ⓑ $x \geq 2$

Ⓒ $x \leq 3$

Ⓓ $x \leq 4$

93. Graph the function $f(x) = 2\sin(3x - \frac{\pi}{2})$.

Ⓐ

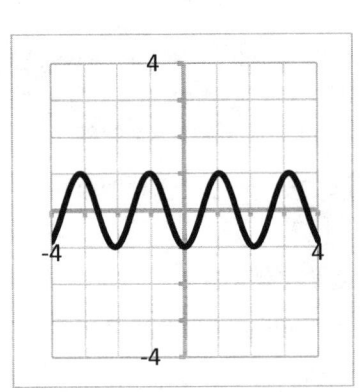

Ⓑ

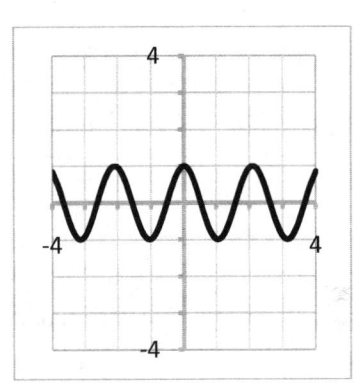

Ⓒ

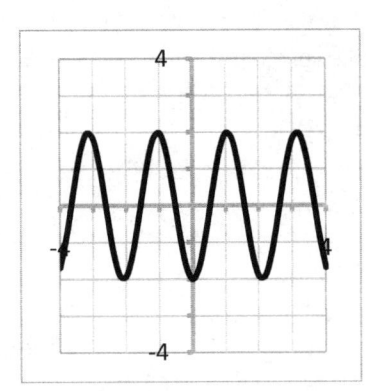

Ⓓ

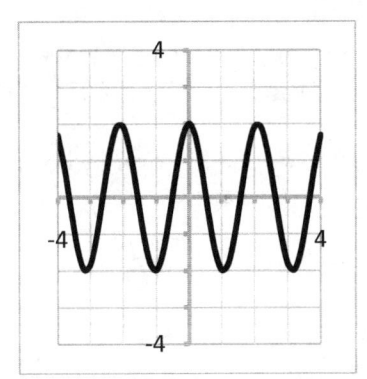

94. The function $f(x) = \cos x$ is not invertible if the domain is all real numbers. Which domain makes the function invertible?

Ⓐ $0 \leq x \leq \pi$

Ⓑ $0 \leq x \leq 2\pi$

Ⓒ $\frac{\pi}{2} \leq x \leq \frac{3\pi}{2}$

Ⓓ $\frac{\pi}{2} \leq x \leq \frac{5\pi}{2}$

Answers and Explanations

1. **C:** Distributing each term in the expression, $x-8$, across each term in the trinomial, gives $4x^4 - 2x^2 + 4x - 32x^3 + 16x - 32$. Writing the expression in standard form gives $4x^4 - 32x^3 - 2x^2 + 20x - 32$.

2. **D:** Since the polynomial has a zero at $x = -4$, it also has a factor of $x + 4$. Therefore, the polynomial may be divided by $(x \mp 4)$, in order to reveal the other factor. Using synthetic division, the other polynomial is determined to be $x^2 - 6x - 16$. This expression may be factored as $(x - 8)(x + 2)$, showing two more zeros at $x = 8$ and $x = -2$.

3. **D:** The denominator of the second rational expression may be factored as $(x + 8)(x + 2)$. Thus, the least common denominator of the two rational expressions is $(x + 8)(x + 2)$. Multiplying the top and bottom of the first fraction by $(x + 8)$, we see that $\frac{3}{x+2} = \frac{3(x+8)}{(x+2)(x+8)}$. The sum may be written as $\frac{3(x+8)+x}{(x+8)(x+2)}$, which simplifies to $\frac{4x+24}{(x+8)(x+2)}$. Factoring out a 4 in the numerator gives: $\frac{4(x+6)}{(x+8)(x+2)}$.

4. **D:** Multiplying each rational expression by the least common denominator of $2(x - 6)$. This procedure can be written as $\frac{x}{x-6} \cdot 2(x-6) + \frac{1}{2} \cdot 2(x-6) = \frac{6}{x-6} \cdot 2(x-6)$. This simplifies to $2x + x - 6 = 12$. Solving for x gives $x = 6$. Substitution of this x-value into the original equation shows division by 0 in the rational expressions, $\frac{x}{x-6}$ and $\frac{6}{x-6}$. Therefore, 6 is an extraneous solution. There is no solution to the rational equation.

5. **B:** The denominator may be factored as $(x^2 - 9)(x - 6)$. The first binomial may be factored as $(x - 3)(x + 3)$. Thus, the given expression may be rewritten as $\frac{x-3}{(x-3)(x+3)(x-6)}$, which simplifies to $\frac{1}{(x+3)(x-6)}$.

6. **D:** The Remainder Theorem states that given a polynomial, $P(x)$, the remainder resulting from dividing the polynomial by the quantity $(x - a)$, is equal to $P(a)$. In other words, the polynomial, evaluated for the value of a, gives the remainder. In this example, $a = 2$. Therefore, the remainder of the polynomial is equal to $2^3 + 4(2) + 7$, or 23.

7. **C:** The least common denominator of $x(x + 4)$ may be multiplied by both rational expressions. Doing so gives $2x = 3(x + 4)$ or $2x = 3x + 12$. Solving for x gives $x = -12$.

8. **A:** After distributing the minus sign across the second trinomial, the expression can be rewritten as $3x^3 - 9x^2 + 6x - 8x^3 - 4x^2 + 3x$. Combining like terms gives $-5x^3 - 13x^2 + 9x$.

9. **B:** A term is a part of an expression that may include a number and/or variable(s) that is separated from other parts of the expression by the operations of addition and/or subtraction. In the given expression, there are four terms, namely $2x^2$, $12x$, -8, and $10x$.

10. A: The expression may be factored as $(x - 8)(x + 5)$. The factorization may be checked by distributing each term in the first factor over each term in the second factor. Doing so gives $x^2 + 5x - 8x - 40$, which can be rewritten as $x^2 - 3x - 40$.

11. B: The quadratic expression may be factored as $(x - 6)(x + 4)$. Setting each factor equal to 0 gives $x - 6 = 0$ and $x + 4 = 0$. Solving for x gives $x = 6$ and $x = -4$.

12. A: A coefficient is the number in front of any term containing a variable or variables. In this case, 6 is the coefficient of $6x^2$. If -9 were distributed across $(x - 4)$ the given binomial, -9 would be the coefficient of $-9x$. However, Choice B is the positive integer, 9. The other two choices represent constants in the expression.

13. A: Irrational numbers cannot be written as fractions. $\sqrt{30}$, $\sqrt[3]{150}$, and $(8)^{1/5}$ are all irrational numbers and remain irrational numbers after addition and multiplication (so that even though $8^{\frac{2}{3}}$ is rational, the sum is not). However, $\sqrt{121} = 11$ is rational and will remain rational after any operation with a rational number, including adding 7. (Further, a sum or product with of a rational number and an irrational number will be irrational.)

14. A: Multiply the terms of the complex binomials using the FOIL method. To FOIL, multiply the First terms, the Outer terms, the Inner terms, and the Last terms, then add all the products together. Next, replace $i^2 = -1$. Finally, combine like terms. $15 + 12i - 30i - 24i^2 = 15 + 12i - 30i + 24 = 39 - 18i$.

15. B: Start by distributing the real numbers. Then combine like terms:
$$3(6 + 2i) - 4(1 + i) = 18 + 6i - 4 - 4i = 14 + 2i$$

16. B: Multiply both numerator and denominator by the denominator's conjugate, which can be found by replacing i with $-i$. Use the FOIL to evaluate these products, remembering $i^2 = -1$, and combine like terms:
$$\frac{3 + 4i}{5 - 2i} \cdot \frac{5 + 2i}{5 + 2i} = \frac{15 + 6i + 20i + 8i^2}{25 - 4i^2} = \frac{15 + 26i - 8}{25 + 4} = \frac{7 + 26i}{29}$$

17. C: The modulus can be found through the formula $|z|^2 = z \cdot \bar{z}$; that is, the square of the modulus of a complex number is equal to the product of that number and its complex conjugate, found by replacing i with $-i$:
$$|z|^2 = (6 + 8i)(6 - 8i) = 36 - 64i^2 = 36 + 64 = 100$$
Therefore, $|z| = \sqrt{100} = 10$.

18. A: Every complex number, a+bi, is comprised of two parts: the real part is a, and the complex part is bi. The complex plane represents the real part, $\mathbb{R}$, on the horizontal axis and the coefficient of the complex part, $\mathbb{C}$, on the vertical. To graph a number on the complex plane, count "a" units to the right(left) for positive(negative) a on the real axis, then up(down) "b" units for positive(negative) b on the complex axis. Therefore, 3+2i is three units to the right and two units up from the origin. Choice A is the correct graph.

19. D: The polar form of a complex number $z = a + bi$ is given by $z = r(cos\theta + isin\theta)$ where $r = \sqrt{a^2 + b^2}$ and $tan\theta = \frac{b}{a}$, so that $\theta = tan^{-1}\frac{b}{a}$. In this case, $r = \sqrt{12^2 + 5^2} = 13$

and $\theta = tan^{-1}\frac{5}{12} = 22.6 \approx 23°$. Substituting r and θ into polar form, $z = 13(cos23° + isin23°)$.

20. D: We could find Mr. Bolt's speed (the distance traveled divided by the elapsed time), but since the question only asks for who wins by how much time, and we already know how much time Mr. Bolt takes, we don't need to. To compare the two runners, then, we just have to convert the deer's speed from km/h to m/s, and calculate how many seconds the deer would take to run the 100 m. Set up conversion fractions so the units will cancel appropriately, and multiply them:
$$\frac{48 \text{ km}}{\text{hr}} \cdot \frac{1000 \text{ m}}{1 \text{ km}} \cdot \frac{1 \text{ hr}}{60 \text{ min}} \cdot \frac{1 \text{ min}}{60 \text{ sec}} = \frac{48 \text{ km}}{\text{hr}} \cdot \frac{1000 \text{ m}}{1 \text{ km}} \cdot \frac{1 \text{ hr}}{60 \text{ min}} \cdot \frac{1 \text{ min}}{60 \text{ sec}} = 13.33 \text{ m/s}$$
The deer's speed is 13.33 m/s, and to find the deer's time, divide the length of the race by its speed: $\frac{100 \text{ m}}{13.33 \text{ m/s}} = 7.5$ seconds, and the deer wins! Compare the two times: 9.58 (Bolt) – 7.5 (Deer) = 2.08. The deer wins by 2.08 seconds.

21. B: Use dimensional analysis to convert the given information to the number of pills needed. Construct conversion fractions based on the given equivalencies. For example, the statement "take 60 mg every 4 hours" corresponds to the fraction $\frac{60 \text{ mg}}{4 \text{ hours}}$. Use these fractions or their reciprocals to make sure the units cancel and leave the desired unit, pills:
$$5 \text{ days} \cdot \frac{24 \text{ hours}}{1 \text{ day}} \cdot \frac{60 \text{ mg}}{4 \text{ hours}} \cdot \frac{1 \text{ pill}}{30 \text{ mg}} = 5 \text{ days} \cdot \frac{24 \text{ hours}}{1 \text{ day}} \cdot \frac{60 \text{ mg}}{4 \text{ hours}} \cdot \frac{1 \text{ pill}}{30 \text{ mg}} = 60 \text{ pills}.$$

22. C: The zeros of an expression are the points at which the corresponding y-values are 0. Thus, the zeros of the expression, represented by the given factors, will occur at the x-values that have corresponding y-values of 0. Setting each factor equal to 0 gives $x + 6 = 0$ and $x - 7 = 0$. Solving for x gives $x = -6$ and $x = 7$. Thus, the zeros of the expression are $x = -6$ and $x = 7$.

23. C: The expression can be written as $(x - 3)(x - 3)$. Distribution gives $x^2 - 3x - 3x + 9$. Combining like terms gives $x^2 - 6x + 9$.

24. A: The slope (or ratio of the change in y-values per change in corresponding x-values) may first be calculated. Using the points, $(-3, -21)$ and $(-1, -3)$, the slope can be written as $\frac{-3-(-21)}{-1-(-3)}$ or 9. The slope can be substituted into the slope-intercept form of an equation, or $y = mx + b$, in order to find the y-intercept. Doing so gives $y = 9x + b$. Substituting the x- and y-values of any ordered pair will reveal the y-intercept. The following may be written: $-21 = 9(-3) + b$; solving for b gives $b = 6$. Thus, the equation that represents the relationship between x and y is $y = 9x + 6$.

25. B: Dividing both sides of the equation by $\frac{1}{3}\pi h$ gives $r^2 = \frac{V}{\frac{1}{3}\pi h}$. Solving for r gives $r = \sqrt{\frac{V}{\frac{1}{3}\pi h}}$ or $r = \sqrt{\frac{3V}{\pi h}}$.

26. C: The power to which 2 is raised to give 64 is 6; $2^6 = 64$. Thus, $x = 6$.

27. D: The radical equation may b0e solved by first subtracting 8 from both sides of the equation. Doing so gives $4\sqrt{x} = 16$. Dividing both sides of the equation by 4 gives $\sqrt{x} = 4$. Squaring both sides gives $x = 16$.

28. D: The literal equation may be solved for x by first subtracting b from both sides of the equation. Doing so gives $ax = c - b$. Dividing both sides of the equation by a gives $x = \frac{c-b}{a}$.

29. A: The inequality may be solved by first subtracting 18 from both sides. Doing so gives $3x > -12$. Dividing both sides of the inequality by 3 gives $x > -4$.

30. D: First, set the right side of the equation equal to zero by subtracting 8 from both sides, yielding $4x^2 - 6x - 8 = 0$. The zeros of the quadratic equation may be determined by using the quadratic formula, $\frac{-b \pm \sqrt{b^2 - 4ac}}{2a}$ Substituting 4 for a, –6 for b, and –8 for c, into the quadratic formula gives: $\frac{6 \pm \sqrt{(-6)^2 - 4(4)(-8)}}{2(4)}$, which reduces to $\frac{6 \pm \sqrt{164}}{8}$. The radical term, $\sqrt{164}$, can be rewritten as $\sqrt{4}\sqrt{41}$. Thus, the expression can now be written as $\frac{6 \pm 2\sqrt{41}}{8}$, which reduces to $\frac{3 \pm \sqrt{41}}{4}$.

31. A: As above, the quadratic equation may be rewritten as $6x^2 - 8x + 8 = 0$. Substituting 6 for a, –8 for b, and 8 for c, into the quadratic formula gives $\frac{8 \pm \sqrt{(-8)^2 - 4(6)(8)}}{2(6)}$, which reduces to $\frac{8 \pm \sqrt{-128}}{12}$. The radical term, $\sqrt{-128}$, can be rewritten as $\sqrt{-64}\sqrt{2}$. Thus, the expression can be written as $\frac{8 \pm 8i\sqrt{2}}{12}$. Factoring out an 8, in the numerator, gives: $\frac{8(1 \pm i\sqrt{2})}{12}$, which reduces to $\frac{2(1 \pm i\sqrt{2})}{3}$.

32. C: In order to complete the square, each term must be divided by the coefficient of 12. Doing so gives $x^2 + 2x = 4$. Dividing the coefficient x of by 2 and squaring it results in the integer, 1. Adding 1 to both sides of the equation gives $x^2 + 2x + 1 = 5$. The left side of the equation can be factored as $(x + 1)(x + 1)$. Thus, the equation, $(x + 1)^2 = 5$, may be used to find the solution.

33. B: Using the method of elimination to solve the system of equations, each term in the top equation may be multiplied by 2, while each term in the bottom equation may be multiplied by –3. Doing so produces two new equations with x-terms that will add to 0; $2(3x + 6y) = 2(36)$ can be written as $6x + 12y = 72$; $-3(2x + 9y) = -3(34)$ can be written as $-6x - 27y = -102$. Thus, the equations, $\begin{matrix} 6x + 12y = 72 \\ -6x - 27y = -102 \end{matrix}$, may be added to find the correct y-value solution.

34. C: The addition property of equality states that any amount added to both sides of an equation does not change the balance of the equation. Adding 9 to both sides of the equation is allowed because of the addition property of equality.

35. C: The division property of equality states that division of both sides of an equation by any amount does not change the balance of the equation. Dividing both sides of the equation by 2 gives $x + 3y = 9$. Therefore, the division property of equality was used.

36. A: Graphing the two equations shows another intersection at the point, $(-3, -3)$. In other words, the line, $y = x$, crosses the graph of $y = x^2 + 4x$ at the points, $(0, 0)$ and $(-3, -3)$.

37. B: Graphing the linear equation and a circle, with a center at $(2, -4)$ and radius of 4, shows points of intersection of $(-2, -4)$ and $(2, -8)$.

38. D: Solving for y, the equation can be rewritten as $y = 3x - 5$. The graph of the equation will have a positive slope of 3 and a y-intercept of -5. Choice D shows a graph with a positive slope that crosses the y-axis at $(0, -5)$.

39. C: The solution of $f(x) = g(x)$ can be determined by setting the two functions equal to one another. Thus, the following may be written $3x + 6 = 2x - 8$. Solving for x gives $x = -14$.

40. A: The green line has a y-intercept of -2 and a slope of $\frac{1}{2}$. Thus, the equation of the line may be written as $y = \frac{1}{2}x - 2$. Multiplying each term by 4 gives $4y = 2x - 8$ or $2x - 4y = 8$. The blue line has a y-intercept of $-\frac{4}{3}$ and a slope of $\frac{1}{3}$. The equation of the blue line may be written as $y = \frac{1}{3}x - \frac{4}{3}$. Multiplying each term by 9 gives $9y = 3x - 12$ or $3x - 9y = 12$. Thus, Choices A and B are the only viable options. If the first inequality, for Choice A, is evaluated for an x-value of 0 and y-value of 0, the equation is false. Thus, the side of the line, not containing the point, $(0, 0)$ would be shaded. If the second inequality, for Choice A, is evaluated for the same x- and y-values, the equation is true. Thus, the side of the line, containing he point, $(0, 0)$ would be shaded. In other words, the region below the green line and above the blue line should be shaded. Since this is indeed the case, the system of inequalities for Choice A is represented by the yellow-shaded region of the graph.

41. A: The function f assigns to each element of the domain exactly one element of the range. Consequently, if x is in the domain $x \geq 3$, then the value of f is in the range $f(x) \geq 0$. Therefore, the correct answer is choice A. On the other hand, choice B is incorrect because f is not defined for some positive values of x, like $x = 1$. Choice C is incorrect because the range of f is $f(x) \geq 0$, not $f(3)$. Finally, choice D is incorrect because the value of $f(3)$ is defined since $x = 3$ is in the domain of f.

42. D: The general form of the interest exponential is $A(t) = P(1 + r)^t$, where P is the initial principal, r the interest rate (as a decimal), and t the number of interest yield periods after the initial investment. Clearly, P is $315 in this case. Furthermore, the exponential function $b(t) = 315(1.05)^t$ starts at 315 when $t = 0$ and is multiplied by 1.05 every time t increases by 1. Therefore, John initially put $315 into the bank account.

43. A: You will need to use the natural logarithm, ln, to solve this equation. First divide both sides of the equation by 3:
$$3e^{2t} = 12$$
$$e^{2t} = 4$$

Next take the natural logarithm of both sides to get rid of the exponent. The natural logarithm is defined as the logarithm to the base e; the natural log is the inverse function of the exponential. Therefore, $\ln e^x = x$.
$$\ln e^{2t} = \ln 4$$
$$2t = \ln 4$$
Finally, divide both sides by 2 to solve for t.
$$t = \frac{\ln 4}{2}$$

44. **C:** The linear function $s(h) = 27h + 720$ starts at 720 when $h = 0$ and increases by 27 every time h increases by 1. Therefore, for every hour after 40, the librarian earns $27, so his salary is $27 per hour.

45. **C:** Linear functions grow by equal differences (rather than equal factors) over equal intervals. In other words, if the linear function $c(f)$ converts a temperature f from Fahrenheit to Celsius, then intervals of equal length (in f) result in equal increases in the value of the function $c(f)$.
From the problem, we know that $c(32) = 0$ and $c(68) = 20$. Thus, we can conclude that intervals of length 36 (like the interval [32,68]) result in an increase of 20 since $20 - 0 = 20$. In addition, since the length of [68,104] is 36, the function $c(f)$ increases by 20 over this interval as well. Use this information to calculate $c(104)$.
$$c(104) = c(68) + 20 = 20 + 20 = 40$$
Therefore, we can conclude that 104°F is equivalent to 40°C.

46. **B:** The domain of a function is the set of all possible input values that can be evaluated by a function. In the given function, the input is n, which represents the month of the year (i.e. $n = 1$ represents January, $n = 2$ represents February, etc.). Since there are only twelve months, and there is no zeroth month, the appropriate domain is $1 \leq n \leq 12$.

47. **B:** Since the theater will sell 500 tickets if it charges $10 per ticket, we know that $t(10) = 500$. Furthermore, because of the way ticket price affects ticket sales, t must be a linear function that decreases by 50 every time d increases by 1. Therefore, the d-term of the function is $-50d$, so the function takes the form $t(d) = -50d + c$. To find the value of c, substitute 10 for d and 500 for $t(10)$ and solve for c.
$$t(10) = -50(10) + c$$
$$500 = -500 + c$$
$$1000 = c$$
Thus, the function is $t(d) = -50d + 1000$.

48. **B:** Since the function is defined recursively, you need to calculate all of the first five terms. The first term is already given in the problem as $f(0) = 2$. To calculate the second term, $f(1)$, which we can write as $f(0 + 1)$ in order to use the recursive definition, substitute 0 for n into the equation $f(n + 1) = 2f(n) - 1$:
$$f(1) = f(0 + 1) = 2f(0) - 1$$
$$f(1) = 2f(0) - 1$$
Since $f(0) = 2$, substitute 2 in for $f(0)$ and simplify the result:
$$f(1) = 2(2) - 1$$
$$= 3$$

Thus, the second term is 3. To calculate the third term, $f(2)$, write this as $f(1 + 1)$ and substitute 1 for n and 3 for $f(1)$ into the same equation $f(n + 1) = 2 \cdot f(n) - 1$ and simplify the result:

$$f(1 + 1) = 2f(1) - 1$$
$$f(2) = 2(3) - 1$$
$$= 5$$

Continuing in this way, you will find that the first five terms of the sequence are 2, 3, 5, 9, 17. Therefore, the fifth term of the sequence is 17.

49. **D:** The situation describes a geometric series, with a common ratio of 2. The formula for finding the sum of a finite geometric series is $S_n = \frac{a_1(1-r^n)}{1-r}$, where S_n represents the sum of n terms, a_1 represents the value of the initial term, r represents the common ratio, and n represents the number of terms. Substituting 2 for a_1, 2 for r, and 18 for n gives: $S_{18} = \frac{2(1-2^{18})}{1-2}$ or $S_{18} = 524{,}286$. Thus, he would save \$524,286 during the course of 18 months.

50. **D:** The situation is another example of a geometric series. This series has a common ratio of 3. Each drawing has 3 times as many red dots as the previous drawing. The formula for finding the sum of a finite geometric series is $S_n = \frac{a_1(1-r^n)}{1-r}$, where S_n represents the sum of n terms, a_1 represents the value of the initial term, r represents the common ratio, and n represents the number of terms. Substituting 4 for a_1, 3 for r, and 20 for n gives: $S_{20} = \frac{4(1-3^{20})}{1-3}$ or $S_{20} = 6{,}973{,}568{,}800$. Thus, he will have drawn 6,973,568,800 red dots in the first 20 drawings.

51. **B:** The situation may be modeled with the following system of equations:
$1.25x + 2.75y = 227.50$
$x + y = 110$, where x represents the number of cupcakes sold and y represents the number of cups of coffee sold. Graphing the system shows an intersection at the point, (50, 60). Thus, he sold 50 cupcakes and 60 cups of coffee.

52. **C:** Using the method of elimination to solve the system of linear equations, each term in the top equation may be multiplied by -2, while each term in the bottom equation may be multiplied by 5. Doing so produces two new equations with x-terms that will add to 0. The sum of $-10x - 18y = 14$ and $10x - 20y = 100$ may be written as $-38y = 114$, where $y = -3$. Substituting the y-value of -3 into the top, original equation gives $5x + 9(-3) = -7$. Solving for x gives $x = 4$. Thus, the solution is $= 4$, $y = -3$.

53. **D:** Check the y-intercepts of each equation by setting $x = 0$ and solving for y. For the top equation, we have $0 + 8y = 8$, and we see that $y = 1$. For the bottom equation $0 + 12y = -96$, and we see that $y = -8$. Comparing graphs, only Choice D has y-intercepts of 1 and -8.

54. **A:** The system can be rewritten to present the x-term, y-term, and z-term of each equation in the same order. Thus, the system can be rewritten as $\begin{aligned} 2x + 4y - 3z &= 26 \\ 3x - 6y + 2z &= -23 \\ 6x + 9y - 4z &= 49 \end{aligned}$. The following matrix equation can now be written: $\begin{bmatrix} 2 & 4 & -3 \\ 3 & -6 & 2 \\ 6 & 9 & -4 \end{bmatrix} \begin{bmatrix} x \\ y \\ z \end{bmatrix} = \begin{bmatrix} 26 \\ -23 \\ 49 \end{bmatrix}$.

55. C: The inverse matrix can be used to solve a system of equations. The product of the inverse matrix and the matrix, containing the constants, on the right side of the equal sign, reveals a matrix, containing the solution. The inverse of the given matrix may first be determined by finding the determinant. The determinant of matrix, $\begin{bmatrix} a & b \\ c & d \end{bmatrix}$ equals $ad - cb$. Thus, the determinant of the matrix, representing the given equations, written $|A|$, is equal to $2(-2) - (-4)(3)$, or 8. The matrix, representing the given equations, must now be transformed by switching the positions of a and d, and reversing the signs on c and b. Doing so gives $\begin{bmatrix} -2 & -3 \\ 4 & 2 \end{bmatrix}$. This transformed matrix may be multiplied by the ratio, $\frac{1}{|A|}$. Thus, the inverse, or A^{-1}, is equal to $\frac{1}{8}\begin{bmatrix} -2 & -3 \\ 4 & 2 \end{bmatrix}$ or $\begin{bmatrix} -\frac{1}{4} & -\frac{3}{8} \\ \frac{1}{2} & \frac{1}{4} \end{bmatrix}$. The solution can now be represented as the product of $\begin{bmatrix} -\frac{1}{4} & -\frac{3}{8} \\ \frac{1}{2} & \frac{1}{4} \end{bmatrix}$ and $\begin{bmatrix} -5 \\ -2 \end{bmatrix}$ or $\begin{bmatrix} 2 \\ -3 \end{bmatrix}$.

56. A: The number of possible combinations of gallons of milk and cartons of eggs may be represented by the inequality, $3.50x + 1.75y \leq 21$, where x represents number of gallons of milk and y represents number of cartons of eggs. Solving for y, the inequality may be written as $y \leq -2x + 12$. The inequality may be graphed as $y = -2x + 12$, with shading shown on the side of the line, containing the point, (0, 0). Note. $0 \leq 12$, so the test point, (0, 0), results in a true statement. Only Choices A and C have a y-intercept of 12. The slope of Choice A may be calculated by using any two points on the line. Using the x- and y-intercepts, the slope can be written as $\frac{0-12}{6-0}$ or -2. Thus, Choice A represents the possible combinations of gallons of milk and cartons of eggs she may purchase.

57. B: The y-intercept is (0, 100) because she opens the account with this constant amount. The slope is 25 because she plans to deposit \$25 into her savings account each month. The equation representing this situation is $y = 25x + 100$, where x represents the number of months and y represents the total amount of money in her savings account. Only Choices A and B have y-intercepts of 100. The slope of each graph must be determined to decide which graph represents the amount of money she will have in her account, after x months. Slope is the ratio of the change in y-values per change in corresponding x-values; $m = \frac{y_2 - y_1}{x_2 - x_1}$. The slope may be determined by choosing any two points on a line. Choosing the points, (5, 200) and (0, 100) for Choice A, gives a slope of $\frac{100-200}{0-5}$ or 20. Choosing the points, (10, 350) and (0, 100) for Choice B, gives a slope of $\frac{100-350}{0-10}$ or 25. Thus, Choice B represents the correct graph.

58. A: The equation is already in standard form, $y = ax^2 + bx + c$. By substituting the coefficients into the quadratic formula, we get $x = \frac{-b \pm \sqrt{b^2 - 4ac}}{2a} = \frac{2 \pm \sqrt{(-2)^2 - 4 \cdot 1 \cdot 10}}{2 \cdot 1} = \frac{2 \pm \sqrt{4 - 40}}{2} = \frac{2 \pm \sqrt{-36}}{2} = \frac{2 \pm 6i}{2} = 1 \pm 3i$.

59. D: A difference of two perfect squares can be factored as: $a^2 - b^2 = (a + b)(a - b)$. When asked to factor the sum of squares, apply the difference of squares rule as follows:

$a^2 + b^2 = a^2 - (-b^2) = (a \pm \sqrt{-b^2})(a \mp \sqrt{-b^2})$. Alternatively, $a^2 + b^2 = a^2 - b^2 i^2 = a^2 - (bi)^2 = (a+bi)(a-bi)$. In this case, then: $4x^2 + 25 = 4x^2 - 25i^2 = (2x)^2 - (5i)^2 = (2x - 5i)(2x + 5i)$.

60. A: A perfect square trinomial is one that can be written as the square of a binomial as follows: $a^2x^2 + 2abx + b^2 = (ax + b)^2$. Notice that $42i = 2 \cdot (3 \cdot 7 \cdot i\ )$ and apply the pattern: $9x^2 + 42ix - 49 = (3x)^2 + 42ix + (7i)^2 = (3x + 7i)^2$.

61. C: Distances on the complex plane are calculated very much like they are on the real plane. To find the distance, use the distance formula $D = \sqrt{(x_1 - x_2)^2 + (y_1 - y_2)^2}$ with $a = x$ and $b = y$:
$$D = \sqrt{((-30) - 12)^2 + (15 - (-3))^2} = \sqrt{(-42)^2 + 18^2} \approx 46$$

62. B: To find the midpoint between two complex numbers, add the complex numbers and divide by 2: $\frac{(-30+15i)+(12-3i)}{2} = \frac{-18+12i}{2} = -9 + 6i$.

63. D: Linear functions can be written in the form $g(x) = ax + b$. To determine the value of a, notice that $g(x)$ decreases by 3 every time x increases by 1: when x goes from 0 to 1, the value of the function goes from 4 to 1; and when x goes from 1 to 2, the function goes from 1 to –2. Since $g(x)$ decreases by 3, the value of a is –3, so the function is $g(x) = -3x + b$. Next calculate the value of b. From the table, you can tell that $g(0) = 4$. Use this to calculate b:

$$g(0) = 4$$
$$-3(0) + b = 4$$
$$0 + b = 4$$
$$b = 4$$

Thus, the function is $g(x) = -3x + 4$.

Alternatively, writing an explicit formula in the form $g(x) = ax + b$ means solving for two variables, a and b. Use the information given in the table to write two equations relating these two variables in terms of x and $g(x)$:
$$4 = a(0) + b$$
$$1 = a(1) + b$$
The first readily solves to $b = 4$, which you can substitute into the second to solve for a:
$$1 = a(1) + 4$$
$$-3 = a(1) = a$$
Thus, the function is $g(x) = -3x + 4$.

64. B: Exponential functions can be written in the form $h(x) = ab^x$. To determine the value of b, notice that $h(x)$ doubles every time x increases by 1. For instance, when x goes from –2 to –1, the value of y goes from 1 to 2; and when x goes from –1 to 0, the value of y doubles from 2 to 4. Since the graph doubles, the value of b is 2, so the function is $h(x) = a \cdot 2^x$. Next calculate the value of a. From the graph, you can tell that $h(0) = 4$. Use this to calculate a:

$$h(0) = 4$$
$$a \cdot 2^0 = 4$$
$$a \cdot 1 = 4$$
$$a = 4$$

Thus, the function is $h(x) = 4 \cdot 2^x$.

Alternatively, from the general form of an exponential $h(x) = ab^x$, notice that if $x = 0$, $h(x) = a$. Therefore, since $y = 4$ when $x = 0$, $a = 4$. You can solve for b from any of the other indicated points, for example:
$$2 = 4b^{-1} = 4/b$$
$$b = 2$$
Therefore, the function is $h(x) = 4 \cdot 2^x$.

65. **C:** The graph of a linear function is a straight line. To graph the given function, first create a table of values.

x	f(x) = 2x − 4	(x,y)
0	2(0) − 4 = −4	(0,−4)
1	2(1) − 4 = −2	(1,−2)
2	2(2) − 4 = 0	(2,0)

Next plot the three points on a coordinate axis and connect them with a straight line. The x- and y-intercepts are the points where the line passes through the x- and y-axes.

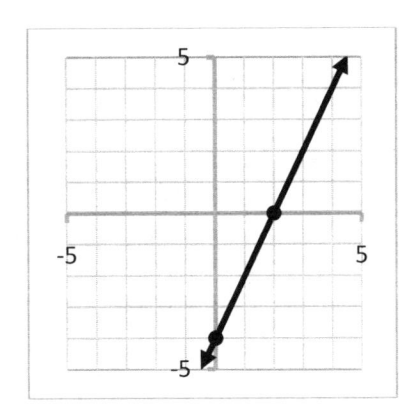

66. **B:** In general, if an initial investment of P dollars earns interest at r percent (expressed as a decimal) per year, then its value V after t years is given by the function $V = P(1 + r)^t$. The given function is $V = 200(1.04)^t$, so the percent interest is 0.04, or 4%, per year.

67. **D:** Exponential functions grow by equal factors over equal intervals. In other words, if the exponential function $n(t)$ represents the number of bacteria in the Petri dish after t days, then intervals of equal length (in t) multiply the value of the function $n(t)$ by equal factors.
From the problem, we know that $n(0) = 160$, $n(2) = 360$, and $n(3) = 540$. Use division to determine how intervals of length 2 (like the interval [0,2]) change the value of $n(t)$.
$$\frac{n(2)}{n(0)} = \frac{360}{160}$$
$$= 2.25$$
Therefore, increasing t by 2 multiplies the value of $n(t)$ by 2.25. Similarly, since the length of [3,5] is 2, the interval [3,5] multiplies the value of $n(t)$ by 2.25 as well. Use this information to calculate $n(5)$:

$$n(5) = n(3) \cdot 2.25 = 540 \cdot 2.25 = 1215$$
Therefore, we can conclude that there are 1215 bacteria in the Petri dish in five days.

68. **B:** The length of an interval is the difference between its endpoints. For example, the length of the interval [2, 4] is 2. To determine how the given function grows over an interval of length 3, determine the value of f at each endpoint of that interval. Since exponential functions grow by equal factors over equal intervals, you can use any interval of length 3, and your answer will apply to all such intervals. For example, you can use the interval [0,3]:

$$f(0) = 3 \cdot 2^{(0)}$$
$$= 3 \cdot 1$$
$$= 3$$

$$f(3) = 3 \cdot 2^{(3)}$$
$$= 3 \cdot 8$$
$$= 24$$

Since $f(0) = 3$ and $f(3) = 24$, the function grows by a factor of $\frac{24}{3} = 8$ over this interval.

69. **D:** The graph of a quadratic function is a parabolic curve. To graph the given function, first create a table of values.

x	$g(x) = x^2 - 2x - 3$	(x,y)
−2	$(-2)^2 - 2(-2) - 3 = 5$	(−2,5)
−1	$(-1)^2 - 2(-1) - 3 = 0$	(−1,0)
0	$(0)^2 - 2(0) - 3 = -3$	(0,−3)
1	$(1)^2 - 2(1) - 3 = -4$	(1,−4)
2	$(2)^2 - 2(2) - 3 = -3$	(2,−3)

Next plot the five points on a coordinate axis and connect them with a curve. The graph will be a U-shaped parabola. Plot the minimum, which is the lowest point on the graph.

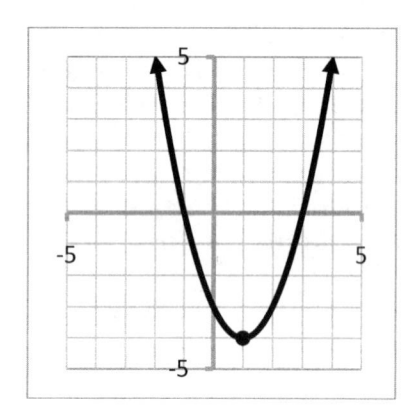

70. A: The metal ball reaches its highest point when h is at its maximum. From the graph, you can tell that the maximum is about 144. Since $h(t) = 144$ when $t = 3$, the ball reaches its highest point 3 seconds after it is thrown.

71. C: Graph the given function by either creating a table of values by hand or by inputting the function $y = x^3 + x^2 - 4x - 4$ into a graphing calculator.

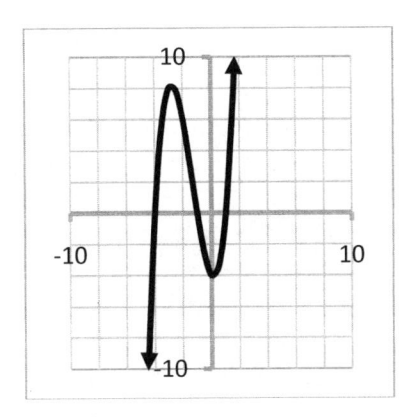

The zeroes of a function are the values where the function equals zero, so in this case, where $f(x) = 0$. You might be able to read these off your table of values. Graphically, the zeroes occur where the graph crosses the x-axis. Notice from the graph above that f crosses the x-axis three times: at the points $(-4,0)$, $(-1,0)$, and $(1,0)$. Plot these points on the graph of f.

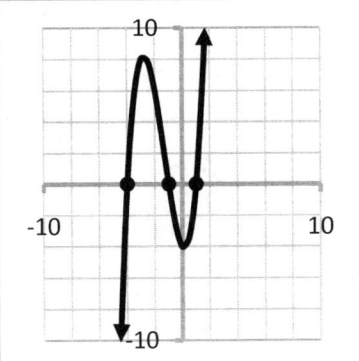

72. D: A piecewise-defined function is a function whose definition changes based on certain conditions. In this case, the given function h is defined as $\frac{1}{2}x$ when x is strictly less than 2 and defined as $4 - x$ otherwise. As a result, the graph is composed of two different straight lines. To graph $h(x)$, first create a table of values for the first half of the function, that is, when x is less than 2:

x	$h(x)$	(x,y)
0	$\frac{1}{2}(0) = 0$	$(0,0)$
1	$\frac{1}{2}(1) = \frac{1}{2}$	$(1,\frac{1}{2})$
2	$\frac{1}{2}(2) = 1$	$(2,1)$

Next plot these three points on a coordinate axis. For the point (2,1), plot an open circle since it is not actually on the graph of h (the first half of the function only applies when x is strictly less than 2). Then connect the points to make a line:

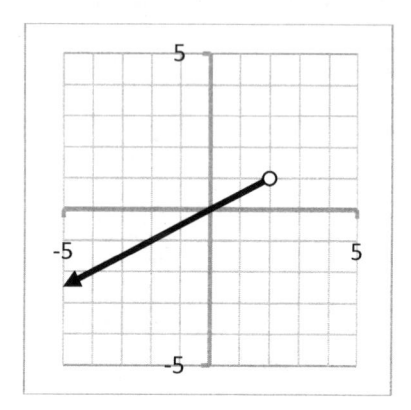

Use a similar procedure to graph the second half of the function. This time use a closed (i.e. filled-in) circle to plot the point at x = 2 since it is part of the second half of the function. Graph this part of h on the same graph.

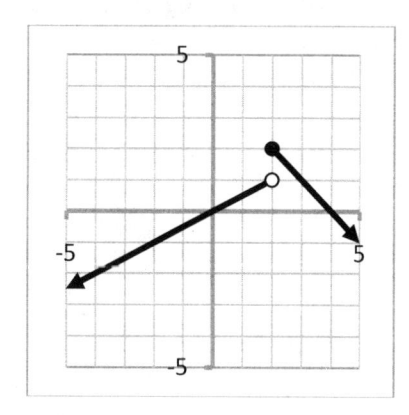

73. A: Examine the graph to determine which graph eventually exceeds the other three. In other words, find the function that eventually goes above the other three as the graph goes from left to right. Notice that the function f goes above the other three when x = 5.

74. B: The x-intercept of a function is the point where the line passes through the x-axis. Since the graph passes through the x-axis at (6,0), its x-intercept is 6. To determine which function has the same x-intercept, substitute 6 for x into each function and see if the result is zero. Start with choice A, $g(x) = -4x - 12$.
$$-4(6) - 12 = -24 - 12$$
$$= -36$$
Since the result is not 6, the x-intercept is not 6. Next try choice B, $g(x) = x^2 - 12x + 36$.
$$(6)^2 - 12(6) + 36 = 36 - 72 + 36$$
$$= 0$$
Thus, the function $g(x) = x^2 - 12x + 36$ has the same x-intercept as the graphed function.

75. D: The cost of the taxi ride is the sum of two functions, a constant function for the first mile and a linear function for the rest of the ride. The constant function is $c_1(d) = 4.25$ since

- 146 -

the cost of the first mile is $4.25. For the linear part, subtract 1 from d to exclude the first mile, and then multiply the result by 0.70 since it costs $0.70 per mile. The result is $c_2(d) = 0.70(d - 1)$. Finally, write the function for the total cost of the taxi ride by adding the two functions.
$$c(d) = c_1(d) + c_2(d)$$
$$= 4.25 + 0.70(d - 1)$$

76. B: The first function $L(g)$ gives the water level after g gallons are pumped into the tank. The second function $w(t)$ gives the number of gallons pumped into the tank after t minutes, which the first function calls g. Consequently, we can have L act on w: the composition of the functions $L(w(t))$ is the water level of the tank after t minutes. Calculate $L(w(t))$.

$$L(w(t)) = 0.3 \cdot w(t)$$
$$= 0.3 \cdot 1.2t$$
$$= 0.36t$$

Thus, the function $L(t) = 0.36t$ represents the water level of the tank after t minutes.

77. D: The number of wheat grains on each square forms a geometric sequence: 1, 2, 4, 8, 16, etc. Notice that these numbers are all powers of two (i.e. $2^0, 2^1, 2^2, 2^3, 2^4$, etc.). Therefore, the sequence can be written as an exponential function in the form $y = 2^x$. Moreover, since this sequence begins (at square number 1) with an exponent of 0 rather than 1, we need to subtract 1 from n to get the correct exponent of 2. Thus, the function $g(n) = 2^{n-1}$ represents the number of wheat grains on the nth square of the chessboard.

78. D: Graph the given function by either creating a table of values by hand or by inputting the function $y = \frac{3}{2x-4}$ into a graphing calculator.

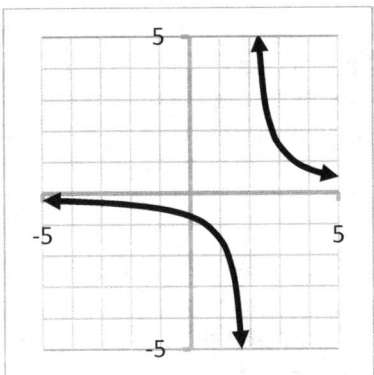

The zeroes of a function are the values where the function equals zero. You might be able to tell from your table of values there are no such points. Graphically, since the graph does not pass through the x-axis at all, g has no zeroes.

An asymptote is a line that the graph of a function gets closer and closer to but never touches. Notice that the function never touches the vertical line $x = 2$. (Check: if $x = 2$, $g(2) = \frac{3}{2(2)-4} = \frac{3}{0}$, which is undefined! There can be no value for the function at this value of x.) Therefore, $x = 2$ is a vertical asymptote of g. In addition, g approaches but never touches the horizontal line $y = 0$. (Check: there is no solution for $g(x) = 0$.) Thus, the second asymptote is $y = 0$. Graph these lines on the same graph with light, dotted lines.

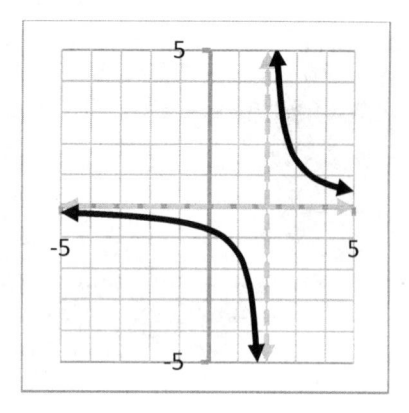

79. A: Graph the given function by either creating a table of values by hand or by inputting the function $y = \log_2 2(x + 3)$ into a graphing calculator. In addition, plot the points where the line passes through the x- and y-axes, which are the x- and y-intercepts of h.

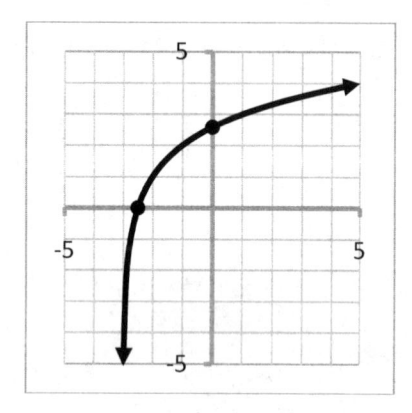

80. B: The zeroes of a function are the domain values where the function equals zero. So in this case, the zeroes are the values of x for which $f(x) = 0$. To find the zeroes of the function, set up an equation and then solve it for x. The first step is to factor the quadratic expression:
$$f(x) = 0$$
$$x^2 + 5x - 24 = 0$$
$$(x + 8)(x - 3) = 0$$
When the coefficient of x^2 is 1, factor the quadratic into a product of binomials $(x + a)(x + b)$, where a and b are chosen so their product is the constant term in the quadratic (including sign), and their sum is the coefficient of the linear term in the quadratic (the x term). Then use the zero-product rule to solve the result. Using that factorization of f, write two equations and solve them both for x:

x + 8 = 0   or   x − 3 = 0
x = −8   x = 3

Therefore, the zeroes of the function are −8 and 3.

81. C: To transform $f(x)$ into $g(x)$, you have to replace x with x + 1. This transformation results in a translation, or shift, of the graph. Specifically, for a particular x, $g(x)$ returns the value of the function $f(x)$ one unit further along the x-axis (to the right). This results in shifting the graph one unit to the left.

82. D: To transform f(x) into g(x), you have to multiply it by 5. This transformation increases the distance between y-values of the same two x values, and so we see it stretches the graph vertically, making it five times "taller".

83. D: The inverse of a function is another function that *undoes* the original one. By convention, the inverse of f(x) is written as $f^{-1}(x)$. To find the inverse of f(x), first replace f(x) with y. Then switch all the x's with all the y's (and vice versa):

$$f(x) = \frac{3-x}{2} \quad \text{(original)}$$

$$y = \frac{3-x}{2} \quad \text{(replaced } f(x) \text{ with } y\text{)}$$

$$x = \frac{3-y}{2} \quad \text{(exchanged } x \text{ and } y\text{)}$$

Next solve the equation for y:
$$2x = 3 - y$$
$$y + 2x = 3$$
$$y = 3 - 2x$$

Finally, replace y with $f^{-1}(x)$ to write the result as an inverse function of f(x):
$$f^{-1}(x) = 3 - 2x$$

84. C: The inverse of a function is another function that *undoes* the original one. By convention, the inverse of f(x) is written as $f^{-1}(x)$. To find the inverse of f(x), first replace f(x) with y. Then switch all the x's with all the y's (and vice versa):

$$f(x) = x^3 + 8 \quad \text{(original)}$$
$$y = x^3 + 8 \quad \text{(replaced } f(x) \text{ with } y\text{)}$$
$$x = y^3 + 8 \quad \text{(exchanged } x \text{ and } y\text{)}$$

Next solve the equation for y:
$$x - 8 = y^3$$
$$\sqrt[3]{x-8} = \sqrt[3]{y^3}$$
$$\sqrt[3]{x-8} = y$$

Finally, replace y with $f^{-1}(x)$ to write the result as an inverse function of f(x):
$$f^{-1}(x) = \sqrt[3]{x-8}$$

85. B: The inverse of a function is another function that *undoes* the original one. By convention, the inverse of g(x) is written as $g^{-1}(x)$. For any value of x, the result of inputting x into g can itself be inputted into g^{-1}, and it will return the original value x. In other words, if g(x) = y, then $g^{-1}(y) = x$.
In regard to the problem, this means that the value of $g^{-1}(3)$ is the value of x for which g(x) = 3. Examining the graph of g, notice that it passes through the point (1,3). Therefore, g(1) = 3, and the value of $g^{-1}(3)$ is 1.

86. D: In 1 s, the weight returns to its previous height, and so the period T of the function is 1. The frequency of a periodic function is the number of cycles of the function per unit time, and is the reciprocal of the period. Thus, the frequency of h is 1.
The amplitude is half the distance between the lowest and highest point: A = ½[5, 25] = 10.
The midline is given by the lowest point plus the amplitude or the highest minus the amplitude: 5 + 10 = 25 – 10 = 15.

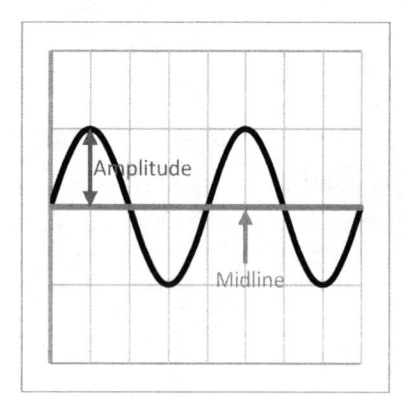

[Graph showing a sine wave with labels "Amplitude" and "Midline"]

Now write the function $h(t)$ by modifying the parent function $y = \cos t$. The amplitude of $\cos t$ is 1. To make the amplitude 10, multiply the parent function by 10.
$$y = 10\cos t$$
The midline of this new function is 0. To move the midline to 15, add 15.
$$y = 10\cos t + 15$$
This function repeats once every 2π, so its period is 2π, and its frequency is therefore $\frac{1}{2\pi}$. To make the frequency 1, multiply t by 2π so the function repeats every second.
$$h(t) = 10\cos(2\pi t) + 15$$
At $t = 0$, the weight is at its lowest point, instead of its highest (where the parent function $\cos t$ starts). To start $h(t)$ at its lowest point, there are two options. Either multiply the amplitude by -1:
$h(t) = -10\cos(2\pi t) + 15$
Or offset the argument by 180°:
$h(t) = 10\cos(2\pi t - \pi) + 15$
Since the latter is not shown, choice D is correct.

87. **B:** First set up an equation for when John's height is 90 m.
$$h(t) = 90$$
$$-60\cos\left(\frac{\pi t}{15}\right) + 70 = 90$$
To solve the equation, isolate $\cos\left(\frac{\pi t}{15}\right)$:
$$-60\cos\left(\frac{\pi t}{15}\right) = 20$$
$$\cos\left(\frac{\pi t}{15}\right) = -\frac{1}{3}$$
Then take the inverse cosine of both sides of the equation:
$$\cos^{-1}\left[\cos\left(\frac{\pi t}{15}\right)\right] = \cos^{-1}\left(-\frac{1}{3}\right)$$
$$\frac{\pi t}{15} = \cos^{-1}\left(-\frac{1}{3}\right)$$
Use a calculator to estimate the right side (in radians):
$$\frac{\pi t}{15} \approx 1.910633$$
Finally, solve for t.
$$t \approx \frac{15(1.910633)}{\pi}$$

$t \approx 9$

Therefore, John is 90 m above the ground after about 9 minutes.

88. **C:** To evaluate $g(2)$, substitute 2 for every occurrence of x in the equation $g(x) = 3x + x + 5$. Then simplify the result using order of operations:
$$g(2) = 3(2) + (2) + 5$$
$$= 6 + 2 + 5$$
$$= 13$$

89. **D:** The surface area will be given by the expression $S(4)$. To calculate this value, substitute 4 for r in the equation $S(r) = 4\pi r^2$. Then simplify the result using order of operations:
$$S(4) = 4\pi(4)^2$$
$$= 4\pi \cdot 16$$
$$= 64\pi$$
Therefore, the surface area of the sphere is 64π.

90. **B:** The average rate of change of a function $f(x)$ from x_1 to x_2 is given by $\frac{f(x_2)-f(x_1)}{x_2-x_1}$. This formula is the same as the one for slope, rewritten in the context of functions. If $x_1 = 1$ and $x_2 = 5$, the average rate of the given function is given by expression below:
$$\frac{f(x_2)-f(x_1)}{x_2-x_1} = \frac{f(5)-f(1)}{5-1}$$
Calculate the values of $f(1)$ and $f(5)$:
$$f(1) = -3(1) + 1 = -2$$
$$f(5) = -3(5) + 1 = -14$$
Then substitute these values into the expression for the average rate of change and simplify the result:
$$\frac{f(5)-f(1)}{5-1} = \frac{(-14)-(-2)}{5-1}$$
$$= \frac{-12}{4}$$
$$= -3$$

91. **B:** The inverse of a function is another function that *undoes* the original one. By convention, the inverse of $h(x)$ is written as $h^{-1}(x)$. For any value of x, the result of inputting x into h can itself be inputted into h^{-1}, and it will return the original value x. In other words, if $h(x) = y$, then $h^{-1}(y) = x$.

In regard to the problem, this means that the value of $h^{-1}(-2)$ is the value of x for which $h(x) = -2$. Examining the table for h, notice that when $x = -1$, $h(x) = -2$. Therefore, $h(-1) = -2$, and the value of $h^{-1}(-2)$ is -1.

92. **B:** A function is invertible if its inverse is a function. The given function f is not invertible if the domain is all real numbers because in some cases different values of x result in the same value of $f(x)$. Graphically, this means that the function does not pass the horizontal line test. That is, at least one horizontal line (like $y = 3$) intersect the graph at more than one point (the points (0,3) and (4,3)).

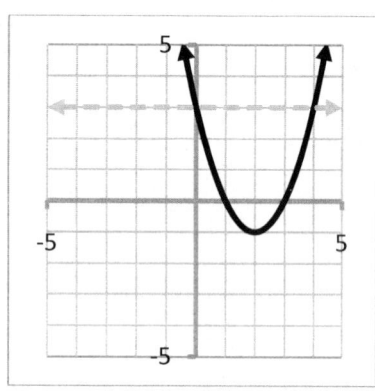

To make the function invertible, restrict the domain so that the new function does pass the horizontal line test. If you restrict the domain to $x \geq 2$, the resulting function will pass the horizontal line test as shown in the graph below.

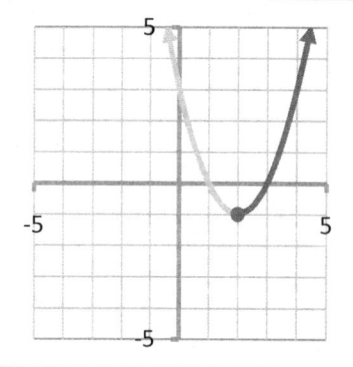

93. **C:** Graph the given function by either creating a table of values by hand or by inputting the function $y = 2\sin(3x - \frac{\pi}{2})$ into a graphing calculator. The graph of a trigonometric function like sine is a periodic function. That is, it repeats its values after a certain interval.

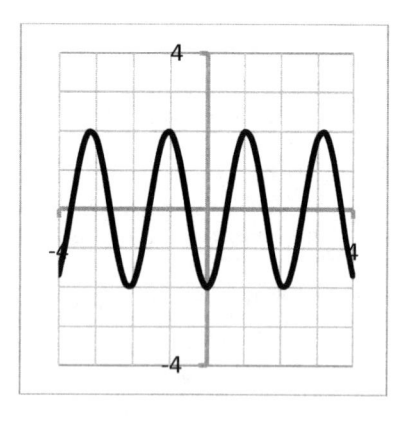

94. **A:** A function is invertible if its inverse is a function. The given function f is not invertible if the domain is all real numbers because, in some cases, different values of x result in the same value of $f(x)$. Graphically, this means that the function does not pass the horizontal line test. That is, at least one horizontal line (like $y = 0.5$) intersect the graph at more than one point.

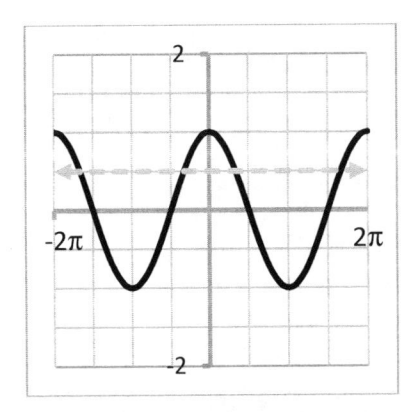

To make the function invertible, restrict the domain so that the new function does pass the horizontal line test. The only choice that accomplishes this is A: if you restrict the domain to $0 \leq x \leq \pi$, the resulting function will pass the horizontal line test as shown in the graph below.

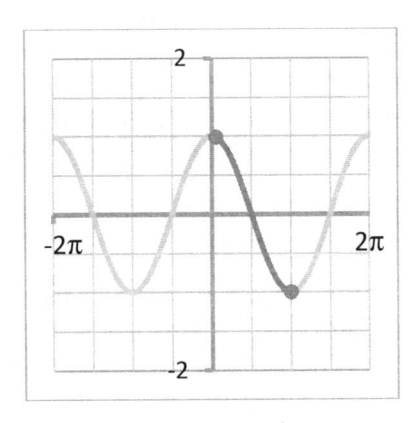

Secret Key #1 - Time is Your Greatest Enemy

Pace Yourself

Wear a watch. At the beginning of the test, check the time (or start a chronometer on your watch to count the minutes), and check the time after every few questions to make sure you are "on schedule."

If you are forced to speed up, do it efficiently. Usually one or more answer choices can be eliminated without too much difficulty. Above all, don't panic. Don't speed up and just begin guessing at random choices. By pacing yourself, and continually monitoring your progress against your watch, you will always know exactly how far ahead or behind you are with your available time. If you find that you are one minute behind on the test, don't skip one question without spending any time on it, just to catch back up. Take 15 fewer seconds on the next four questions, and after four questions you'll have caught back up. Once you catch back up, you can continue working each problem at your normal pace.

Furthermore, don't dwell on the problems that you were rushed on. If a problem was taking up too much time and you made a hurried guess, it must be difficult. The difficult questions are the ones you are most likely to miss anyway, so it isn't a big loss. It is better to end with more time than you need than to run out of time.

Lastly, sometimes it is beneficial to slow down if you are constantly getting ahead of time. You are always more likely to catch a careless mistake by working more slowly than quickly, and among very high-scoring test takers (those who are likely to have lots of time left over), careless errors affect the score more than mastery of material.

Secret Key #2 - Guessing is not Guesswork

You probably know that guessing is a good idea. Unlike other standardized tests, there is no penalty for getting a wrong answer. Even if you have no idea about a question, you still have a 20-25% chance of getting it right.

Most test takers do not understand the impact that proper guessing can have on their score. Unless you score extremely high, guessing will significantly contribute to your final score.

Monkeys Take the Test

What most test takers don't realize is that to insure that 20-25% chance, you have to guess randomly. If you put 20 monkeys in a room to take this test, assuming they answered once per question and behaved themselves, on average they would get 20-25% of the questions correct. Put 20 test takers in the room, and the average will be much lower among guessed questions. Why?
   1. The test writers intentionally write deceptive answer choices that "look" right. A test taker has no idea about a question, so he picks the "best looking" answer, which is often

wrong. The monkey has no idea what looks good and what doesn't, so it will consistently be right about 20-25% of the time.

2. Test takers will eliminate answer choices from the guessing pool based on a hunch or intuition. Simple but correct answers often get excluded, leaving a 0% chance of being correct. The monkey has no clue, and often gets lucky with the best choice.

This is why the process of elimination endorsed by most test courses is flawed and detrimental to your performance. Test takers don't guess; they make an ignorant stab in the dark that is usually worse than random.

$5 Challenge

Let me introduce one of the most valuable ideas of this course—the $5 challenge:

You only mark your "best guess" if you are willing to bet $5 on it.
You only eliminate choices from guessing if you are willing to bet $5 on it.

Why $5? Five dollars is an amount of money that is small yet not insignificant, and can really add up fast (20 questions could cost you $100). Likewise, each answer choice on one question of the test will have a small impact on your overall score, but it can really add up to a lot of points in the end.

The process of elimination IS valuable. The following shows your chance of guessing it right:

If you eliminate wrong answer choices until only this many remain:	Chance of getting it correct:
1	100%
2	50%
3	33%

However, if you accidentally eliminate the right answer or go on a hunch for an incorrect answer, your chances drop dramatically—to 0%. By guessing among all the answer choices, you are GUARANTEED to have a shot at the right answer.

That's why the $5 test is so valuable. If you give up the advantage and safety of a pure guess, it had better be worth the risk.

What we still haven't covered is how to be sure that whatever guess you make is truly random. Here's the easiest way:

Always pick the first answer choice among those remaining.

Such a technique means that you have decided, **before you see a single test question**, exactly how you are going to guess, and since the order of choices tells you nothing about which one is correct, this guessing technique is perfectly random.

This section is not meant to scare you away from making educated guesses or eliminating choices; you just need to define when a choice is worth eliminating. The $5 test, along with a pre-defined random guessing strategy, is the best way to make sure you reap all of the benefits of guessing.

Secret Key #3 - Practice Smarter, Not Harder

Many test takers delay the test preparation process because they dread the awful amounts of practice time they think necessary to succeed on the test. We have refined an effective method that will take you only a fraction of the time.

There are a number of "obstacles" in the path to success. Among these are answering questions, finishing in time, and mastering test-taking strategies. All must be executed on the day of the test at peak performance, or your score will suffer. The test is a mental marathon that has a large impact on your future.

Just like a marathon runner, it is important to work your way up to the full challenge. So first you just worry about questions, and then time, and finally strategy:

Success Strategy

1. Find a good source for practice tests.
2. If you are willing to make a larger time investment, consider using more than one study guide. Often the different approaches of multiple authors will help you "get" difficult concepts.
3. Take a practice test with no time constraints, with all study helps, "open book." Take your time with questions and focus on applying strategies.
4. Take a practice test with time constraints, with all guides, "open book."
5. Take a final practice test without open material and with time limits.

If you have time to take more practice tests, just repeat step 5. By gradually exposing yourself to the full rigors of the test environment, you will condition your mind to the stress of test day and maximize your success.

Secret Key #4 - Prepare, Don't Procrastinate

Let me state an obvious fact: if you take the test three times, you will probably get three different scores. This is due to the way you feel on test day, the level of preparedness you have, and the version of the test you see. Despite the test writers' claims to the contrary, some versions of the test WILL be easier for you than others.

Since your future depends so much on your score, you should maximize your chances of success. In order to maximize the likelihood of success, you've got to prepare in advance. This means taking practice tests and spending time learning the information and test taking strategies you will need to succeed.

Never go take the actual test as a "practice" test, expecting that you can just take it again if you need to. Take all the practice tests you can on your own, but when you go to take the official test, be prepared, be focused, and do your best the first time!

Secret Key #5 - Test Yourself

Everyone knows that time is money. There is no need to spend too much of your time or too little of your time preparing for the test. You should only spend as much of your precious time preparing as is necessary for you to get the score you need.

Once you have taken a practice test under real conditions of time constraints, then you will know if you are ready for the test or not.

If you have scored extremely high the first time that you take the practice test, then there is not much point in spending countless hours studying. You are already there.

Benchmark your abilities by retaking practice tests and seeing how much you have improved. Once you consistently score high enough to guarantee success, then you are ready.

If you have scored well below where you need, then knuckle down and begin studying in earnest. Check your improvement regularly through the use of practice tests under real conditions. Above all, don't worry, panic, or give up. The key is perseverance!

Then, when you go to take the test, remain confident and remember how well you did on the practice tests. If you can score high enough on a practice test, then you can do the same on the real thing.

General Strategies

The most important thing you can do is to ignore your fears and jump into the test immediately. Do not be overwhelmed by any strange-sounding terms. You have to jump into the test like jumping into a pool—all at once is the easiest way.

Make Predictions

As you read and understand the question, try to guess what the answer will be. Remember that several of the answer choices are wrong, and once you begin reading them, your mind will immediately become cluttered with answer choices designed to throw you off. Your mind is typically the most focused immediately after you have read the question and digested its contents. If you can, try to predict what the correct answer will be. You may be surprised at what you can predict.

Quickly scan the choices and see if your prediction is in the listed answer choices. If it is, then you can be quite confident that you have the right answer. It still won't hurt to check the other answer choices, but most of the time, you've got it!

Answer the Question

It may seem obvious to only pick answer choices that answer the question, but the test writers can create some excellent answer choices that are wrong. Don't pick an answer just because it sounds right, or you believe it to be true. It MUST answer the question. Once you've made your selection, always go back and check it against the question and make sure that you didn't misread the question and that the answer choice does answer the question posed.

Benchmark

After you read the first answer choice, decide if you think it sounds correct or not. If it doesn't, move on to the next answer choice. If it does, mentally mark that answer choice. This doesn't mean that you've definitely selected it as your answer choice, it just means that it's the best you've seen thus far. Go ahead and read the next choice. If the next choice is worse than the one you've already selected, keep going to the next answer choice. If the next choice is better than the choice you've already selected, mentally mark the new answer choice as your best guess.

The first answer choice that you select becomes your standard. Every other answer choice must be benchmarked against that standard. That choice is correct until proven otherwise by another answer choice beating it out. Once you've decided that no other answer choice seems as good, do one final check to ensure that your answer choice answers the question posed.

Valid Information

Don't discount any of the information provided in the question. Every piece of information may be necessary to determine the correct answer. None of the information in the question is there to throw you off (while the answer choices will certainly have information to throw you off). If two seemingly unrelated topics are discussed, don't ignore either. You can be confident there is a relationship, or it wouldn't be included in the question, and you are probably going to have to determine what is that relationship to find the answer.

Avoid "Fact Traps"

Don't get distracted by a choice that is factually true. Your search is for the answer that answers the question. Stay focused and don't fall for an answer that is true but irrelevant. Always go back to the question and make sure you're choosing an answer that actually answers the question and is not just a true statement. An answer can be factually correct, but it MUST answer the question asked. Additionally, two answers can both be seemingly correct, so be sure to read all of the answer choices, and make sure that you get the one that BEST answers the question.

Milk the Question

Some of the questions may throw you completely off. They might deal with a subject you have not been exposed to, or one that you haven't reviewed in years. While your lack of knowledge about the subject will be a hindrance, the question itself can give you many clues that will help you find the correct answer. Read the question carefully and look for clues. Watch particularly for adjectives and nouns describing difficult terms or words that you don't recognize. Regardless of whether you completely understand a word or not, replacing it with a synonym, either provided or one you more familiar with, may help you to understand what the questions are asking. Rather than wracking your mind about specific detailed information concerning a difficult term or word, try to use mental substitutes that are easier to understand.

The Trap of Familiarity

Don't just choose a word because you recognize it. On difficult questions, you may not recognize a number of words in the answer choices. The test writers don't put "make-believe" words on the test, so don't think that just because you only recognize all the words in one answer choice that that answer choice must be correct. If you only recognize words in one answer choice, then focus on that one. Is it correct? Try your best to determine if it is correct. If it is, that's great. If not, eliminate it. Each word and answer choice you eliminate increases your chances of getting the question correct, even if you then have to guess among the unfamiliar choices.

Eliminate Answers

Eliminate choices as soon as you realize they are wrong. But be careful! Make sure you consider all of the possible answer choices. Just because one appears right, doesn't mean that the next one won't be even better! The test writers will usually put more than one good answer choice for every question, so read all of them. Don't worry if you are stuck between two that seem right. By getting down to just two remaining possible choices, your odds are now 50/50. Rather than wasting too much time, play the odds. You are guessing, but guessing wisely because you've been able to knock out some of the answer choices that you know are wrong. If you are eliminating choices and realize that the last answer choice you are left with is also obviously wrong, don't panic. Start over and consider each choice again. There may easily be something that you missed the first time and will realize on the second pass.

Tough Questions

If you are stumped on a problem or it appears too hard or too difficult, don't waste time. Move on! Remember though, if you can quickly check for obviously incorrect answer choices, your chances of guessing correctly are greatly improved. Before you completely give up, at least try to knock out a couple of possible answers. Eliminate what you can and then guess at the remaining answer choices before moving on.

Brainstorm

If you get stuck on a difficult question, spend a few seconds quickly brainstorming. Run through the complete list of possible answer choices. Look at each choice and ask yourself, "Could this answer the question satisfactorily?" Go through each answer choice and consider it independently of the others. By systematically going through all possibilities, you may find something that you would otherwise overlook. Remember though that when you get stuck, it's important to try to keep moving.

Read Carefully

Understand the problem. Read the question and answer choices carefully. Don't miss the question because you misread the terms. You have plenty of time to read each question thoroughly and make sure you understand what is being asked. Yet a happy medium must be attained, so don't waste too much time. You must read carefully, but efficiently.

Face Value

When in doubt, use common sense. Always accept the situation in the problem at face value. Don't read too much into it. These problems will not require you to make huge leaps of logic. The test writers aren't trying to throw you off with a cheap trick. If you have to go beyond creativity and make a leap of logic in order to have an answer choice answer the question, then you should look at the other answer choices. Don't overcomplicate the problem by creating theoretical relationships or explanations that will warp time or space. These are normal problems rooted in reality. It's just that the applicable relationship or explanation may not be readily apparent and you have to figure things out. Use your common sense to interpret anything that isn't clear.

Prefixes

If you're having trouble with a word in the question or answer choices, try dissecting it. Take advantage of every clue that the word might include. Prefixes and suffixes can be a huge help. Usually they allow you to determine a basic meaning. Pre- means before, post- means after, pro - is positive, de- is negative. From these prefixes and suffixes, you can get an idea of the general meaning of the word and try to put it into context. Beware though of any traps. Just because con- is the opposite of pro-, doesn't necessarily mean congress is the opposite of progress!

Hedge Phrases

Watch out for critical hedge phrases, led off with words such as "likely," "may," "can," "sometimes," "often," "almost," "mostly," "usually," "generally," "rarely," and "sometimes." Question writers insert these hedge phrases to cover every possibility. Often an answer choice will be wrong simply because it leaves no room for exception. Unless the situation calls for them, avoid answer choices that have definitive words like "exactly," and "always."

Switchback Words

Stay alert for "switchbacks." These are the words and phrases frequently used to alert you to shifts in thought. The most common switchback word is "but." Others include "although," "however," "nevertheless," "on the other hand," "even though," "while," "in spite of," "despite," and "regardless of."

New Information

Correct answer choices will rarely have completely new information included. Answer choices typically are straightforward reflections of the material asked about and will directly relate to the question. If a new piece of information is included in an answer choice that doesn't even seem to relate to the topic being asked about, then that answer choice is likely incorrect. All of the information needed to answer the question is usually provided for you in the question. You should not have to make guesses that are unsupported or choose answer choices that require unknown information that cannot be reasoned from what is given.

Time Management

On technical questions, don't get lost on the technical terms. Don't spend too much time on any one question. If you don't know what a term means, then odds are you aren't going to get much further since you don't have a dictionary. You should be able to immediately recognize whether or not you know a term. If you don't, work with the other clues that you have—the other answer choices and terms provided—but don't waste too much time trying to figure out a difficult term that you don't know.

Contextual Clues

Look for contextual clues. An answer can be right but not the correct answer. The contextual clues will help you find the answer that is most right and is correct. Understand the context in which a phrase or statement is made. This will help you make important distinctions.

Don't Panic

Panicking will not answer any questions for you; therefore, it isn't helpful. When you first see the question, if your mind goes blank, take a deep breath. Force yourself to mechanically go through the steps of solving the problem using the strategies you've learned.

Pace Yourself

Don't get clock fever. It's easy to be overwhelmed when you're looking at a page full of questions, your mind is full of random thoughts and feeling confused, and the clock is ticking down faster than you would like. Calm down and maintain the pace that you have set for yourself. As long as you are on track by monitoring your pace, you are guaranteed to have enough time for yourself. When you get to the last few minutes of the test, it may seem like you won't have enough time left, but if you only have as many questions as you should have left at that point, then you're right on track!

Answer Selection

The best way to pick an answer choice is to eliminate all of those that are wrong, until only one is left and confirm that is the correct answer. Sometimes though, an answer choice may immediately look right. Be careful! Take a second to make sure that the other choices are not equally obvious. Don't make a hasty mistake. There are only two times that you should stop before checking other answers. First is when you are positive that the answer choice you have selected is correct. Second is when time is almost out and you have to make a quick guess!

Check Your Work

Since you will probably not know every term listed and the answer to every question, it is important that you get credit for the ones that you do know. Don't miss any questions through careless mistakes. If at all possible, try to take a second to look back over your answer selection and make sure you've selected the correct answer choice and haven't made a costly careless mistake (such as marking an answer choice that you didn't mean to mark). The time it takes for this quick double check should more than pay for itself in caught mistakes.

Beware of Directly Quoted Answers

Sometimes an answer choice will repeat word for word a portion of the question or reference section. However, beware of such exact duplication. It may be a trap! More than likely, the correct choice will paraphrase or summarize a point, rather than being exactly the same wording.

Slang

Scientific sounding answers are better than slang ones. An answer choice that begins "To compare the outcomes..." is much more likely to be correct than one that begins "Because some people insisted..."

Extreme Statements

Avoid wild answers that throw out highly controversial ideas that are proclaimed as established fact. An answer choice that states the "process should used in certain situations, if..." is much more likely to be correct than one that states the "process should be discontinued completely." The first is a calm rational statement and doesn't even make a definitive, uncompromising stance, using a hedge word "if" to provide wiggle room, whereas the second choice is a radical idea and far more extreme.

Answer Choice Families

When you have two or more answer choices that are direct opposites or parallels, one of them is usually the correct answer. For instance, if one answer choice states "x increases" and another answer choice states "x decreases" or "y increases," then those two or three answer choices are very similar in construction and fall into the same family of answer choices. A family of answer choices consists of two or three answer choices, very similar in construction, but often with directly opposite meanings. Usually the correct answer choice will be in that family of answer choices. The "odd man out" or answer choice that doesn't seem to fit the parallel construction of the other answer choices is more likely to be incorrect.

Special Report: How to Overcome Test Anxiety

The very nature of tests caters to some level of anxiety, nervousness, or tension, just as we feel for any important event that occurs in our lives. A little bit of anxiety or nervousness can be a good thing. It helps us with motivation, and makes achievement just that much sweeter. However, too much anxiety can be a problem, especially if it hinders our ability to function and perform.

"Test anxiety," is the term that refers to the emotional reactions that some test-takers experience when faced with a test or exam. Having a fear of testing and exams is based upon a rational fear, since the test-taker's performance can shape the course of an academic career. Nevertheless, experiencing excessive fear of examinations will only interfere with the test-taker's ability to perform and chance to be successful.

There are a large variety of causes that can contribute to the development and sensation of test anxiety. These include, but are not limited to, lack of preparation and worrying about issues surrounding the test.

Lack of Preparation

Lack of preparation can be identified by the following behaviors or situations:

Not scheduling enough time to study, and therefore cramming the night before the test or exam
Managing time poorly, to create the sensation that there is not enough time to do everything
Failing to organize the text information in advance, so that the study material consists of the entire text and not simply the pertinent information
Poor overall studying habits

Worrying, on the other hand, can be related to both the test taker, or many other factors around him/her that will be affected by the results of the test. These include worrying about:

Previous performances on similar exams, or exams in general
How friends and other students are achieving
The negative consequences that will result from a poor grade or failure

There are three primary elements to test anxiety. Physical components, which involve the same typical bodily reactions as those to acute anxiety (to be discussed below). Emotional factors have to do with fear or panic. Mental or cognitive issues concerning attention spans and memory abilities.

Physical Signals

There are many different symptoms of test anxiety, and these are not limited to mental and emotional strain. Frequently there are a range of physical signals that will let a test taker know that he/she is suffering from test anxiety. These bodily changes can include the following:

Perspiring
Sweaty palms
Wet, trembling hands
Nausea
Dry mouth
A knot in the stomach
Headache
Faintness
Muscle tension
Aching shoulders, back and neck
Rapid heart beat
Feeling too hot/cold

To recognize the sensation of test anxiety, a test-taker should monitor him/herself for the following sensations:

The physical distress symptoms as listed above
Emotional sensitivity, expressing emotional feelings such as the need to cry or laugh too much, or a sensation of anger or helplessness
A decreased ability to think, causing the test-taker to blank out or have racing thoughts that are hard to organize or control.

Though most students will feel some level of anxiety when faced with a test or exam, the majority can cope with that anxiety and maintain it at a manageable level. However, those who cannot are faced with a very real and very serious condition, which can and should be controlled for the immeasurable benefit of this sufferer.

Naturally, these sensations lead to negative results for the testing experience. The most common effects of test anxiety have to do with nervousness and mental blocking.

Nervousness

Nervousness can appear in several different levels:

The test-taker's difficulty, or even inability to read and understand the questions on the test
The difficulty or inability to organize thoughts to a coherent form
The difficulty or inability to recall key words and concepts relating to the testing questions (especially essays)
The receipt of poor grades on a test, though the test material was well known by the test taker

Conversely, a person may also experience mental blocking, which involves:

Blanking out on test questions
Only remembering the correct answers to the questions when the test has already finished.

Fortunately for test anxiety sufferers, beating these feelings, to a large degree, has to do with proper preparation. When a test taker has a feeling of preparedness, then anxiety will be dramatically lessened.

The first step to resolving anxiety issues is to distinguish which of the two types of anxiety are being suffered. If the anxiety is a direct result of a lack of preparation, this should be considered a normal reaction, and the anxiety level (as opposed to the test results) shouldn't be anything to worry about. However, if, when adequately prepared, the test-taker still panics, blanks out, or seems to overreact, this is not a fully rational reaction. While this can be considered normal too, there are many ways to combat and overcome these effects.

Remember that anxiety cannot be entirely eliminated, however, there are ways to minimize it, to make the anxiety easier to manage. Preparation is one of the best ways to minimize test anxiety. Therefore the following techniques are wise in order to best fight off any anxiety that may want to build.

To begin with, try to avoid cramming before a test, whenever it is possible. By trying to memorize an entire term's worth of information in one day, you'll be shocking your system, and not giving yourself a very good chance to absorb the information. This is an easy path to anxiety, so for those who suffer from test anxiety, cramming should not even be considered an option.

Instead of cramming, work throughout the semester to combine all of the material which is presented throughout the semester, and work on it gradually as the course goes by, making sure to master the main concepts first, leaving minor details for a week or so before the test.

To study for the upcoming exam, be sure to pose questions that may be on the examination, to gauge the ability to answer them by integrating the ideas from your texts, notes and lectures, as well as any supplementary readings.

If it is truly impossible to cover all of the information that was covered in that particular term, concentrate on the most important portions, that can be covered very well. Learn these concepts as best as possible, so that when the test comes, a goal can be made to use these concepts as presentations of your knowledge.

In addition to study habits, changes in attitude are critical to beating a struggle with test anxiety. In fact, an improvement of the perspective over the entire test-taking experience can actually help a test taker to enjoy studying and therefore improve the overall experience. Be certain not to overemphasize the significance of the grade - know that the result of the test is neither a reflection of self worth, nor is it a measure of intelligence; one grade will not predict a person's future success.
To improve an overall testing outlook, the following steps should be tried:

Keeping in mind that the most reasonable expectation for taking a test is to expect to try to demonstrate as much of what you know as you possibly can.
Reminding ourselves that a test is only one test; this is not the only one, and there will be others.

The thought of thinking of oneself in an irrational, all-or-nothing term should be avoided at all costs.
A reward should be designated for after the test, so there's something to look forward to. Whether it be going to a movie, going out to eat, or simply visiting friends, schedule it in advance, and do it no matter what result is expected on the exam.

Test-takers should also keep in mind that the basics are some of the most important things, even beyond anti-anxiety techniques and studying. Never neglect the basic social, emotional and biological needs, in order to try to absorb information. In order to best achieve, these three factors must be held as just as important as the studying itself.

Study Steps

Remember the following important steps for studying:

Maintain healthy nutrition and exercise habits. Continue both your recreational activities and social pass times. These both contribute to your physical and emotional well being. Be certain to get a good amount of sleep, especially the night before the test, because when you're overtired you are not able to perform to the best of your best ability.
Keep the studying pace to a moderate level by taking breaks when they are needed, and varying the work whenever possible, to keep the mind fresh instead of getting bored. When enough studying has been done that all the material that can be learned has been learned, and the test taker is prepared for the test, stop studying and do something relaxing such as listening to music, watching a movie, or taking a warm bubble bath.

There are also many other techniques to minimize the uneasiness or apprehension that is experienced along with test anxiety before, during, or even after the examination. In fact, there are a great deal of things that can be done to stop anxiety from interfering with lifestyle and performance. Again, remember that anxiety will not be eliminated entirely, and it shouldn't be. Otherwise that "up" feeling for exams would not exist, and most of us depend on that sensation to perform better than usual. However, this anxiety has to be at a level that is manageable.

Of course, as we have just discussed, being prepared for the exam is half the battle right away. Attending all classes, finding out what knowledge will be expected on the exam, and knowing the exam schedules are easy steps to lowering anxiety. Keeping up with work will remove the need to cram, and efficient study habits will eliminate wasted time. Studying should be done in an ideal location for concentration, so that it is simple to become interested in the material and give it complete attention. A method such as SQ3R (Survey, Question, Read, Recite, Review) is a wonderful key to follow to make sure that the study habits are as effective as possible, especially in the case of learning from a textbook. Flashcards are great techniques for memorization. Learning to take good notes will mean that notes will be full of useful information, so that less sifting will need to be done to seek out what is pertinent for studying. Reviewing notes after class and then again on occasion will keep the information fresh in the mind. From notes that have been taken summary sheets and outlines can be made for simpler reviewing.

A study group can also be a very motivational and helpful place to study, as there will be a sharing of ideas, all of the minds can work together, to make sure that everyone understands, and the studying will be made more interesting because it will be a social occasion.

Basically, though, as long as the test-taker remains organized and self confident, with efficient study habits, less time will need to be spent studying, and higher grades will be achieved.

To become self confident, there are many useful steps. The first of these is "self talk." It has been shown through extensive research, that self-talk for students who suffer from test anxiety, should be well monitored, in order to make sure that it contributes to self confidence as opposed to sinking the student. Frequently the self talk of test-anxious students is negative or self-defeating, thinking that everyone else is smarter and faster, that they always mess up, and that if they don't do well, they'll fail the entire course. It is important to decreasing anxiety that awareness is made of self talk. Try writing any negative self thoughts and then disputing them with a positive statement instead. Begin self-encouragement as though it was a friend speaking. Repeat positive statements to help reprogram the mind to believing in successes instead of failures.

Helpful Techniques

Other extremely helpful techniques include:

Self-visualization of doing well and reaching goals
While aiming for an "A" level of understanding, don't try to "overprotect" by setting your expectations lower. This will only convince the mind to stop studying in order to meet the lower expectations.
Don't make comparisons with the results or habits of other students. These are individual factors, and different things work for different people, causing different results.
Strive to become an expert in learning what works well, and what can be done in order to improve. Consider collecting this data in a journal.
Create rewards for after studying instead of doing things before studying that will only turn into avoidance behaviors.
Make a practice of relaxing - by using methods such as progressive relaxation, self-hypnosis, guided imagery, etc - in order to make relaxation an automatic sensation.
Work on creating a state of relaxed concentration so that concentrating will take on the focus of the mind, so that none will be wasted on worrying.
Take good care of the physical self by eating well and getting enough sleep.
Plan in time for exercise and stick to this plan.

Beyond these techniques, there are other methods to be used before, during and after the test that will help the test-taker perform well in addition to overcoming anxiety.

Before the exam comes the academic preparation. This involves establishing a study schedule and beginning at least one week before the actual date of the test. By doing this, the anxiety of not having enough time to study for the test will be automatically eliminated.

Moreover, this will make the studying a much more effective experience, ensuring that the learning will be an easier process. This relieves much undue pressure on the test-taker.

Summary sheets, note cards, and flash cards with the main concepts and examples of these main concepts should be prepared in advance of the actual studying time. A topic should never be eliminated from this process. By omitting a topic because it isn't expected to be on the test is only setting up the test-taker for anxiety should it actually appear on the exam. Utilize the course syllabus for laying out the topics that should be studied. Carefully go over the notes that were made in class, paying special attention to any of the issues that the professor took special care to emphasize while lecturing in class. In the textbooks, use the chapter review, or if possible, the chapter tests, to begin your review.

It may even be possible to ask the instructor what information will be covered on the exam, or what the format of the exam will be (for example, multiple choice, essay, free form, true-false). Additionally, see if it is possible to find out how many questions will be on the test. If a review sheet or sample test has been offered by the professor, make good use of it, above anything else, for the preparation for the test. Another great resource for getting to know the examination is reviewing tests from previous semesters. Use these tests to review, and aim to achieve a 100% score on each of the possible topics. With a few exceptions, the goal that you set for yourself is the highest one that you will reach.

Take all of the questions that were assigned as homework, and rework them to any other possible course material. The more problems reworked, the more skill and confidence will form as a result. When forming the solution to a problem, write out each of the steps. Don't simply do head work. By doing as many steps on paper as possible, much clarification and therefore confidence will be formed. Do this with as many homework problems as possible, before checking the answers. By checking the answer after each problem, a reinforcement will exist, that will not be on the exam. Study situations should be as exam-like as possible, to prime the test-taker's system for the experience. By waiting to check the answers at the end, a psychological advantage will be formed, to decrease the stress factor.

Another fantastic reason for not cramming is the avoidance of confusion in concepts, especially when it comes to mathematics. 8-10 hours of study will become one hundred percent more effective if it is spread out over a week or at least several days, instead of doing it all in one sitting. Recognize that the human brain requires time in order to assimilate new material, so frequent breaks and a span of study time over several days will be much more beneficial.

Additionally, don't study right up until the point of the exam. Studying should stop a minimum of one hour before the exam begins. This allows the brain to rest and put things in their proper order. This will also provide the time to become as relaxed as possible when going into the examination room. The test-taker will also have time to eat well and eat sensibly. Know that the brain needs food as much as the rest of the body. With enough food and enough sleep, as well as a relaxed attitude, the body and the mind are primed for success.

Avoid any anxious classmates who are talking about the exam. These students only spread anxiety, and are not worth sharing the anxious sentimentalities.

Before the test also involves creating a positive attitude, so mental preparation should also be a point of concentration. There are many keys to creating a positive attitude. Should fears become rushing in, make a visualization of taking the exam, doing well, and seeing an A written on the paper. Write out a list of affirmations that will bring a feeling of confidence, such as "I am doing well in my English class," "I studied well and know my material," "I enjoy this class." Even if the affirmations aren't believed at first, it sends a positive message to the subconscious which will result in an alteration of the overall belief system, which is the system that creates reality.

If a sensation of panic begins, work with the fear and imagine the very worst! Work through the entire scenario of not passing the test, failing the entire course, and dropping out of school, followed by not getting a job, and pushing a shopping cart through the dark alley where you'll live. This will place things into perspective! Then, practice deep breathing and create a visualization of the opposite situation - achieving an "A" on the exam, passing the entire course, receiving the degree at a graduation ceremony.

On the day of the test, there are many things to be done to ensure the best results, as well as the most calm outlook. The following stages are suggested in order to maximize test-taking potential:

Begin the examination day with a moderate breakfast, and avoid any coffee or beverages with caffeine if the test taker is prone to jitters. Even people who are used to managing caffeine can feel jittery or light-headed when it is taken on a test day.
Attempt to do something that is relaxing before the examination begins. As last minute cramming clouds the mastering of overall concepts, it is better to use this time to create a calming outlook.
Be certain to arrive at the test location well in advance, in order to provide time to select a location that is away from doors, windows and other distractions, as well as giving enough time to relax before the test begins.
Keep away from anxiety generating classmates who will upset the sensation of stability and relaxation that is being attempted before the exam.
Should the waiting period before the exam begins cause anxiety, create a self-distraction by reading a light magazine or something else that is relaxing and simple.

During the exam itself, read the entire exam from beginning to end, and find out how much time should be allotted to each individual problem. Once writing the exam, should more time be taken for a problem, it should be abandoned, in order to begin another problem. If there is time at the end, the unfinished problem can always be returned to and completed.

Read the instructions very carefully - twice - so that unpleasant surprises won't follow during or after the exam has ended.

When writing the exam, pretend that the situation is actually simply the completion of homework within a library, or at home. This will assist in forming a relaxed atmosphere, and will allow the brain extra focus for the complex thinking function.

Begin the exam with all of the questions with which the most confidence is felt. This will build the confidence level regarding the entire exam and will begin a quality momentum. This will also create encouragement for trying the problems where uncertainty resides.

Going with the "gut instinct" is always the way to go when solving a problem. Second guessing should be avoided at all costs. Have confidence in the ability to do well.

For essay questions, create an outline in advance that will keep the mind organized and make certain that all of the points are remembered. For multiple choice, read every answer, even if the correct one has been spotted - a better one may exist.

Continue at a pace that is reasonable and not rushed, in order to be able to work carefully. Provide enough time to go over the answers at the end, to check for small errors that can be corrected.

Should a feeling of panic begin, breathe deeply, and think of the feeling of the body releasing sand through its pores. Visualize a calm, peaceful place, and include all of the sights, sounds and sensations of this image. Continue the deep breathing, and take a few minutes to continue this with closed eyes. When all is well again, return to the test.

If a "blanking" occurs for a certain question, skip it and move on to the next question. There will be time to return to the other question later. Get everything done that can be done, first, to guarantee all the grades that can be compiled, and to build all of the confidence possible. Then return to the weaker questions to build the marks from there.

Remember, one's own reality can be created, so as long as the belief is there, success will follow. And remember: anxiety can happen later, right now, there's an exam to be written!

After the examination is complete, whether there is a feeling for a good grade or a bad grade, don't dwell on the exam, and be certain to follow through on the reward that was promised...and enjoy it! Don't dwell on any mistakes that have been made, as there is nothing that can be done at this point anyway.

Additionally, don't begin to study for the next test right away. Do something relaxing for a while, and let the mind relax and prepare itself to begin absorbing information again.

From the results of the exam - both the grade and the entire experience, be certain to learn from what has gone on. Perfect studying habits and work some more on confidence in order to make the next examination experience even better than the last one.

Learn to avoid places where openings occurred for laziness, procrastination and day dreaming.

Use the time between this exam and the next one to better learn to relax, even learning to relax on cue, so that any anxiety can be controlled during the next exam. Learn how to relax the body. Slouch in your chair if that helps. Tighten and then relax all of the different muscle groups, one group at a time, beginning with the feet and then working all the way up to the neck and face. This will ultimately relax the muscles more than they were to begin with. Learn how to breathe deeply and comfortably, and focus on this breathing going in and out as a relaxing thought. With every exhale, repeat the word "relax."
As common as test anxiety is, it is very possible to overcome it. Make yourself one of the test-takers who overcome this frustrating hindrance.

Special Report: Additional Bonus Material

Due to our efforts to try to keep this book to a manageable length, we've created a link that will give you access to all of your additional bonus material.

Please visit http://www.mometrix.com/bonus948/dsstfundcolalg to access the information.